REVISIONING THE TREE OF LIFE

REVISIONING THE TREE OF LIFE
A New Cabala for Magic, Pathworking, and Meditation

John Michael Greer

AEON

First published in 2025 by
Aeon Books

Copyright © 2025 by John Michael Greer

The right of John Michael Greer to be identified as the author of this work has been asserted in accordance with §§ 77 and 78 of the Copyright Design and Patents Act 1988.

All rights reserved. No part of this publication may be reproduced, stored in a retrieval system, or transmitted, in any form or by any means, electronic, mechanical, photocopying, recording, or otherwise, without the prior written permission of the publisher.

British Library Cataloguing in Publication Data

A C.I.P. for this book is available from the British Library

ISBN-13: 978-1-80152-194-9

Typeset by Medlar Publishing Solutions Pvt Ltd, India

www.aeonbooks.co.uk

Dedicated to the memory of

Sara-Ellen Clare Greer

1961–2024

CONTENTS

FOREWORD	ix
INTRODUCTION: A CABALA FOR TODAY	xiii
PART ONE: PRINCIPLES OF THE CABALA	
The Tree of Life	7
Numbers and archetypes	13
Pillars, worlds, and paths	19
The religious dimension	35
Macrocosm and microcosm	41
Awakening to the inner worlds	53
PART TWO: SYMBOLISM OF THE CABALA	
Correspondences of the spheres	69
Correspondences of the paths	81
The tarot as symbolic synthesis	93
PART THREE: PRACTICE OF THE CABALA	
Stage one: discursive meditation	109
Stage two: the sanctum ceremonies	123

Stage three: active imagination and dreamwork	147
Stage four: the Tree of Life in the body	159
Stage five: the bridge of light	169
Stage six: sphere workings	177
Stage seven: the magical images	195
Stage eight: pathworkings	199
BIBLIOGRAPHY	209
INDEX	213

FOREWORD

It seems like a very long time now since the last years of the 1980s. That was when I first set out to formulate my understanding of the Cabala, the heart of the occult philosophy I have studied and practiced since my teen years. As my ideas took shape, I wrote a study course on the Cabala as I then understood it. Several years later, after the course had been shared with a small number of students, I revised it thoroughly with the help of my wife Sara and turned it into the manuscript for my first book, *Paths of Wisdom*, which was published in 1996.

As an introduction to the Cabala as practiced in the tradition of the Hermetic Order of the Golden Dawn, it still seems useful to me, and the fact that it still has steady sales almost 30 years since its first publication suggests that I am not alone in that assessment. That said, a good deal can be learned in 30 years. I wrote the original draft of *Paths of Wisdom* before I met any of my teachers, when I was still working entirely with what I could learn from books and my own experiences. Above all, it was before I met and studied with John Gilbert, whose distinctive Cabalistic teachings are central to what follows, and before I plunged into the Pythagorean, Platonic, and Gnostic roots of the Cabala, which are equally central to this book.

Readers who are familiar to any degree with the current literature on the occult end of the Cabala will find this a very odd book. I make no apologies for this. I have tried to present the Cabala, in the version I learned from John Gilbert, in a way that avoids some of the awkward traps and blind alleys that so often interfere with understanding. I have attempted throughout to start from first principles, to make the meaning and purpose of the system understandable, and to show how certain practices unfold naturally from those principles and lead to the heights of human possibility. I have made some modifications to the symbolism, philosophy, and practices that John taught; since John himself constantly edited and revised his own teachings, and what I received from him was simply the version he happened to be passing on during the years that I knew him, this is entirely in keeping with his legacy!

Readers of my other books may wish to know that the practices in this volume are entirely compatible with those of the Golden Section Fellowship and the Fellowship of the Hermetic Rose, two systems of practice also based on the material I learned from John Gilbert.[1] The ritual work of both these systems may be substituted for the simpler ritual forms I have given in the pages that follow. The practical material given in the pages that follow may also be reworked to fit other versions of the occult Cabala, though this will take some significant revisions of certain parts of the work, and should only be attempted by those who already have a solid practical grasp of whatever system of Cabalistic symbolism they intend to use.

A note on spelling is probably just as necessary here as it was in my earlier book on the Cabala. All those years ago when I was first studying the Cabala, people would pick fights now and then over the proper spelling of the word. I take a certain wry amusement in the fact that the same thing still happens online today. There is good reason why the spelling has never been settled: the sounds of Semitic languages such as Hebrew are very hard to transliterate clearly into Indo-European languages such as English, and so there are three common spellings—Cabala, Kabbalah, and Qabalah—none of which do a very good job of expressing the pronunciation of the Hebrew word קבלה.

That said, the spelling "Cabala" has been standard in English since the 16th century, and I know of no good reason not to use it. Furthermore,

---

[1] See Greer 2021 and Greer 2022b for more about these systems.

it has been the standard Latin spelling all along and remained the standard English spelling until a century ago. For reasons that will be made clear in the introduction, it makes a good label for the particular approach to the Cabala presented in this book.

Finally, the dedication of this book deserves a few words. When I originally conceived this book, I intended to dedicate it to John Gilbert, who as teacher, initiator, and friend passed on to me much of the material included here, and made an immeasurable contribution to my occult work more generally. Though we only saw each other in person a handful of times, we carried on a lively correspondence by email, punctuated by phone calls, for most of ten years before his failing health and a range of other factors sent us both along different paths. It was still a shock to hear in 2021 that he had died, and I miss the man to this day. A more immediate and pressing grief, however, requires acknowledgment here.

My late wife Sara, a longtime and serious occultist who put as much time and effort into studying the Cabala as I have, was a constant source of good advice, assistance, and loving support to me throughout my writing career and my work as an occultist, from the first days of our relationship to the last weeks of the long illness that ended her life. It was her encouragement, all those years ago, that gave me the confidence to turn that original Cabala study course into a book, and she put many hours into helping me revise and rework the manuscript of *Paths of Wisdom* until it was publishable. She hoped to contribute the same kind of help to this project. Instead, it is the first book I have written after her death. I dedicate it to her memory.

—John Michael Greer

INTRODUCTION: A CABALA FOR TODAY

Paul Foster Case, an influential 20th-century American writer on the Cabala, liked to refer to his subject as the Ageless Wisdom. It's a colorful label but an inaccurate one. Like every other spiritual tradition, the Cabala is anything but ageless. The insights at its core are enduring, but the forms chosen by each generation of authors and teachers to communicate those insights change constantly in response to shifts in language and culture. Take any Cabalistic work you like, whether it be Moses de Leon's *Sefer ha-Zohar*, Dion Fortune's *The Mystical Qabalah*, or the one in your hands: it bears the imprint of its time and place of origin on every page.

To accept a spiritual tradition such as the Cabala as a living, growing, changing reality, however, is to run afoul of a fusillade of deep-rooted prejudices in our time. The cult of progress that functions as a state religion in most modern societies has inevitably generated pushback from those unwilling to buy into the dubious claim that what is new is always better. That pushback, however, has too often taken the form of an equally problematic insistence that what is old is always better. Applied to spiritual traditions, this typically yields a fundamentalist approach in which some older form of the tradition is treated as the one and only one option.

In the Cabala, much more often than not, that amounts to a fixation on the specifically Jewish forms of the tradition and an angry rejection of its Christian and occult forms. Inevitably that has gotten tangled up with a selectively applied rhetoric of cultural appropriation, in which modern students of other forms of the Cabala are lambasted in tones of high outrage because six centuries ago certain European intellectuals, most of them at least nominally Christian, studied the Cabala with Jewish teachers and then adapted the teachings they received to their own religious visions.

There is one great difficulty with all this heated rhetoric, however: the Cabala is not originally Jewish. The Jewish version was created in the 11th century in rabbinical circles in southern France. As Gershom Scholem pointed out many decades ago in his magisterial *The Origins of the Kabbalah*, those circles drew their inspiration for the Cabala from the flowering of the Gnostic tradition then under way in southern France. The borrowings that brought the Cabala into being are not minor; they involve core elements of the Cabalistic tradition—and many of these core elements can be traced back in Gnosticism many centuries before their first documented appearance in Jewish writings. The Gnostic tradition, in turn, had its origins in Hellenistic Greek culture, and so the Cabala was originally Greek, not Jewish.

The borrowings found in the Jewish tradition of the Cabala extend to some of the most basic concepts of the tradition. The word *sephirah*, for example, the standard term for the ten spheres or powers of the Tree of Life, is not originally a Hebrew word. It's the Hebrew pronunciation of the Greek word *sphaera*, "sphere." *Gematria*, the standard Cabalistic term for the mathematical analysis of Hebrew words, is not a Hebrew word either; scholars are divided on whether it comes from Greek *geometria*, "geometry," or *grammateia*, "having to do with writing," but it's certainly Greek in origin and may have been framed as it was in Hebrew as a clever reference to both. To cite only one more of the many examples, the greatest of the angels in Jewish Cabalistic literature, Metatron or Mittraton, does not have a Hebrew name; his name is Greek *meta thronos*, "before the throne."

The Tree of Life itself, the essential diagram of the Cabala, is an even more significant example. It was already in circulation in Gnostic circles in the late 2nd century, some 900 years before its first appearance in Jewish tradition. Celsus included a version of it in *The True Discourse*, his essay attacking Christianity. Origen's defense of the Christian faith some 70 years later, *Against Celsus*, refers in detail to the same diagram.

The broader idea of the universe as a tree with its roots in heaven, the basic metaphor underlying the Tree of Life, is found all through the mystical end of Greek philosophy; Cicero cites it in *On the Nature of the Gods*, for example, and Plotinus returns to it over and over again in the *Enneads*.

Once established in Greek mystical circles, the Tree of Life diagram seems to have spread very far. There is even a Chinese version of the Tree of Life, the *Taijitu*, which adapts the same overall structure to the needs of Chinese mysticism. This diagram first appears in the writings of the important Neo-Confucian philosopher Zhou Dunyi (1017–1073). The presence of a Gnostic diagram in China at that time comes as no surprise to those who know their way around the remarkable diffusion of mystical traditions in ancient times.

Gnostic Christianity had won a foothold in China by the 6th century, and philosophical and mystical traditions had been flowing back and forth along the Silk Route since at least the 2nd century BC, when Buddhist missionaries preached their faith in Alexandria and Hellenistic art styles found their way to northern India and western China. The point that matters for our purposes is that Chinese intellectuals were already studying a version of the Tree of Life by the time that the first version of the Jewish Cabala came into being.

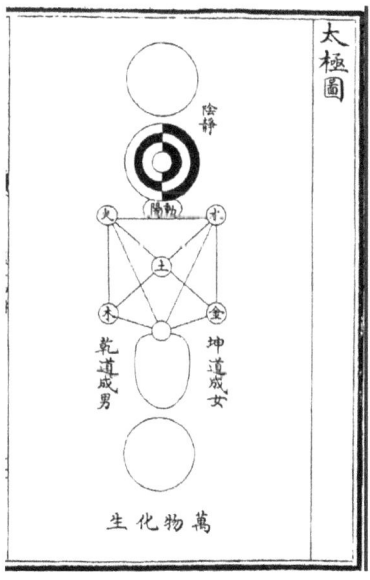

Taijitu

The origins of the Cabala reach back before Gnosticism, however. Trace them further and a fascinating story emerges. As John Dillon pointed out many years ago in his essential volume *The Middle Platonists*, Gnosticism and the parallel movement of Hermeticism can best be understood as offshoots of the Platonist tradition, adapting the refined ideas of Platonist philosophers to more robust magical and mystical uses. Long before the rise of Gnosticism, Platonists such as Philo of Alexandria, Plutarch of Chaeroneia, and Apuleius of Madaura had already worked out a remarkable share of the core concepts of the Cabala in detail.

Consider the doctrine of the primal worlds, one of the most distinctive teachings of the later Cabala. According to this doctrine, developed in its classic Jewish form by Rabbi Isaac Luria (1534–1572), the powers of evil in the cosmos today are the remnants of a universe that preceded our own, a realm of unbalanced force symbolized by "the kings that reigned in the land of Edom, before there reigned any king over the children of Israel" (Genesis 26:31). It's an intriguing concept and has been developed into a core theme of later Cabalistic theory, but it was not original to Luria, or to Judaism.

Some 15 centuries before Luria's time, Plutarch of Chaeroneia had already referred to an earlier form of the same theory in his essay *On Isis and Osiris*. "Before this world became manifest and was brought to completion by the Logos," Plutarch wrote, "Matter, being shown by its nature to be incomplete of itself, brought forth the first creation"[2]—a creation that was necessarily imperfect, an image and phantom rather than a world, and was swept away by the creative force of the Logos descending into matter. Plutarch did not invent this teaching; he was not an original thinker in philosophical terms. He referred to it in passing, while explaining the allegorical meaning of an ancient Egyptian myth, and expected the reader to recognize the idea. This shows that it was already current in the Platonist teachings of his time.

His version of the teaching and Isaac Luria's version are of course not the same, and this is exactly the point that matters here. Plutarch drew on the diverse and evolving body of philosophy and spirituality historians of ideas now call Middle Platonism. Luria also drew on a much later generation of that same body of ideas, which had already been adopted by influential Jewish thinkers such as Philo of Alexandria

---

[2] I have used John Dillon's translation here; see Dillon 1996, p. 204.

many centuries earlier and has continued to provide philosophers and mystics of all the Western faiths with an abundant source of ideas for two and a half millennia. Both men took a concept that was already part of that body of ideas and put it to work for their own religious and philosophical purposes. Many other people did the same thing all through the history of the traditions we are tracing.

Platonism, especially in its Middle Platonic forms, was thus the common philosophical language of spiritually minded intellectuals all over the Mediterranean world from ancient times until the end of the Renaissance, and it still has no shortage of students today. Judaism was of course far from the only religious tradition to draw heavily from it. The concept of a single god who manifests in three forms, for example, was widespread in Middle Platonism long before it became the central theological vision of Christianity.

The role of Platonism in the Western esoteric traditions that descended from Gnosticism and Hermeticism is even more profound. For the last century and a half, those traditions have been given the label "occultism." That term has been a source of quite a bit of unnecessary confusion. It has nothing to do with the word "cult"; the word "occult" comes from the Latin *occultus*, and means "hidden." Occult philosophy, as it was called in the Renaissance, got its name partly because of the legal penalties its students then risked and partly because it deals with the hidden sides of the universe and the individual human being. The intellectual framework of occultism comes straight out of the Platonic tradition, partly by way of the Cabala, but also through Gnostic and Hermetic teachings. In its philosophical and intellectual dimensions, in fact, it's fair to say that Western occultism is simply Middle Platonism dressed in wizard's robes.

It makes perfect sense, in the context of ancient thought, that Platonism should have evolved in this direction. One of the core insights of ancient philosophy, developed in various ways by the diverse schools and thinkers of the age, is that under ordinary conditions the individual human being controls only two things: his voluntary actions and his personal judgments. Everything else is at best a crapshoot and at worst a function of immovable fate. Each school offered its own response to the human situation set out in these terms. It was through the interpenetration of Middle Platonism with magical teachings and practices that the traditions ancestral to the Cabala came to see that there was a third factor that the human individual can control: his interactions with the world through those deep levels of consciousness in which rational thought cannot function and symbol, archetype, and dream take its place. That was the insight that opened the way to classic Western occultism in all its forms.

Behind the Platonist engagement with this deeper realm of human experience, in turn, stands another, older tradition, the one set in motion by Pythagoras of Crotona more than two centuries before Plato's time, when he took the teachings he had learned in Egypt and reworked them extensively for a Western audience. Ultimately, then, the Cabala—like the whole tradition of Western esoteric spirituality—has its roots in ancient Egypt. It was through the work of Pythagoras that this tradition found its way from the ancient temples of the Nile valley to the young cultures of the West, but his teachings were not strictly Egyptian by any means. He synthesized what he had learned in Egypt with the indigenous Greek Mysteries, traditional initiation rituals which each had their own mystical lore and symbolism to pass on to initiates.

It was through the teachings of Pythagoras, as formulated and developed by generations of ancient scholars, that the Western world encountered the idea that the first ten numbers—the *sephiroth*, in Cabalistic terminology—are the essential principles on which the world is founded. The Pythagoreans liked to arrange these ten numbers into geometrical diagrams. The most famous of them was the tetractys, a triangle of ten points, as shown here.

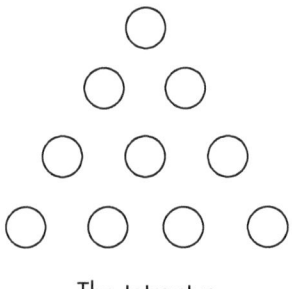

The tetractys

In later Pythagorean teachings, this basic diagram was expanded and reworked in various ways. The 2nd-century Greek mathematician Theon of Smyrna, in his book *Mathematics Useful for Understanding Plato*, described 11 forms of the tetractys, of which the third and fourth had the most significant impact on later traditions. The fourth tetractys assigns the levels of the tetractys to the four elements of ancient Greek tradition:

INTRODUCTION: A CABALA FOR TODAY   xix

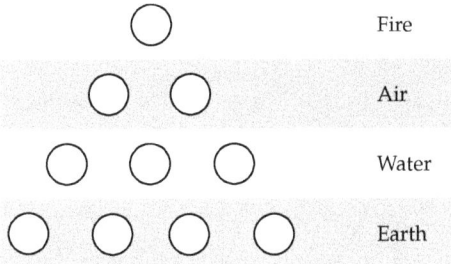

Tetractys of the elements

Here we have the ancestor of all the various ways of mapping the four elements onto the Tree of Life. Yet it is the third tetractys that is arguably the most important in the history of the Cabala, as it assigns those same four levels to geometrical figures: the first to the point, the second to the line, the third to the plane, and the fourth to the three-dimensional solid.

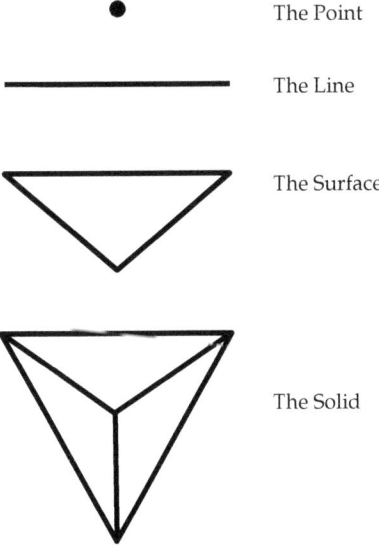

Tetractys of geometry

In Greek geometry the triangle is the essential plane figure and the tetrahedron is the essential solid figure. Put a point, a line, a triangle, and a tetrahedron in descending order and the diagram it produces will seem very familiar to Cabalists.

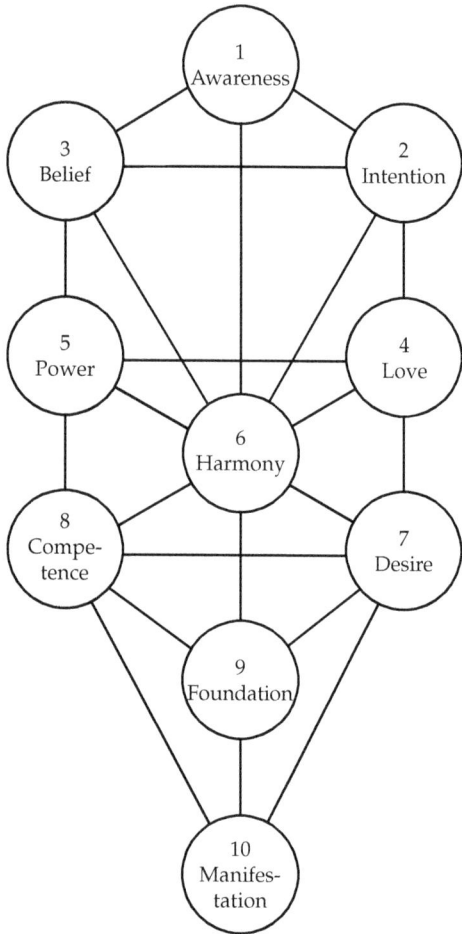

The Tree of Life

Does any of this make the Jewish Cabala invalid or inauthentic? Of course not. The creators of the Jewish Cabala took up a set of teachings familiar to mystics and esotericists across the early medieval Mediterranean world, adapted those teachings in a creative manner to the needs of their faith, and enriched it with the treasures of Judaism's own liturgical, contemplative, and magical traditions. The result was and still is one of the world's great mystical systems, and an important part of Jewish tradition. The mere fact that its creators built on older Greek foundations hardly negates the value of their achievement.

An equivalent process, after all, gave rise to the Hebrew alphabet. That was not a Jewish invention either. Its earliest form was borrowed from the Phoenicians, who spoke a related Semitic language. Thereafter it evolved along with the Hebrew language and became the vehicle for richly developed literary and calligraphic traditions. In due time it became the focus of mythic narratives that projected it into infinite distance, portraying the Hebrew letters as principles that existed in the mind of God before the world was made.

The same process of backdating, in turn, happened with the Cabala as well. In Jewish Cabalistic literature the Cabala is said to have been taught to Adam in Paradise by angels, passed on to the patriarchs, and completed by Moses, who communicated it to an inner circle of students. Historically speaking, this isn't what happened, but that matters only from within the context of the historian. Mythic narratives of the sort we're discussing have their own kind of truth, and that kind of truth is important in its own right. Problems creep in only when the truths of myth are confused with the facts of history.

The Jewish Cabala thus remains a live option in every sense for observant Jews, and also for those gentiles who are drawn to it and are willing to embrace the laws that, according to Jewish tradition, were handed down to Noah. Long before Jews took up the traditions that became the Cabala, however, plenty of people were studying and practicing their own versions of those traditions outside Judaism. Another large group of gentiles took up versions of the same traditions in the Renaissance, partly influenced by the Jewish Cabala but also profoundly influenced by the Platonic, Hermetic, and Gnostic traditions that had come down to them via other routes. Their creation was the Christian Cabala. From that in turn, by way of further generations of innovators, came the occult Cabala.

The Jewish Cabala, in other words, has always been one branch of a great and spreading tree, not the trunk, much less the root. It has always been one option among many—or, rather, a collection of several options, for there are distinct traditions within the Jewish Cabala, which disagree with one another about important issues of philosophy and practice. The Christian and occult branches of the Cabala are at least as diverse as the Jewish branch. Again, this is as it should be, since the Cabala is a living tradition and not an embalmed corpse.

This book is about one of the forms of the occult Cabala. At its core is a set of Cabalistic teachings I received during the first decade of this century from my late teacher John Gilbert. These teachings differ in important ways from the Golden Dawn system of occult Cabala, the most common version practiced in the English-speaking world these days, and in equally important ways from the European system of occult Cabala set in motion by Eliphas Lévi and brought to maturity by Papus, Oswald Wirth, and their heirs, which remains widely practiced in Europe and the Latin diaspora. Each of these is a distinct system with its own symbolism and its own practical methods.

John Gilbert was an American occultist of what was once a classic type, initiated into an assortment of rites and traditions from various sources, which he then adapted and modified in response to his own experiences. The Cabala he taught was based on material he received from two of his teachers, the occultist Dr. Juliet Ashley and the dissident Universalist Rev. Matthew Shaw, who taught under the name Rhodonn Starrus (an idiosyncratic spelling of "Rose Cross" in Greek). Where Ashley and Shaw got it is anyone's guess—the bubbling cauldron of 20th-century American occultism is still too poorly documented and too scantily researched for such questions to be easily answered.

The religious vision that undergirded John's teachings is hard to classify in terms of religious orthodoxies but instantly familiar to those who know their way around American alternative culture. Experiential and inclusive rather than dogmatic, it relied on the term "the Divine" as a placeholder for the unknowable reality at the heart of religious experience, and went out of its way to avoid trying to set out hard and fast rules about the nature of that reality. The first line of the *Tao Te Ching*, "The Tao that can be described is not the eternal Tao," was music to John's ears. It may offer some sense of the seriousness with which he took this point that he consecrated me as a bishop in the Universal Gnostic Church, one of the traditions he had received, even though he was more or less a monotheist and I am a polytheist.

The Cabala he taught was equally flexible and equally open to personal experience. It is not quite like any other set of Cabalistic teachings I have encountered in my studies. Such basic factors as the profound distinction between the first three spheres of the Tree of Life and the lower seven, the relationship between the Tree and the four traditional elements, and the symbolism of the 22 paths of the Tree are distinctive—not to say idiosyncratic—though they work in practice just as well as the more widely known systems.

The practical applications of John's version of the Cabala are just as distinctive. He used much less ritual and much more meditation than most of the currently popular systems of occult Cabala, and the rituals he did use were in a tradition of their own, equally distant from the more popular methods of the present and recent past. Among other differences, they use much less in the way of ritual hardware than many other methods, and can be practiced with perfect success given a spare corner of a bedroom or the like, a convenient chair, and a few other easily obtained objects. The result is an effective system, and one well suited for a time when many people are struggling with economic hardship and other practical issues.

This book is thus in part an attempt to preserve and pass on a unique and highly practical tradition of American alternative spirituality. It is a little more than that, however. As I write these words, the Western world is stumbling through a cascade of difficult cultural transformations set in motion by the failure of the cult of progress mentioned earlier to make good on its promises. The rationalist materialism that provided that cult with its impetus has begun to crumple as it became clear to too many people that the artificial world cobbled together by human reason in the service of collective ego has turned out to be unfit for human habitation.

The most common response to that realization is a flight back to the dogmatic religious ideologies of an earlier day. Too few people have noticed that it was precisely those belief systems, with their inevitable abuses in the hands of entrenched and often despotic hierarchies, that made rationalist materialism inevitable and built the foundations for its temporary triumph. Returning to the old claim that religious institutions ought to tell people what they are and are not allowed to believe simply makes a second pass through rationalist materialism more likely.

There are other options. One of them—to my mind, the most promising—is to turn to the living Spirit itself and there seek visions that will be appropriate for the needs of our time. It seems to me, in other words, that we would be well advised to stop trying to tell the Divine what we expect it to be, and start listening instead to what it has to say. Through the ages, traditions of experiential spiritual practice have been used to foster that act of listening. The Cabala in all its many forms embodies one such set of traditions, and it seems likely to be that some people at least will find the version I learned from John Gilbert well suited to the work ahead.

It is not the only approach well suited to that work, in or out of the Cabala. That is why I subtitled this book "A New Cabala for Magic, Meditation, and Pathworking" and not "*The* New Cabala for Every Imaginable Purpose." The Cabala—any version of the Cabala, from any source—is a set of tools, not a collection of truths; for those who are ready to get past the outward trappings of human existence and go deeper, it provides concepts and techniques, and these inevitably will be better suited to some than to others. Those who find this path appropriate, however, will discover a wealth of possibilities in the pages ahead. More to the point, they will find those possibilities once they use the material that follows as a launching point their own practices, and a way of making sense of their personal experiences of the Divine in its many forms. It is for these adventurers in the realms of the spirit that these pages have been written.

PART ONE

PRINCIPLES OF THE CABALA

It is easy to misunderstand the Cabala, and the quickest road to misunderstanding is to treat it as an ideology—a set of beliefs or opinions about this or that subject. Plenty of Cabalistic writers have contributed to confusions of that kind by equating the Cabala too closely with the teachings of whatever religious or spiritual tradition they themselves practice. Even in its ancestral Pythagorean and Platonist forms, however, the Cabala was something subtler, more abstract, and more useful than a belief system.

Contemporary Gnostic bishop and Cabalist Stephan A. Hoeller has proposed a useful way of thinking about the Tree of Life, the diagram at the heart of the Cabala. He suggests that it can be described in three different ways.[3] First, it is an archetype—that is, one of the primordial patterns at the foundation of consciousness, equivalent to the Ideas or Forms of Platonic teaching. Second, it is a filing system, in which whatever images and ideas we encounter can be sorted out into their proper places. Third, it embodies a method of using the mind: in other words, it is a practical technique as well as a way of making sense of the world.

The second of these ways will occupy most of our attention in the earlier sections of this book. One way of understanding this approach is to see the Tree of Life as a filing cabinet with ten drawers and 32 file folders. The drawers and folders can be used to store and organize anything you choose. Once you know how the drawers and folders work, they organize the material in a way that reveals unexpected connections and provides easy access from one file or drawer to another.

This metaphor is an effective method to communicate some part of the way the Cabala works, but another approach drawn from the mathematical vision of reality that Pythagoras introduced to Western esoteric spirituality may be just as useful. In this way of thinking, the spheres and paths of the Tree of Life function like the x, y, and z of a mathematical formula. Take the familiar Pythagorean formula relating the short sides of a right triangle to its longest side: $x^2 + y^2 = z^2$. You can replace those letters with any numbers you wish, so long as all three of them are in the right relationship to one another, and you can apply the result to define a right triangle on any scale you choose, from molecules to galaxies. The formula remains just as valid in each case.

---

[3] Hoeller 1975, p. 28.

In the same way, the ten spheres and 22 paths of the Tree of Life set out a pattern of relationships that can be found throughout the universe of human experience. The chief difference between the pattern set forth by the Tree of Life and those that are used in mathematics can be described simply enough: mathematics works with quantities that are represented by signs, while the Cabala works with qualities that are represented by symbols.

These distinctions are worth a few words. Quantity is the answer to the question "how many?" It abstracts this one feature from the buzzing, blooming confusion of experience, and the results can then be handled with ordinary mathematics. That has many advantages, but it also has drawbacks, because the world is not as simple as a purely quantitative vision makes it look. We all learn in school that $1 + 1 = 2$. Is this true, though? Here is one apple, here is another apple, and over there are two more apples. Is this one apple plus that one really equal to those others? It depends on their size, condition, and variety, doesn't it?

Quality is everything that is left behind when quantity is abstracted. Quantities can be represented by signs, which are abstract labels—x, y, and z, for example, are signs used in mathematics. You know that you're dealing with signs when one can be replaced by another without any loss of meaning: $a^2 + b^2 = c^2$ means exactly the same thing as $x^2 + y^2 = z^2$.

Qualities, by contrast, are best represented by symbols, which are concrete sensory images rather than abstract labels, and which cannot be replaced by others without a loss of meaning. The Tree of Life is a symbol; each of its ten spheres and 22 paths is an anchor for a constellation of symbols. Those symbols express meanings that, to switch metaphors, provide our filing cabinet with the labels and folders that allow all of the richness of human experience to be brought into a single structure of consciousness.

The ten spheres, as we will see, can be traced in the simplest actions of the human will. They can be found in the inner structure of the human psyche and in the vast sweep of the solar system. Cabalists since ancient times have held that they also provide a glimpse into the Divine itself. This very broad applicability comes from the sheer simplicity of the pattern the Cabala deploys. Eliphas Lévi, whose epochal 1855 volume *Dogme et Rituel de la Haute Magie* (*Doctrine and Ritual of*

High Magic) played a crucial role in reshaping the occult Cabala for the modern world, described this in his usual exuberant prose:

> We are seized with admiration, when we penetrate the sanctuary of the Cabala, by the sight of a doctrine so logical, so simple and at the same time so absolute. The necessary union of ideas and of signs; the consecration of the most fundamental realities with primitive characters, the trinity of words, of letters and of numbers; a philosophy as simple as the alphabet, profound and infinite as the Verb; theorems more complete and illuminating than those of Pythagoras; a theology which we summarize by counting on our fingers; an infinity that could be held in the hollow of a child's hand; ten numbers and 22 letters, a triangle, a square and a circle: those are the whole of the elements of the Cabala. They are the elementary principles of the written Verb, the reflection of that spoken Verb which created the world![4]

Is the Cabala the only system of symbolic relationships that can be used in this way? Of course not. The universe of human experience is so intricate in its structure and so multifarious in its expressions that any system like the Cabala must be an oversimplification, an attempt to bring the tremendous complexity of the cosmos within reach of mere human minds. No such simplification can ever be final. The world's spiritual traditions thus include many such systems, and no two of them try to make sense of the cosmos in the same way.

Yet for two and a half millennia, mystics and occultists across the Western world have put the Cabala in its various forms to work in the quest for understanding, and many of them have found it a valuable tool. Its long history, and the way that it has been adapted for the needs of many different religious traditions over the course of that history, have given it a clarity and a flexibility that can be matched by few other equivalent systems. These qualities make it a valid option even, or especially, in a period of confusion and disarray such as the present.

In the pages ahead I attempt to set out the philosophy and practice of the Cabala as I learned it from my teacher John Gilbert, expanded and enriched by my reading and study in more traditional Cabalistic literature, in the Pythagorean and Platonist traditions, and in the

---

[4] Lévi 2017, p. 21.

work of some more recent philosophies as well. I have also made use of some of the insights of Carl Jung, though I have had to free those from the weight of 19th-century scientific materialism that Jung's historical circumstances forced him to load atop them. Finally, I have woven in a few discoveries of my own.

As this suggests, what follows should not be taken as any kind of definitive statement of Cabalistic philosophy. It is my attempt to make sense of one way of understanding an ancient, complex, and richly detailed set of tools for exploring the universe of human experience. If you choose to study and practice the Cabala, using this system or any other, you will discover that your own insights will shape the way you understand the system, and this is as it should be. Where an ideology is an attempt to replace individual insights with some standardized set of opinions, the Cabala is a toolkit that different people can use to organize and work with their individual insights in uniquely personal ways.

The Tree of Life

"In the beginning God created the heavens and the earth," the Book of Genesis starts out. "The Tao created one, one created two," wrote Lao Tsu. These are two forms of an ancient and widespread insight into the origin of the world we experience. A unity unfolds into a polarity of two opposing but complementary forces: that is how the cosmos comes into being.

Pythagoras, who stands at the fountainhead of Western occultism, taught that the two principles of existence were Limit and the Unlimited. Later Pythagorean philosophers took this analysis further, and saw Limit and the Unlimited as the paired manifestations of a unity that stands behind them, unseen but inescapable. This is reflected in the words of Genesis just cited: the heavens are infinite, the earth is finite, and both are the creations of a divine power which transcends both.

In this vision of the creative process, therefore, there are three fundamental principles in the cosmos: the hidden unity and its two children or creations. You can think of these latter two principles as form and the formless, limit and the limitless, yang and yin, energy and matter, self and environment, or any other duality or polarity you wish. These varied sets of paired concepts are not identical or even interchangeable, but like the variables in an equation, they stand in relation to each other and to their common source in the same manner. Take any phenomenon you wish in the universe of human experience, and you can conceive of it as a unity that expresses itself in terms of a pair of polarized expressions.

The three drawers of the Cabalistic filing cabinet that are assigned to this aspect of human experience are the first three spheres of the Tree of Life. Their traditional numerical labels are 1, 2, and 3, the first three natural numbers. In Platonist and Pythagorean circles they were called the Monad, the Dyad, and the Triad. In the Jewish Cabala they were assigned more colorful Hebrew names: Kether, the Crown; Chokmah, Wisdom; and Binah, Understanding. In the teachings I received from John Gilbert, which centered with laser intensity on human consciousness and its practical applications, their names are Awareness, Intention, and Belief. Many other names could be assigned to them, but these will do for the time being.

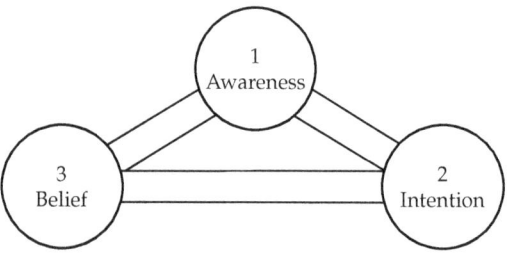

The primal triad

The three spheres just named form the primal triad, or as it is also called, the supernal triad or the Upper World. They are the first principles of the Tree of Life, and a division always separates them from the seven remaining spheres, which are the secondary principles or the Lower World. Our Cabalistic filing cabinet thus has three upper drawers and seven lower drawers. Between them is a gap, which is traditionally called the Abyss, a change of planes or a shifting of gears between the primary and secondary principles of the cosmos.

One way to understand the Abyss is to think of the difference between the way of thinking about the cosmos sketched out above and the way we normally perceive things. While it is true that every pair of opposites unfolds from a hidden unity, that's not what most of us experience. Instead, we are confronted by opposites in conflict, and if there is to be any unity between the opposites it usually has to be constructed with much labor.

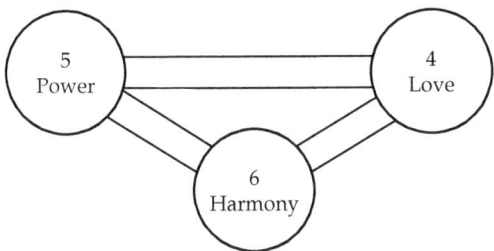

The reflected triad

Thus what lies below the Abyss, at the summit of the reality we experience directly, is an imperfect reflection of the primal triad. Like an image mirrored in water, it is reversed, with the two opposites above the third factor that unites them. At this level of the Tree of Life, the opposites no longer have the hidden unity present to hold them in balance. Instead, a harmony must be created between them.

The opposites and the harmony they create are the next three spheres of the Tree of Life. Their traditional numerical labels are 4, 5, and 6. Their names in Pythagorean and Platonist traditions are the Tetrad, the Pentad, and the Hexad; in the Jewish Cabala, they are Chesed, Mercy; Geburah, Severity; and Tiphareth, Beauty. In the Cabala I learned from John Gilbert they are Love, Power, and Harmony. They form the reflected triad of the Tree.

Once the opposites have entered into balance they begin to combine with each other and with the balanced state that has been born of their union. This produces the last four spheres of the Tree of Life, in which potential passes over into action. These are sometimes portrayed as a third triad, reflected from the second, with a fourth sphere left over below it. At other times they are understood as a tetrad of four linked principles of manifestation.

Each of these four spheres unfolds from those in the triad immediately above. In the terms I was taught, Love plus Harmony produces Desire; Power plus Harmony produces Competence; Love plus Power produces Foundation; and Love, Power, and Harmony all together produce Manifestation. Desire, Competence, Foundation, and Manifestation are of course John Gilbert's names for the last four spheres; the Pythagoreans and Platonists called them the Heptad, the Octad, the Ennead, and the Decad. In the Jewish Cabala they are Netzach, Victory; Hod, Glory; Yesod, Foundation; and Malkuth, Kingdom.

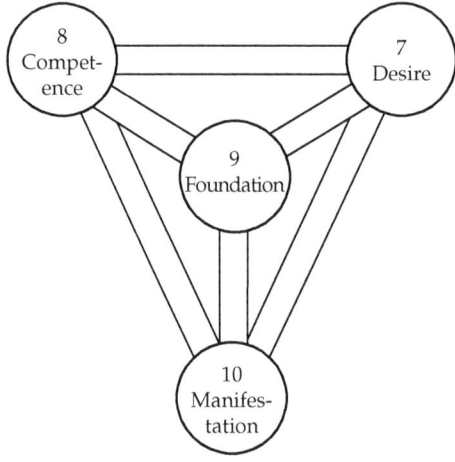

The tetrad

There is also an additional archetypal factor in this structure. In the middle of the Abyss, between the primal triad and the reflected triad, there is an additional factor which is not called a sphere but in certain very limited ways functions like one. In Hebrew this not-sphere is called Daath, which means Knowledge; in John Gilbert's Cabala it is simply called Knowledge. The Sepher Yetzirah, the oldest surviving work in the Jewish Cabalistic tradition, provides an important warning here: "10 is the number of the ineffable Sephiroth, 10 and not 9, ten and not 11." To say "10 and not 9" is to stress that the material world, the sphere of Manifestation, is a reality and not simply an illusion. To say "ten and not eleven" is to say that the knowledge we have, or claim to have, about the Tree of Life is less real than the Tree itself.

All this doubtless seems very bare and abstract, but then the same thing is true of an empty filing cabinet or a mathematical equation. Let's take a moment to put something into each of the drawers of the cabinet, or to suggest one value for each variable in the equation, before we proceed further.

The example I have in mind here is any action whatsoever that you or any other person consciously wills and performs. In order to begin any such action, you need three things. First, you need to be aware that the action is possible: this is Awareness, the first sphere. Second, you need to intend to do the action: this is Intention, the second sphere. Third, you need to believe that you can do the action: this is Belief,

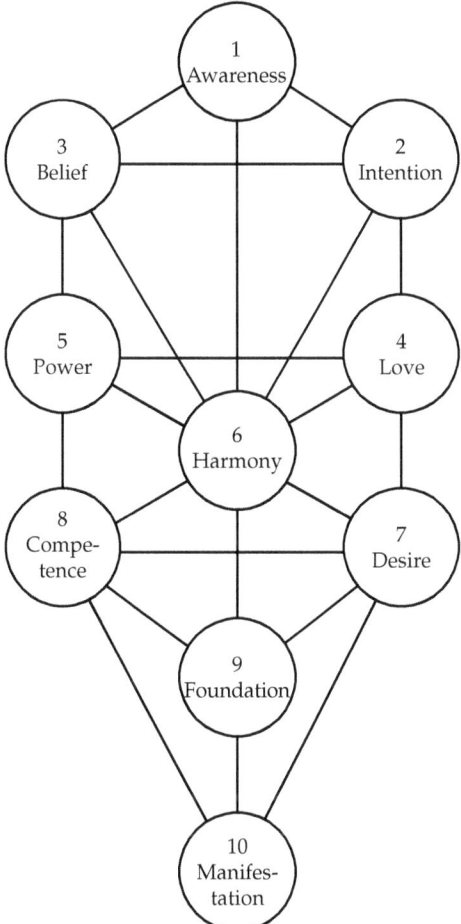

The Tree of Life

the third sphere. Without all three factors of the primal triad, you cannot even attempt the action.

Now comes the inevitable gap between the realm above the Abyss and the other, wholly different realm below it: in this case, between the factors that make an action possible and the factors that make it happen. In the middle of the gap is placed Knowledge, which belongs to neither side of the Abyss. Seen from above, it represents the factors that are below; seen from below, it represents the factors that are above. It is at once a bridge and a barrier, the gate and the guardian of the gate. It hovers like a phantom in the void.

Once below the Abyss, we reach the realm where possibility becomes actuality. What makes you attempt an action at a given place and time? First, you value the action or its intended results enough to pursue it then and there: this is Love, the fourth sphere. Second, you have the capacity to carry out the action then and there, or at least to attempt it: this is Power, the fifth sphere. Third, you assess the circumstances and decide that the balance of motive and capacity, of love and power, favors the attempt: this is Harmony, the sixth sphere. This gives you the reflected triad.

Now the powers of the reflected triad combine to create the tetrad of action. Motive plus circumstances give rise to a specific Desire. Power plus circumstances provide the capacity to act, which is an expression of Competence. Desire and Competence provide a Foundation for the action. When all three spheres of the second triad combine to make the action happen, it takes place, and its results become a Manifestation of the potential of the primal triad.

Once you have learned the names and basic meanings of the ten spheres, take the time to work through this process a few times with specific examples. Get a sense of how the Tree of Life functions as a map for the process by which an ordinary human action moves from possibility to reality. Doing this will make it much easier for you to grasp how the Tree works when you apply it more generally.

Numbers and archetypes

Treated as a simple sequence of numbered stages, the Tree of Life can seem dry and lifeless. It is when we take the next step and begin exploring the deeper meaning of numbers themselves that an inner life begins to flow through the Tree.

This requires a leap of consciousness for most students. People in modern industrial cultures generally think of numbers strictly in terms of quantity: so many of this, so many of that. Each of the first ten natural numbers, however, also has a qualitative dimension. It is through numbers as symbols, representing qualities, that we approach the archetypes of the ten spheres.

Nowadays most people associate the word "archetype" with the theories of the Swiss psychotherapist Carl Jung. Jung did not invent either the word or the concept, however. Behind his use of the term, as hinted earlier, lies the same Platonist traditions that gave rise to the Cabala itself. Jung himself studied those traditions closely by way of his well-known interest in Gnosticism and alchemy. Here as so often in his work, he was less a pioneer than a translator, taking ancient magical concepts and restating them in terms that could slip through the filters of the scientific materialism of his day and ours.

We can describe an archetype as one of the basic patterns of meaning that underlie all human thought. It is through participation in archetypes that anything means anything at all. Consider the experience of falling in love. A constellation of perceptions, thoughts, feelings, intuitions, and actions flows together into a single insight: "I love this person." An archetype—we can call it Eros, as Plato did in his dialogue *The Symposium*, or the anima or animus, as Jung did in his writings—has gathered up all these disparate raw materials and given them a new and potent meaning.

The same thing happens with numbers. Think of what happens when you realize that a set of apparently separate things are all connected. This is as much an archetypal experience as falling in love. As any Platonist could tell you, the archetype of the One has gathered all these seemingly separate phenomena up into itself and showed you that in a real and important sense, they are all one thing.

The archetypes are hardwired into the foundations of human consciousness. This does not mean, as Jung himself pointed out repeatedly in his writings, that they are purely psychological; as a scientist, he simply preferred to talk about their psychological dimension. Human beings and human consciousness are after all part of the wider world, not some alien presence shoved into the world from outside. Religious and occult traditions around the world and throughout time have pointed out in turn that the world we know through our ordinary senses is itself simply one part of a much greater world which we may as well call "spiritual." Cabalistic tradition from the time of Pythagoras on has held that the ten number-archetypes are basic not only to human consciousness but to the cosmos as a whole, in its spiritual, mental, and material aspects alike.

It is impossible to define an archetype: the archetypes are too abstract, too fundamental, and too all-encompassing for that. The best that the human mind can do is to point to some of the ways an archetype expresses itself in human experience, as I have done above with the archetypes of the Lover and the One. The natural numbers from one to ten, in their bare simplicity, are nothing more than indications of the same kind.

With this in mind, we can attempt a first pass through the ten archetypes of the Tree of Life. The first has already been mentioned: the Monad, the archetype of unity. This is the principle by which we can experience anything at all as one thing, and it is also the principle by which we can experience everything taken all together as one thing. It is expressed in human consciousness by awareness, because to be aware of anything is to be aware of it as a thing, as a unity and thus something that participates in the Monad.

The second is the Dyad, the archetype of duality, polarity, and division. This is the principle by which we can distinguish any individual thing from everything else—the principle that permits any one thing to stand apart from its background. It is inseparable from the Monad, since the thing it distinguishes becomes one thing as distinct from everything else, but it is also the division and disruption of the Monad, the breach that divides 1 into 2. It is therefore the principle of change. It is expressed in human consciousness by intention, because every intention aims at a goal to the exclusion of all other things.

The third is the Triad, the archetype of completion and perfection, and also of time, since the flow of time always involves the triad of past, present, and future. This is the stabilizing principle that joins together what the Dyad has disrupted, bringing the object and its background together into a new unity. It is therefore the principle of rest. It is expressed in human consciousness by belief, because our beliefs are the framework we use to make sense of ourselves and the universe.

If we proceed beyond the Triad, once again we encounter Knowledge, the presence that hovers in the Abyss. In terms of the archetypes we have been tracing, it is represented by a number between 3 and 4. Among the natural numbers, of course, there is no such thing, and this again points out that Knowledge is not a reality in its own right: Lao Tsu's saying, "The Tao that can be described is not the eternal Tao," is especially relevant here. A cryptic passage in the Bible describes Knowledge as "a time, and times, and half a time," that is, three and a half times. It is perhaps better represented by the irrational number π, which is between 3 and 4 and can never be calculated exactly.

Once we are below the Abyss we are back in the world of the natural numbers as archetypes. The fourth of these is the Tetrad, the archetype of structure and form, and also of space, since human beings always tend to think of space in terms of four directions extending out from the individual as center. This is the principle that allows a universe to come into being, since every object, no matter how tiny, exists in the three dimensions of space and the one dimension of time. The Pythagoreans used to symbolize this by adding the first four numbers—$1 + 2 + 3 + 4 = 10$—and later Cabalists used a similar additive process as one of the ways to assign the spheres of the Tree to four worlds. The Tetrad is the generative number, because once the Tetrad exists the rest of the Tree of Life unfolds inevitably to its completion. It is expressed in human consciousness by love, the generative principle among human beings.

The fifth is the Pentad, the archetype of conflict and force. Now that space and time have come into being, conflict between different things cannot be avoided. A Cabalistic tradition holds that the Pentad is a door through which both good and evil enter the newborn universe. Thus the Pentad represents the universe in all its moral complexity, and it brings with it the power and necessity of choice. The Pentad is also the archetype of marriage, which is of course also a choice, and the Pythagoreans taught that this is demonstrated by the fact that $5 = 2 + 3$, the marriage of the Dyad and the Triad. It is expressed in human consciousness by power, the capacity to sustain conflict and to achieve our goals.

The sixth is the Hexad, the archetype of harmony and balance. The conflicts set in motion by the Pentad are not eternal. As they unfold in space and time, they eventually achieve a balance, and from that balance emerges harmony. From harmony, in turn, it becomes possible to glimpse worlds or dimensions higher than the realm of conflict between opposites. The Hexad is the great balancing factor in the Tree of Life, the point at which time and space, force and form, and all the other dualities set in motion by the Dyad achieve rest through their integration in a larger realm. The Pythagoreans taught that this is shown by the fact that $6 = 2 \times 3$, the progeny of the marriage of the Dyad and Triad. It is expressed in human consciousness by harmony itself.

The seventh is the Heptad, traditionally the most sacred of numerical archetypes. It is on the seventh day, according to the Book of Genesis, that the Divine rested from its labors and declared that the world was very good. In many traditions around the world, similarly, there are seven heavens above the earth and seven underworlds below it. The Heptad is also the archetype of spontaneity and the unexpected. From the harmony of the Hexad, new things emerge that cannot be known in advance in any way accessible to human thought, as the higher dimension glimpsed from the Hexad becomes an active force. Thus the universe becomes complex and richly textured. The unexpected nature of the Heptad is shown, according to the Pythagoreans, by the fact that, alone among the first ten natural numbers, 7 has no divisors but 1 and no multiples at all. It is expressed in human consciousness by desire, which is spontaneous and often unexpected, following rules of its own that are not the rules of conscious reason.

The eighth is the Octad, the archetype of communication, synthesis, and equilibrium. As the universe becomes complex, each of the things in it enters into interaction with the others. Patterns are formed, dissolved, and reformed in a process of constant change and interchange which leads to a state of equilibrium or moving balance, in which change itself becomes the guarantor of stability. Its complexity is shown numerically by 8's place as the only cubic number in the first ten natural numbers, the product of $2 \times 2 \times 2$. Since it goes beyond the Heptad, it also represents the emergence of capacities beyond the normal human range. It is expressed in human consciousness by competence, the principle that enables us to deal effectively with a complex universe, but which also requires us to develop capacities that are not inborn in us.

The ninth is the Ennead, the archetype of completion and limitation. Just as the conflicts set in motion by the Pentad come to rest in the harmony of the Hexad, the teeming complexity of the Heptad passes through the synthesis and equilibrium of the Octad into the stability of the Ennead. At this stage all the changes have been rung, all the interactions have worked themselves out, and the universe settles into a steady state. The Pythagoreans held that this is shown by the fact that $9 = 3 \times 3$, the product of the archetype of rest multiplied by itself. It is expressed in human consciousness as the foundation of thought, feeling, and action established by all eight of the previous principles.

It is with the tenth archetype, the Decad, that the cycle begins anew, because 10 is simply 1 raised to a higher decimal power. This is the archetype of manifestation, of the world as it actually exists around us, in which the first nine archetypes each unfold their full potential and flow into one another. Thus the Decad completes the sequence of the archetypes on the Tree of Life by closing the circle. Like the ouroboros, the symbolic serpent that devours its own tail, the Tree of Life is cyclical in nature. Its basic archetypes set out the ten steps by which the universe comes into being and reestablishes its original unity within a new complexity. It is expressed in human consciousness by the ever-changing manifestation that the universe presents to the self at every moment.

As with the material introduced already, it is useful to take the time to think through each of these archetypal patterns until you are familiar with them. Be sure to associate them with the sphere that represents them and the patterns that relate them to one another and the Tree as a whole. As you do this, the diagram of the Tree will stop being a mere abstract pattern and start turning into a framework of basic concepts you can use to understand the universe and yourself. Keep all this in mind as we move on to the ways that these ten archetypes are arranged and brought into relationship with one another.

Pillars, worlds, and paths

Since early on in the history of the tradition, Cabalists have traced out various patterns on the Tree of Life. These can be used to help the mind of the student to grasp the subtler meanings of the principles just described. They also play an important role in the meditative exercises central to the tradition's practical applications.

One of the most basic and most important of these is defined by three pillars formed by the vertical columns of spheres in the conventional diagram of the Tree. Here the metaphor comes from the Old Testament descriptions of the Temple of Solomon, as interpreted symbolically in initiatory traditions such as Freemasonry. According to the Biblical accounts, the Temple had two huge brass pillars standing in front of it, one on each side of the entrance. They were named Jachin, "established," and Boaz, "strength."

Jewish Cabalists associated these symbolically with the pillars of fire and cloud that guided the Israelites on their flight from Egypt. From there, they developed into symbols of duality in general, playing the same role in the Cabala that the yin-yang symbol plays in Taoism and Chinese philosophy generally. On Pythagorean principles, these two pillars were completed with the addition of a third, and all three were then set out on the Tree of Life diagram, as shown in the illustration.

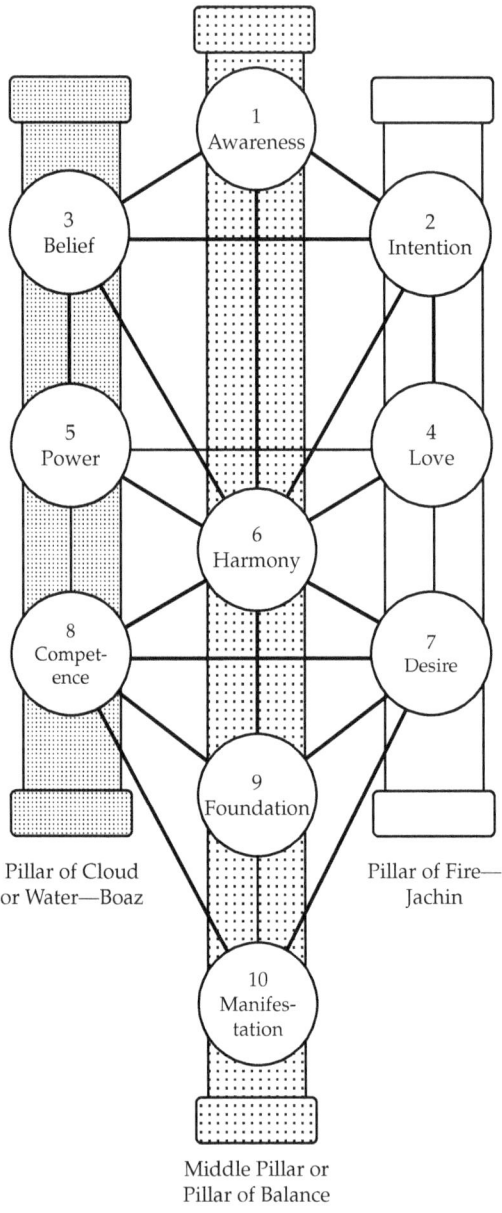

Three pillars

The right-hand pillar, the pillar of force descending from Intention through Love to Desire, represents the active, transforming, outward-moving energies of the Tree, and of everything in the cosmos represented by the Tree. The left-hand pillar, the pillar of form descending from Belief through Power to Competence, represents the receptive, stabilizing, inward-moving energies of the Tree and the cosmos. Between them, held in balance by both of them and holding them both in balance, is the middle pillar, the pillar of balance descending from Awareness through Harmony and Foundation to Manifestation.

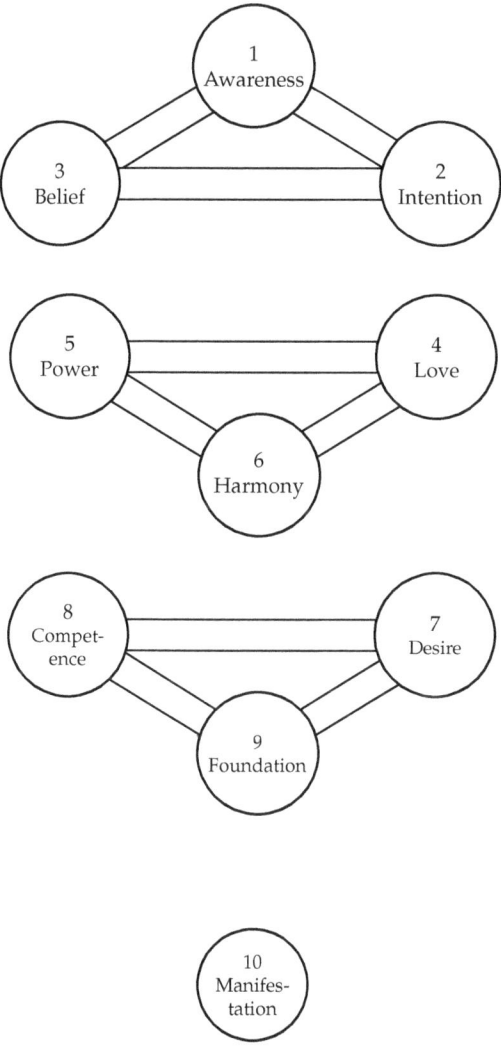

Three triads

Notice how the three columns help sort the Tree into the triads discussed earlier. In the first triad, above the Abyss, a sphere on the middle pillar gives rise to a pair of spheres, one on each of the two pillars to the side;

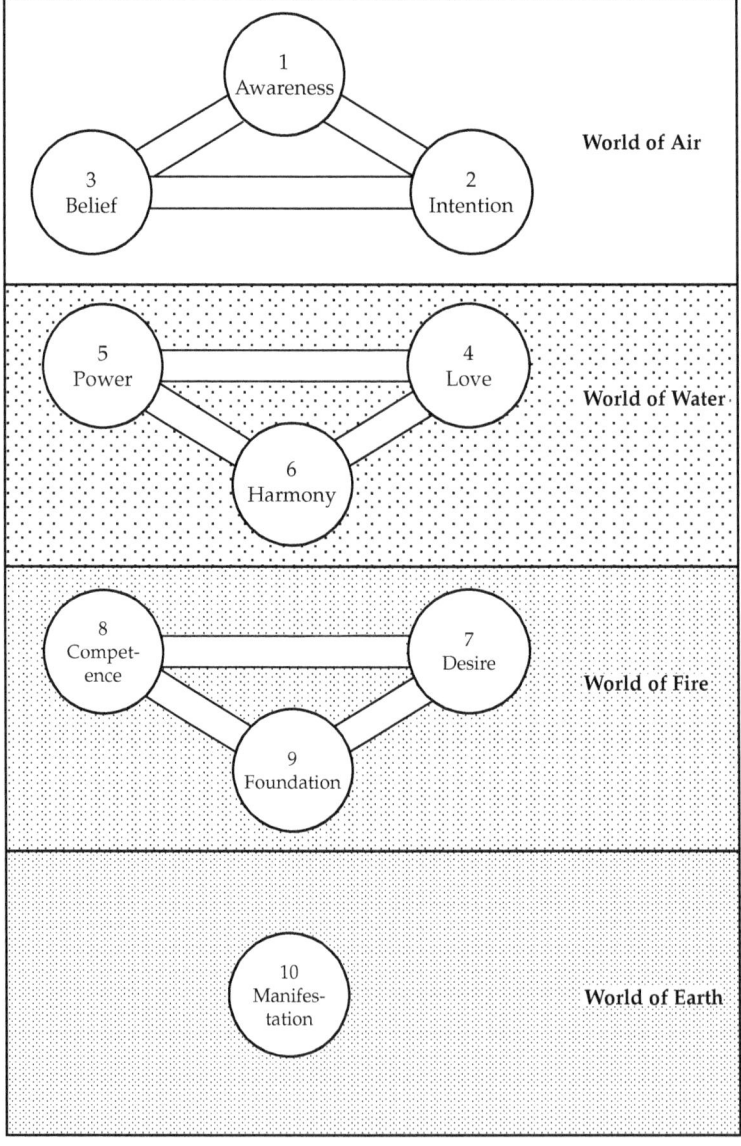

Four worlds

in each of the following triads, below the Abyss, two spheres, one on each of the two side pillars, give rise to a single sphere on the middle pillar.

This same principle can be applied to every adjacent pair of spheres on the Tree, providing an even richer set of symbolic triads for meditation and practice. The rule here is simple. Take any set of three spheres on the Tree; provided that they are connected directly to one another by paths, they can be understood and explored in meditation as a triad. Some—for example, Harmony, Desire, and Competence—belong to the "one creates two" type; others—for example, Desire, Competence, and Foundation—belong to the "two creates one" type; while still others—for example, Love, Harmony, and Desire—belong to both types and can and should be investigated in meditation from both perspectives.

This same pattern of triads can also be interpreted in a different way, as a set of four worlds in which the spheres of the Tree of Life have their places. These worlds correspond to the planes or levels of being in other esoteric spiritual traditions, and they are traditionally assigned to the four elements of ancient cosmology: air, water, fire, and earth. Different Cabalistic traditions, however, assign elements to worlds in different ways. Every such assignment known to me gives the fourth world and the tenth sphere to the element of earth, but other than that, disagreement reigns.

The teachings I received from John Gilbert take their elemental pattern from the Sepher Yetzirah. In the first chapter of the Sepher Yetzirah, the elements proceed from the spirit of the Divine in this order: first air, then water, then fire, and then the six directions of space, which correspond to the world of ordinary experience and therefore to earth. This order, as shown in the diagram above, is applied to the four worlds.

Interestingly, this same order has an unexpected echo in the geometry of the tattwas, a set of symbols assigned to the four elements in Hindu tradition and borrowed from there by Western occultists in the heyday of the Hermetic Order of the Golden Dawn. The tattwas of the four material elements are Vayu, representing air; Apas, representing water; Tejas, representing fire; and Prithivi, representing earth. Notice the number of line segments in each of the tattwa symbols: Vayu is a circle, made from one continuous line; Apas is a crescent, made from two curved lines; Tejas is a triangle, made from three straight lines; and Prithivi is a square, made from four straight lines.

Each of the four worlds is a mode or manifestation of existence. The first and highest world, which is formed from the primal triad, is therefore the world of air, corresponding to the tattwa Vayu. This is the realm of spirit, and in fact the word "spirit" comes from a Latin word meaning "breath" or "air;" it can also be seen as the realm of the unconscious self, the aspect of the individual which lies deeper than consciousness can reach. This is the world of archetypes, the ultimate source of all our thoughts and ideas. It is the first created reality to come forth from the unmanifest Divine, bearing with it the divine manifestations to humanity, and so it can be considered the divine world, or the world of God or the gods.

The second world, which is formed from the reflected triad, is the world of water, corresponding to the tattwa Apas. This is the reflection of the first world, the world of creation where archetypes first take on specific forms, and it is the realm of soul and the subconscious self. It is also the world of the higher reaches of thought and emotion. It is associated in various traditions with the archangels, logoi, or spirits who serve the Divine, and so can be considered the archangelic world or the world of higher or protective spirits.

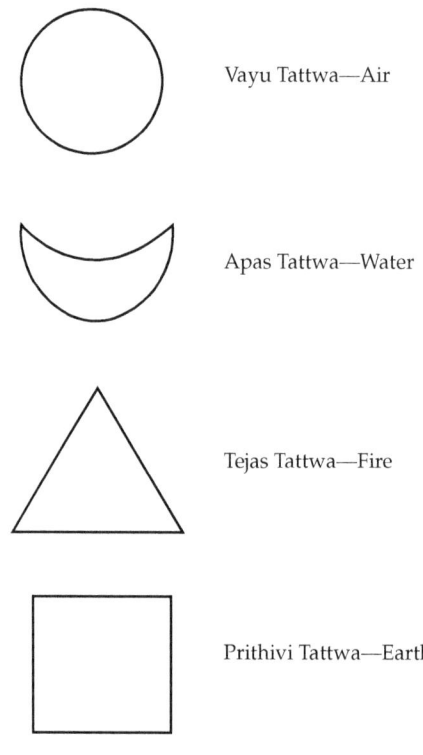

Four tattwas

The third world, the second reflection of the primal triad, is the world of fire, corresponding to the tattwa Tejas. This is the world of formation, where forces descending from the creative processes of the world of water are shaped and reshaped in constant flux. It includes the third triad and is the realm of ego and of the conscious self. As such, it is also the world of desire and aversion, and of all the expressions of the life force. The lower dimensions of human thought and emotion belong here, and so do their equivalents throughout the natural world. It can thus be considered the world of the macrocosm or of nature.

The fourth world, the final result of the creative process, is the world of earth, corresponding to the tattwa Prithivi. This is the world of action, where the archetypal, creative, and formative forces from higher on the Tree finish their descent into the world of space and time. It includes only the tenth sphere Manifestation and is the realm of matter

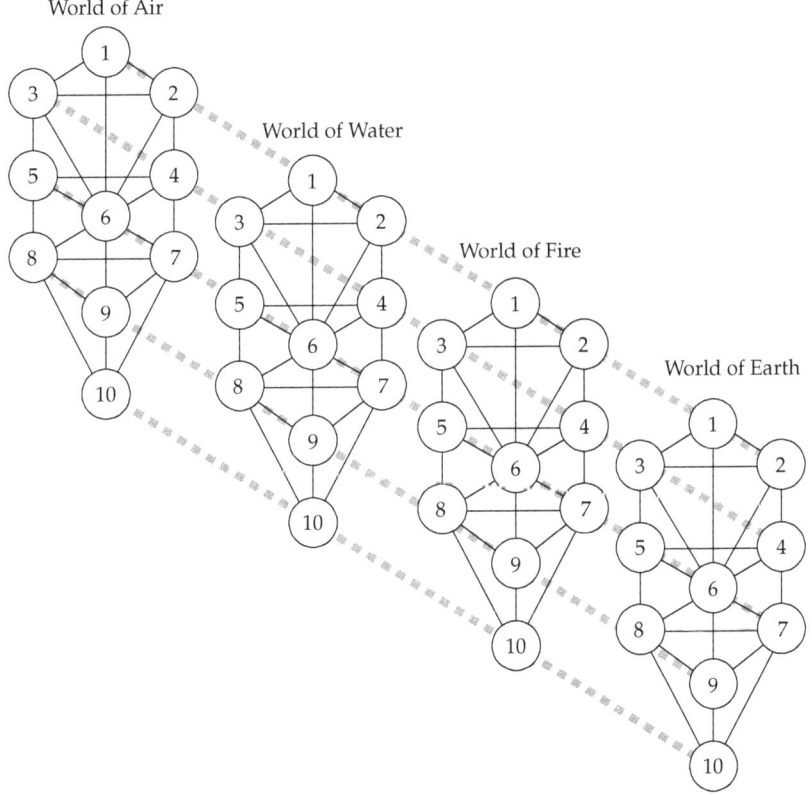

Four trees

and the material body. Since each individual is a unique manifestation of the primal triad, this world can also be considered the world of the microcosm or the individual human being.

While each of these worlds has a special relationship with certain spheres, as just discussed, in another sense each sphere exists in all four worlds. For some purposes it is therefore useful to think of the four worlds as four Trees of Life, each with its own ten spheres. This way of thinking about the cosmos goes back very far into Pythagorean and Platonist tradition, and may have its origins in the Egyptian teachings Pythagoras brought to Europe.

In a richly symbolic passage, to cite one ancient example, the Christian Platonist Clement of Alexandria portrayed the wisdom of ancient Egypt as a collection of 42 sacred scrolls written by the legendary initiate Hermes Trismegistus. The first ten scrolls were in the keeping of the oracle-priests, and dealt with gods, laws, and the training of priests; the second set of ten was in the keeping of the priests who had custody of the images of the gods, and dealt with hymns and offerings; the third set of ten was kept by the scribe, and dealt with cosmography, topography, and geography; and the fourth set of 12 included four scrolls on horoscopes kept by the astrologers, six scrolls on medicine kept by the healers, and two scrolls on the duties and rites of kingship kept by the sacred chanters. Forty of those scrolls had to be present in the hall where the pharaoh's vizier gave his judgments.

No such set of 42 scrolls has turned up anywhere in the ample written records of ancient Egypt. Clearly Clement was speaking in the allegorical style common among Platonists. Each set of ten scrolls represents a Pythagorean tetractys or, in modern Cabalistic terms, one of the four worlds. The first is the world of air, which corresponds to the gods, the basic principles or laws of existence, and thus to the training of those who deal with the Divine directly. The second is the world of water, which deals with the spiritual helpers and reflections of the Divine—in ancient Egypt, as in most other ancient societies, images of gods and goddesses were ceremonially empowered so that a spirit-messenger from the deity they represented would be present in them. The third is the world of fire, the macrocosm or world of nature, and thus includes humanity's knowledge of the heavens and the earth.

As for the fourth, the fact that there were 12 scrolls but only ten of them had a place in the judgment hall had a specific lesson in ancient times. In Middle Platonism and the Gnostic traditions that developed from it, the number 12 represented the signs of the zodiac and the world of everyday life ruled by astrological forces, while the number ten represented the spiritual world governed by the tetractys. In one of the surviving Hermetic treatises from ancient times, for that reason, moving from the 12 to the ten becomes a metaphor for awakening to the spiritual realm.

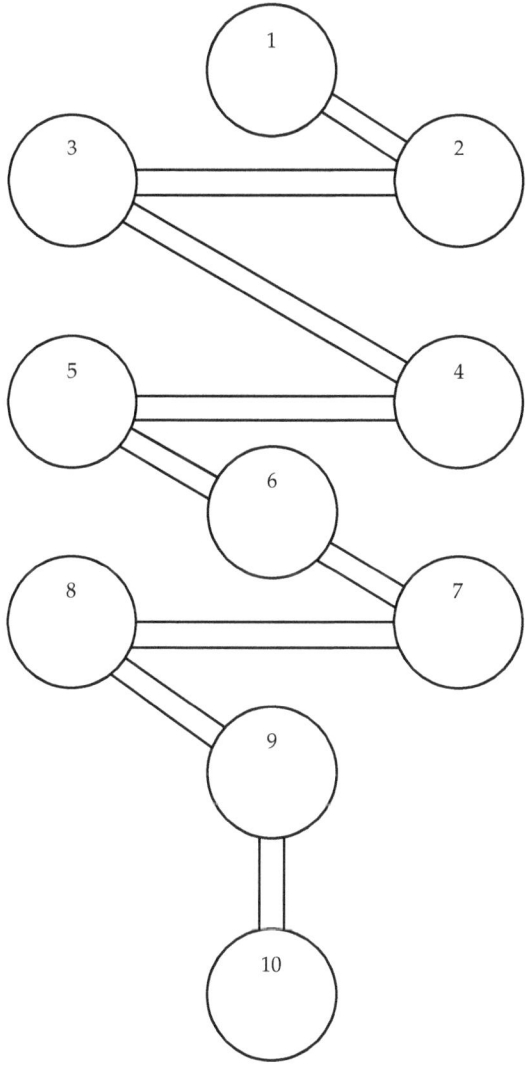

Lightning flash

This same symbolism underlies Clement's metaphor and provides the key to the fourth world. Set aside the two scrolls that were reserved for royalty, and the ten that remain deal with things relevant to the life of the individual: on the one hand, the astrological factors that shape the personality; on the other, the factors of health and disease that affect the body. Thus the world of earth is the microcosm, the individual human being in which all these worlds manifest.

Another important pattern structuring the Tree of Life is formed by the ten spheres in the order of their unfolding. This is called the lightning flash, drawing on an image from the *Sepher Yetzirah*, or the flaming sword, which borrows from the Book of Genesis. The lightning flash traces out the process by which every created thing comes into being—and this is true whether the thing is created by the Divine or by a created being such as you or me. This process deserves close attention and study, so that the process of creation can be well understood and used as a guide in everyday life. This pattern also plays an important role in the practical applications of this system of Cabala, as will be explained in a later chapter.

Yet the metaphor of the flaming sword also makes this pattern a warning. In the allegory of the Book of Genesis, a flaming sword is placed before the gate of Eden to keep fallen humanity out. This teaches that the process of creation is also the process by which we become enmeshed in the tenth sphere, the world of everyday life. It must therefore be overcome in order to awaken to the spheres and worlds that lie beyond.

The response to the lightning flash, the route by which we rise up out of our entanglement in ordinary existence, forms another pattern, one of immense importance. This pattern is formed by the 22 paths of the Tree of Life. Where the lightning flash relates the spheres to one another from above downward, the paths relate them to one another from the bottom upward. They are the routes that the Cabalist uses to ascend through the spheres and worlds from the realm of material existence to the highest plane that the human soul can reach.

Where the basic pattern and meanings of the spheres is fixed in nearly all versions of the Cabala, the pattern and meanings of the paths vary significantly from tradition to tradition and school to school. In her influential work on the Tree of Life, *The Mystical Qabalah*, English occultist Dion Fortune summarized this distinction in a memorable way, pointing out that the spheres are objective but the paths are subjective. Another way to say the same thing is that the spheres exist independently of us but the paths—or, more precisely, those paths that we are capable of traversing—have to be made by us.

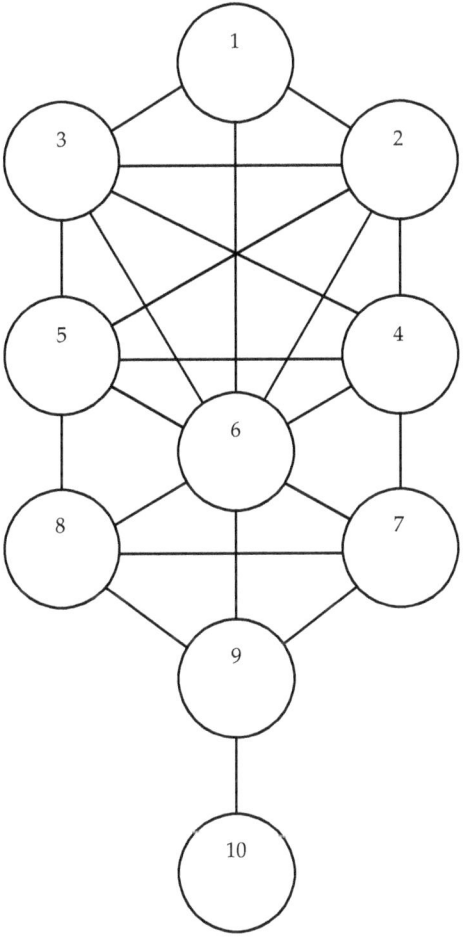

Rabbinic tree of life

By tradition there are 22 paths connecting the ten spheres. Not all Cabalistic schools put the paths in the same places; some Jewish Rabbinic schools, for example, arrange the paths on the Tree as shown above, while Arthur Edward Waite, in his Christian mystical version of the Golden Dawn system, used the version shown below as the basis for its degree work:

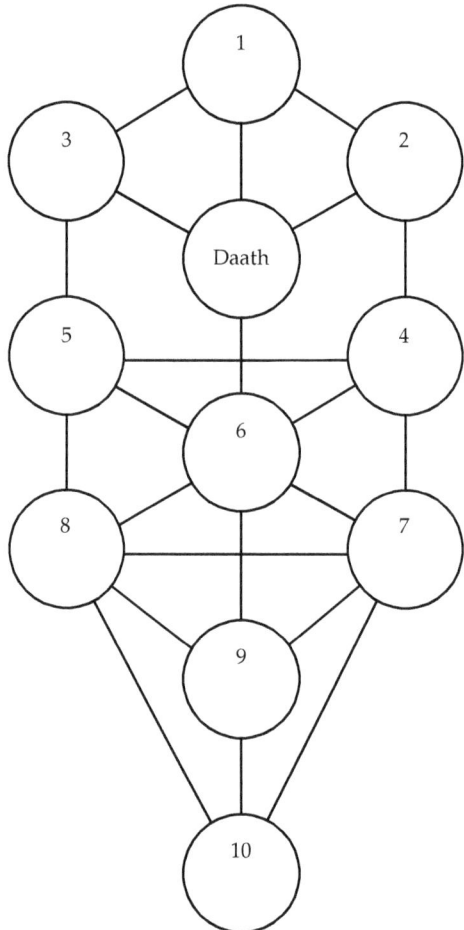

Waite tree of life

Most other Western occult schools use the arrangement set out in the earlier diagrams in this book, as shown below. This is the version that John Gilbert used in his Cabalistic teaching, and I have followed his lead here as in most other things. How the various symbols of the Paths—letters, numbers, tarot cards, and more—are assigned to the

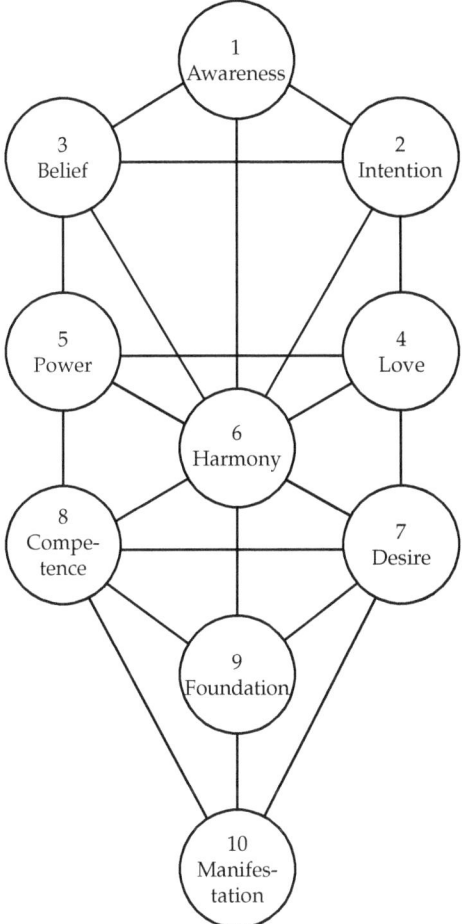

The Tree of Life

paths varies even more wildly, with many different systems in use and considerable variation within those systems. We will explore this when we start sorting out the symbolism of the Tree later on.

Of these paths, the most important are the three that rise straight up the central axis of the Tree. In some Cabalistic literature the paths connecting the eighth, sixth, and seventh spheres in that order are portrayed symbolically as a bow, and the paths connecting the seventh and eighth spheres to the tenth are the bowstring. The path of the arrow, then, is formed by the middle pillar of the Tree of Life, rising straight up from the tenth sphere through the ninth and sixth spheres to the highest attainment possible to the human soul. The preliminary work on the Tree of Life is likened to the winding path of a serpent climbing through the boughs and branches of a tree. At a certain point, however, it becomes possible—and indeed necessary—to leave the path of the serpent and become the archer who shoots straight up to and through the sun.

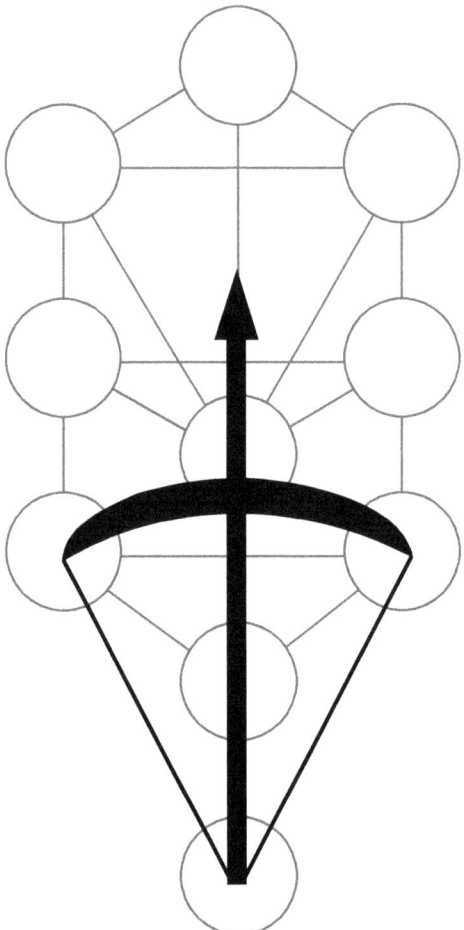

The path of the arrow

The sword or dagger is therefore the symbol of creation or involution, the process of descent into matter. The arrow or spear is accordingly the symbol of initiation or evolution, the process of rising up out of matter. Approach a great many myths and legends with this in mind and unexpected depths open up; to cite only one example, it is anything but accidental that in Christian mythology John the Baptist, who was born at midsummer, was killed by a sword, while Jesus, who was born at midwinter, was stabbed with a spear. Mythic images such as these make good themes for meditation.

All these patterns will come into their own once you begin practical work with the Cabala. For now, it can be useful to go over the Tree of Life sphere by sphere in your mind, reminding yourself of how each sphere relates to these patterns. Which pillar includes the sphere? Which triad embraces it? Which world gives it its context? Where does it fit on the lightning flash? What spheres connect to it through the paths, and how does it relate to the path of the arrow? Once you can think through such questions easily you will be prepared for the work to come.

The religious dimension

In the Jewish versions of the Cabala it became standard practice very early on to assign the ten spheres of the Tree of Life to the ten titles assigned to the God of Israel in the Old Testament. That custom was carried over intact into the Christian Cabala and passed from there into most of the earlier versions of the occult Cabala. At the hands of several leading members of the Hermetic Order of the Golden Dawn, and then of the Golden Dawn's eccentric alumnus Aleister Crowley, that habit became the template on which pantheons were applied wholesale to the Tree of Life like so many sets of interchangeable parts.

The difficulty with this approach is that deities are not merely arbitrary symbols to be plugged into the available slots of the Tree of Life. Gods and goddesses are persons, not abstractions, and it is a mistake to include them in your Cabalistic work unless you are prepared to accept the issues and responsibilities that accompany dealings with persons: persons who, it might be added, are considerably wiser and more powerful than you are.

To invoke a deity is to enter into a relationship. If you have such a relationship or want to establish one, including deities among the symbolism of the Tree of Life you use in your personal Cabalistic practice is entirely appropriate. In the system of Cabala I was taught by

John Gilbert, however, whether to do this—and of course which deity or deities to include if you do this—must always be a personal choice. That choice, in turn, is best made on the basis of your own personal religious beliefs.

It is useful here to keep in mind that the Cabala was not originally a religious teaching. It emerged from Pythagorean and Platonist circles that blended philosophy and spirituality in a way our modern cultural categories have a hard time addressing. We tend to divide the world into two realms, a religious realm that includes the Divine and the spiritual side of life, and a secular realm that includes everything else. The Platonist perspective, by contrast, traces out a third realm between spirit and matter.

That third realm is the realm of mind. It includes what modern cultures call psychology, but it recognizes that mind is present everywhere and in all things, not simply an oddity that occurs in certain lumps of meat called human brains. It blends with the world of spirit on one side and the world of matter on the other; it is the proper realm of many kinds of spiritual practice, including magic—in the definition given it by Dion Fortune, the art and science of causing changes in consciousness in accordance with will. This is the realm where the Cabala has its proper place, exploring the ways that human consciousness mediates between spirit and matter and experiences the influences of both.

Properly speaking, then, the Cabala does not claim to define the religious realm any more than it sets out rules for the realm of physical matter. You will not be able to solve theological disputes using it, any more than you can use it to assess the value of a scientific theory. This is why it can be used with nearly any religion. It can also be practiced in the absence of any religion, so long as the person who practices it keeps an open mind concerning spiritual things. It works poorly with dogmatic religious fundamentalism, or with the equally dogmatic kind of atheism that insists that there can be no gods. Given any set of beliefs that include an openness to religious experience, on the other hand, it works well.

In the teachings I studied with John Gilbert, the three realms we have just been discussing map out neatly onto the Tree of Life. The religious realm, the realm of the Divine and of transcendent spiritual realities, corresponds to the primal triad. The secular realm is primarily the tenth sphere of Manifestation, but it also includes the rest of the lower tetrad: the desires we direct toward the material world, the competence with which we approach it, and the life force that provides a foundation for our work there. The realm between, the realm of mind proper, is the reflected triad of Love, Power, and Harmony. In terms of the division of the Tree into four elemental worlds, in turn, the Divine and all that pertains to it belongs to the world of air, the Cabala and its practices to the world of water, the various arts and sciences our species uses to deal with the material realm to the world of fire, and the realities of everyday existence to the world of earth.

As noted in the previous section, it is entirely possible to assign each of these four worlds ten spheres of its own, and so the ten titles of the God of Israel (or any other set of divine names you happen to prefer) can be assigned to the ten spheres of the world of air. For the purposes of Cabalistic practice, however, it is generally more useful to work with a single Tree of Life, to assign the world of air and the realm of the Divine to the primal triad, and to leave the seven lower spheres to the realms below the Divine.

For the purposes of teaching, and in his own spiritual practices as well, John Gilbert liked to assign the three highest spheres of the Tree a set of abstract labels: the Divine Creator, the Divine Father, and the Divine Mother. These echo a common pattern found in the Jewish tradition of the Cabala, in which Abba, "father," is a title of the second sphere and Aima, "mother," a title of the third. At the same time, John freely admitted that the first three spheres can also be assigned just as well to the three persons of the Christian Trinity, the Father, the Son, and the Holy Spirit.

Go back to the older Platonist traditions and the possibilities multiply further. In Pythagorean writings about the tetractys, the number 1, was always seen as male and the number 2 as female—in the Pythagorean text *The Theology of Arithmetic*, for instance, they are identified with the god Zeus and the goddess Demeter, respectively.[5] This text goes out of its way not to mention the deity assigned to the number 3, but in the Greek mystery traditions Pythagoras studied so closely, the child of Zeus and Demeter was Dionysus. That triad—Zeus for the first sphere, Demeter for the second, and Dionysus for the third—can be used by modern Cabalists just as effectively as those already discussed, provided that the Cabalists in question either have a relationship with these three deities or are willing to enter into one.

---

[5] Waterfield 1988, p. 46.

Triads including a god, a goddess, and a child of either sex were quite common in ancient Pagan traditions and are far from uncommon in modern polytheist faiths. If Raphael Patai's well-researched book *The Hebrew Goddess* is correct, for that matter, Jews in the days when Solomon's temple still stood worshipped a triad that included the god Yahweh, the goddess Asherah, and their daughter the goddess Anath.

Yet this is far from the only form of divine triad found in ancient or modern times. Some ancient faiths worshipped a god and two goddesses, others a goddess and two gods, and still others three gods or three goddesses. Nor is it necessary that all three figures be divine: a triad formed by the God of Israel and the two supreme archangels Metatron and Sandalphon is documented in some esoteric Jewish sources.

In modern Hinduism, the most popular and prolific of the surviving polytheist religions, the Trimurti—the triad of the three great gods Brahma, Vishnu, and Shiva—is only one of a bumper crop of triads described in the scriptures and reverenced by worshippers. In Buddhism, meanwhile, it is extremely common to see images of the Buddha flanked by two bodhisattvas, most often Avalokiteshvara the bodhisattva of compassion and Manjushri the bodhisattva of wisdom.[6] Here again, the triadic pattern is alive and well.

Note here again that these triads do not follow any particular pattern of gender. In many books on the occult Cabala, the second sphere of the Tree of Life is defined as male and the third sphere as female. John Gilbert used this pattern when he assigned the second sphere to the Divine Father and the third to the Divine Mother. Yet the number 2 was considered feminine in Pythagorean teaching, as noted above, so the Greek triad of Zeus, Demeter, and Dionysus can be assigned readily enough to the first three spheres in order, as can the ancient Hebrew triad of Yahweh, Asherah, and Anath; the same pattern is suggested by the first three trumps of the tarot, the Magician followed by the High Priestess and the Empress. Nor is it unworkable, if you happen to follow a religion with one great goddess and two lesser gods, to assign the goddess to the first sphere and the gods to the two others.

Which of these many triads should you place at the summit of the Tree of Life in your own personal work? The one that receives your prayers, of course. If you are a Christian, the Father, the Son, and the

---

[6] A bodhisattva ranks just below a buddha in Buddhist teaching.

Holy Spirit belong in those places. If you are a Hindu, whichever triad of deities you worship primarily can be placed there.

The same rule applies equally to any other religion you may happen to follow. If yours is a strictly monotheistic religion, place your god in the first and highest sphere and conceive of the second and third spheres as the two most important manifestations of the god's power. If yours is a religion that reveres a pair of deities rather than a triad, place your deities in the second and third spheres and assign the first to the divine unity that lies beyond them. The Tree is flexible that way.

And if you have not found a religious faith that appeals to you, but you are open to the possibility of religious experience? John Gilbert's preferred labels, Divine Creator for the first sphere, Divine Father for the second, and Divine Mother for the third, are suitable in that case. Leave them as abstractions if you wish, and see what happens as you begin working with the practical material in this book.

Ultimately, the opinions you have about the Divine are much less important than the purveyors of prefabricated ideologies would like you to think. As you proceed in the work and explore the inner realms to which your consciousness has access, your opinions may change, and if you reach the summit of human possibility and stand on the brink of the Abyss, awaiting the descending grace of the Divine, the response you get may or may not be anything remotely like what you expect. The Divine is not subject to human opinions, after all, or anything else apart from its own inscrutable will.

Macrocosm and microcosm

The Tree of Life is among other things a map of the process by which the cosmos and everything in it comes into being. Since the nature of everything reflects the process by which it is born—the English word "nature," after all, comes ultimately from the Latin word *nascor*, "to be born"—the Tree is also a diagram of the nature of every created thing. In the language of Renaissance occultism, every individual thing in the universe is a *microcosm*, literally a little universe, and reflects the *macrocosm*, the greater universe.

In Cabalistic teachings one standard way to make sense of the Tree of Life is to see it as a map shared by both these universes, each in its own way. There are various ways to map each of them onto the Tree. For example, it used to be standard to assign the nested spheres of the old Earth-centered cosmology onto the Tree of Life as an image of the macrocosm, and this habit remains in place today, even among people who are well aware that the Earth circles the Sun.

Here again, however, it is important to remember the image of the Tree of Life as a filing cabinet, and not to mistake it for a fixed set of doctrines. Any way of understanding the macrocosm or the microcosm can be mapped onto the Tree of Life and used as file folders, to continue the metaphor, in the ten drawers of our filing cabinet.

42   REVISIONING THE TREE OF LIFE

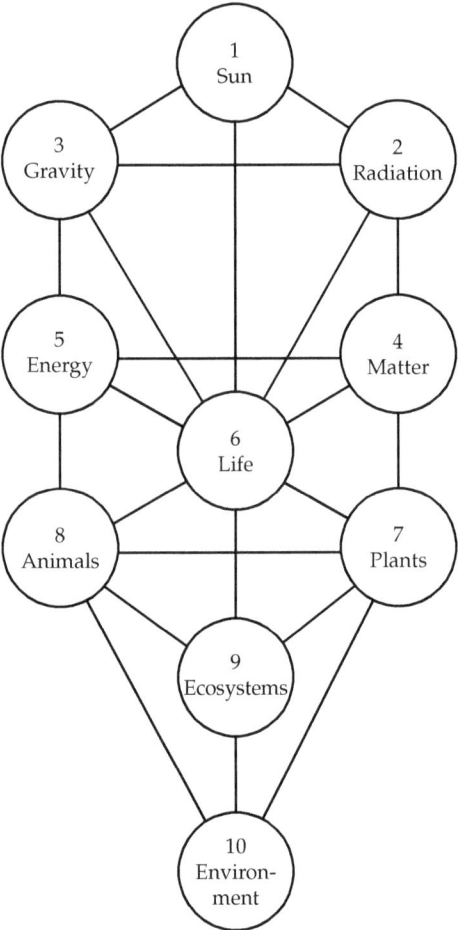

The Tree of Life in ecology

An example may help communicate this point better than any amount of abstract discussion. The science of ecology is at least as suitable as a source of Cabalistic metaphor as any other. Arguably, if our species intends to survive on this planet for very much longer, a certain amount of attention to this science is appropriate! The diagram above shows how the basic concepts of ecology can be assigned to the ten spheres of the Tree.

At the top of the Tree, the first sphere represents the Sun, the source of all light and life on our planet. It has two major effects that shape our lives: the light, heat, and other forms of radiation that stream out from it, and the mighty gravitational force that holds the Earth in its orbit and keeps it from spinning out into the eternal cold and darkness of interstellar space. These correspond neatly to the second and third spheres of the Tree, and complete the primal triad.

Below this is the Abyss, well represented by the 93 million miles of lethal, radiation-soaked vacuum that separate us from the Sun. Below that, in turn, is the reflected triad here on Earth. The fourth sphere is represented by the solids, liquids, gases, and plasmas (hot, electrically charged particles) that form Earth's stock of matter, sorting themselves out into the four elemental spheres of the planet itself, its seas and waters, its atmosphere, and the fiery magnetosphere that shields it from the Sun's harmful rays. The fifth sphere is represented by the energy that filters through these layers of matter to set things in motion. The sixth, drawing on all five of the spheres above it, is the phenomenon of biological life.

Now we descend into the tetrad, where life differentiates itself and then recombines. The seventh sphere consists of plant life. More precisely, it represents all those living things that ecologists call autotrophs, literally "self-feeders," which synthesize the food they need from the energy and material substances of their environments. (Plants and chemosynthetic organisms belong to this category.) The eighth sphere consists of animal and fungal life—here again there is a more precise term, heterotrophs or "other-feeders," those living things that survive on other living things. The ninth sphere represents all the connections and relationships that weave living things together into ecosystems. The tenth sphere, finally, stands for each individual environment—this hillside, say, or that pond—and the plants, animals, and ecological relationships that make that environment what it is.

It would be just as easy to use the Tree of Life to make sense of any other way of understanding the macrocosm, scientific or otherwise. Doing this with any system of thought familiar to you is a good exercise, and will help you grasp some of the potentials of the Tree of Life. It's also possible, and in some contexts useful, to work out the expressions of the ten spheres, three pillars, and four worlds in various microcosms. For practical purposes, however, the microcosm that matters most to students of the Cabala is the human microcosm, the individual human being. The Tree of Life can be used as a diagram of the manifestations and levels of yourself. Doing so is essential as a first step toward making sense of the spiritual path—the practical side of all these names and symbols.

It is important to realize first that the human microcosm is exactly that, a miniature reflection of the cosmos, rather than being somehow equal to the cosmos. Some Cabalistic teachings hold that there are ten spheres in every one of the spheres of the Tree of Life. Seen in this way, all the spheres and paths you will be experiencing in the work given in this book—or in any book on the Cabala—are in the tenth sphere, Manifestation, and in fact are found in the lower seven spheres of Manifestation. Reflecting on this will help you keep your sense of proportion and avoid the inflation of the ego that sometimes burdens incautious practitioners.

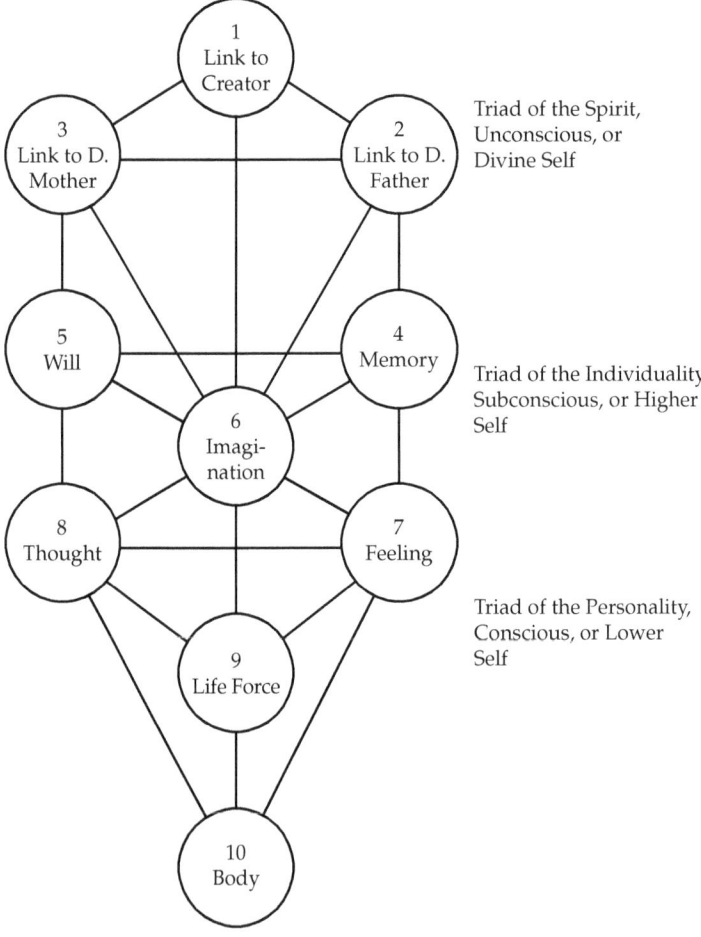

The Tree of Life in the microcosm

In exploring these spheres we can start from the bottom of the Tree, with the aspect of ourselves each of us knows best, our own material body. This corresponds to the tenth sphere of the Tree. The material body is not a prison or a burden; rather, it is the manifestation in matter of all the forces and influences of the spheres above it. If you want to understand what it is and how it works, textbooks on anatomy and physiology are good resources. Here as elsewhere in occult philosophy, it's important to realize that the sciences aren't wrong, they're simply incomplete. They have focused so tightly on the small part of reality that we experience as physical matter and energy that they mistake it for the whole of existence.

The ninth sphere of the microcosm, the closest of the less obvious realities to matter, is thus the one that materialists have denounced most frantically. It is therefore the great stumbling block for many people in the modern industrial world. Nearly all of us have been taught from infancy on that there is no such thing as the life force, and that life is nothing but a complicated set of chemical reactions. (Watch that phrase "nothing but"—it is almost always an attempt to erase some part of human experience and replace it with some soulless and lifeless simulacrum. As psychologist Victor Frankl pointed out trenchantly, these days nihilism is obsessed less with nothingness than with nothing-but-ness.)

We can explore a less blinkered perspective by way of a common experience. Back some years ago, members of my generation used to talk about the "vibe" of a place, a person, or an activity. This is one way of speaking of the mode of perception we're discussing. People who pay little attention to their feelings tend to mistake that mode of perception for feeling, while people who pay little attention to their thoughts tend to mistake it for thought. It is neither. It is the normal, natural, healthy human perception of the life force. Most cultures around the world and throughout time treat it as an ordinary part of everyday reality.

The cultures of the industrial Western world, by contrast, have been so caught up in their obsession with the conquest of matter that they have done their best to ignore and revile this side of human experience. Many people who had inconveniently clear perceptions of the life force in childhood still carry the emotional scars from the bullying they received from parents, teachers, and other children when they were unwise enough to mention their experiences aloud. Those scars are among the burdens that students of the Cabala may have to contend with.

The next two spheres in the microcosm, by contrast, are well known to everyone. The eighth sphere corresponds to the thinking (or, more often, chattering) mind, while the seventh sphere corresponds to the whole range of our feelings. As the diagram of the Tree shows, these two are on the same level; neither is superior or inferior to the other. Because thought and feeling are both unbalanced—each on its own pillar of the Tree, off to one side of the central pillar—they usually fall into conflict with each other.

These four lowest spheres—the body, the life force, thought, and feeling—complete the tetrad of the ordinary, unawakened human personality. This is the level on which most people spend their lives. It is called the lower self in many occult writings and the conscious self in many psychological systems.

It is when we proceed to the next three spheres, the reflected triad in the microcosm, that we come within reach of the less ordinary aspects of human consciousness. This triad includes three capacities that exist in all of us but, in most of us, are not fully conscious: the sixth sphere corresponds to the imagination, the fifth sphere to the will, and the fourth sphere to the memory. In the unawakened person, these belong to the subconscious self, not the conscious self; this is why we so often cannot call up some specific memory when we want it, for example, but have to wait for the subconscious self to produce it for us. The same is true of will and imagination.

The subconscious nature of will is particularly important to understand, because it goes far to explain the confusions over the concept of free will that have troubled the philosophically minded for so long. From a Cabalistic standpoint, whether a given person has free will depends entirely on the focus of that person's consciousness. Those who are solely conscious of the material world, and have not yet turned their attention inward even far enough to explore their inner resources of life, thought, and feeling, have no free will worth mentioning. They respond mechanically to whatever stimulus is strongest, and believe whatever their parents, their peers, or the media tell them to believe.

The path that leads beyond this initial state requires turning toward the inner world, and realizing how much of the world we experience is the product of our own consciousness. Those who do this discover, among other things, a source of will and purpose within themselves that can free them of the habit of automatic response to stimuli. In the language of psychology, they stop being other-directed and become inner-directed. At this stage the experience of freedom of the will is a real one, and worth cultivating. Only later on, when the third triad has become fully conscious and the second triad becomes the focus of study, does the seeker begin to discover that the will within them is not exactly theirs—that it is one facet of the will of the Divine, rather than an arbitrary personal factor, and that their true freedom is found by learning to perceive and express that will as completely and richly as possible.

While a good general grasp of the powers and possibilities of the third triad is an essential preliminary, and many schools teach exercises that focus on these, the mastery of the second triad is therefore the main focus of occult training. This is why, as a student of occultism, you can expect to spend so much time using your imagination, developing your will, and committing things to memory! This higher triad or subconscious self has a deeper importance, however. It is also what some occult schools call the individuality and others call the higher self; it is the potential for greatness that sleeps in all of us, and it is also the lowest aspect of the self that survives the death of the material body. To awaken this level of the self out of its sleep into full waking awareness is therefore to pass through death with no interruption of consciousness and no loss of memory.

Beyond the higher self lies the Abyss, and beyond the Abyss lies the primal triad, the Upper World of the microcosm. These three spheres are the transcendent principles from which the self has unfolded into space and time, and to which the self will eventually return. Beyond time, space, and any mode of consciousness we are capable of conceiving, they are the unseen roots of our being. Where the tetrad is the conscious self and the reflected triad is the subconscious self, the primal triad is the unconscious self. It corresponds in a certain sense to the collective unconscious in the theories of Carl Jung. It can be known only in its effects, never in itself.

In practical terms, we can think of these three spheres as the links connecting us to the three highest principles of the macrocosm. As discussed in the previous section, the terms John Gilbert liked to use for these were the Divine Creator, the Divine Father, and the Divine Mother, but these labels can be replaced if you wish by any suitable triad from your own religious or spiritual tradition.

These same distinctions between phases of the macrocosm can be understood in another way, one that follows the pattern of the four

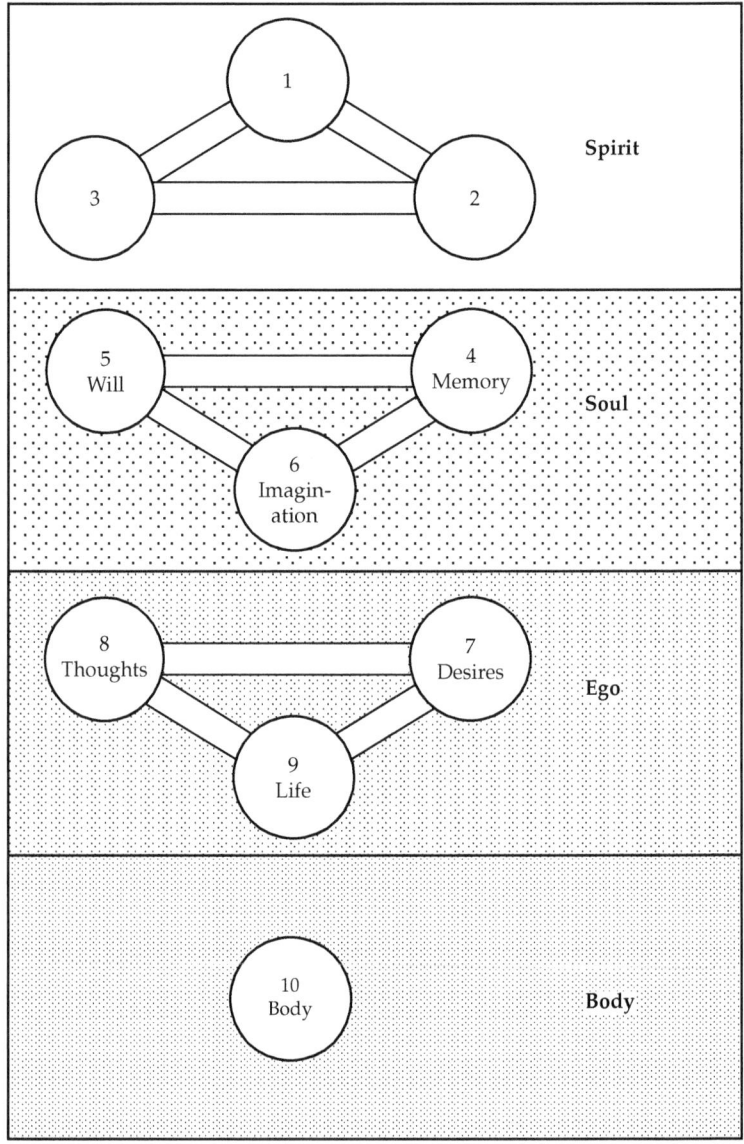

Four worlds in the microcosm

worlds discussed earlier. This scheme, which John used constantly in his teaching, assigned a familiar label to each of the divisions of the Tree of Life. The first world in the microcosm, which includes the primal triad and forms the eternal, unchanging root of the self, he called the spirit. The second world in the microcosm, which includes the reflected triad and represents the individuality, the aspect of the self that endures from life to life and gathers up the experience of each incarnation, he called the soul. The third world in the microcosm, which includes the third triad and represents the personality, the aspect of the self that exists only in a single life, he called the ego. The fourth world, finally, which includes only the tenth sphere, he assigned to the body, the temporary vehicle of spirit, soul, and ego in incarnation.

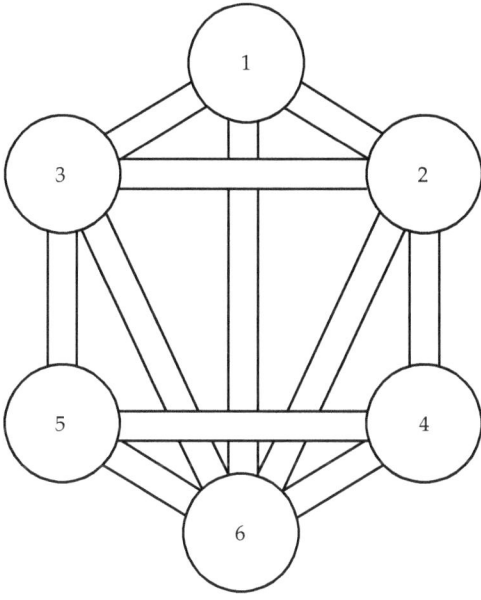

The hexad

In this way the entire Tree can be identified with either the macrocosm or the microcosm. There is another way to trace the relationship between macrocosm and microcosm in the Tree, however, and this is to map both into a single diagram. In this approach the six higher spheres form a hexad that represents the macrocosm, and the five lower spheres form a pentad that represents the macrocosm. This reflects a common tradition in ceremonial magic, in which a hexagram (six-pointed star) is used as an emblem of the macrocosm and a pentagram (five-pointed star) as an emblem of the microcosm.

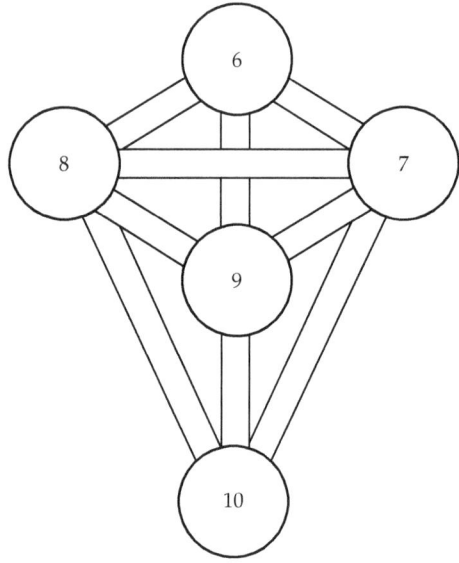

The pentad

Four points worth noting follow from this way of dividing the Tree. First, the pentad of the microcosm includes everything that belongs to the conscious self—that is, the ego and the body—while the hexad of the macrocosm includes everything that belongs to the subconscious and unconscious selves—that is, the soul and the spirit. Thus the pentad represents what we have to start with as we begin the inward path, and the hexad represents what we have to deal with as we proceed.

Second, this division opens the way to a different sense of the movement of energy through the Tree of Life. The hexad of the macrocosm belongs to what we may call the way of creation; it is the realm of impersonal descending energy, through which the Divine brings the worlds into being. The pentad of the macrocosm, by contrast, belongs to what we may call the way of initiation; it is the realm of personalized ascending consciousness, through which souls make their way back toward the Divine.

These downward and upward currents will have an important practical role to play in the practical side of our work. They correspond to the two great currents of subtle force that come into manifestation in the world we experience, the solar current descending from the heavens and the telluric current rising up from the center of the earth.

Some systems of Cabalistic practice work with one or the other of these. It was one of the distinctive features of John Gilbert's teachings that he always worked with both, uniting celestial and terrestrial, macrocosm and microcosm, the grace of the Divine and the focused effort and intention of the individual in a single process.

Third, the lower pentad includes all of the spheres and paths that belong to the symbolic bow and arrow discussed in an earlier section. This teaches that all the capacities necessary to rise to the summit of attainment possible to the human soul are present within the microcosm. Meditation on the diagram of the path of the arrow, and the way the spheres and paths of the microcosmic pentad relate to the process of spiritual unfoldment, has much to teach the attentive student of the Cabala.

Finally, one sphere—the sixth sphere—belongs to both the hexad and the pentad, both the macrocosm and the microcosm. Imagination, the microcosmic expression of the sixth sphere, is dismissed as an irrelevance by many people in the modern industrial world. It is revealing that the word "imaginary" is so often treated as though it means "unreal." The imagination, though, is the power through which we assemble the inputs of our sense organs, our life force, our thoughts, and our feelings into our perception of a world.

Use your imagination without conscious awareness and you get whatever world you have been taught to construct by your culture, your family, and your own habits of thought and feeling. Do it deliberately and intentionally, and within certain very broad limits, you can have the world you choose. How this is done—how the ordinary person caught in a world of random circumstances becomes an extraordinary person capable of shaping the world through memory, will, and imagination—is the theme of the next section of this book.

Awakening to the inner worlds

The uses of the Tree of Life in relation to the human microcosm are not limited to the kind of orientation you can get from the "You Are Here" marking on a map. It also provides a diagram of the route that you, as a practitioner of the Cabala, can use for guidance in the work of individual transformation.

It is essential here to realize that most of us do not perceive the full extent of our own beings. At the beginning of the spiritual path, we may not be aware of ourselves at all. Many people are so intent on the material world around them that they never stop to pay attention to the worlds within them—much less to the ways that inner patterns of thought and feeling shape how they experience the world around them. As Jung liked to point out, most people are utterly unaware of how much of what they think is objective truth about the outside world consists of their own mental and emotional contents projected on the blank screen of the world. Then they wonder why their lives are such a mess.

Many people, for example, go through life longing for love and wealth, and never succeed in finding either one. Meanwhile, the world around them is chock-full of opportunities for both, which they never succeed in embracing. The barriers that stand in the way of their dreams are in themselves, not in the world. Some have beliefs that keep them from perceiving opportunities, some have attitudes that keep them from being able to pursue those that they do notice, still others have habits that guarantee that their pursuit will fail, while some unfortunate people have all three. To change lives of frustration and misery into lives of happiness and success, what is needed is not a change in the world but a change in themselves.

It was with this in mind that the oracle at Delphi, the most sacred of the holy places of ancient Greece, had the words *Gnothi Seauton*—"Know Yourself"—carved above its portal. This is also the reason why meditation and other exercises for turning awareness inward to the self are so central to every spiritual path worth the name. In order to take even the first step in genuine spirituality, it is essential to pay a little less attention to the material world and a little more attention to the inner resources we use to understand and cope with the material world. In the teachings I received, this crucial first step in the inner path is called the awakening of the third triad—or, with a slight change of emphasis, the awakening *to* the third triad.

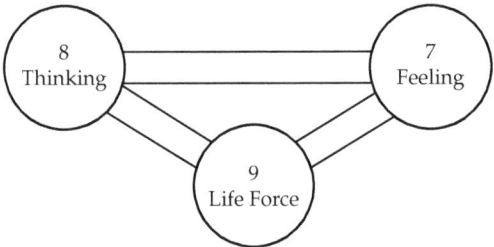

The third triad in the microcosm

The third triad embraces the seventh, eighth, and ninth spheres of the Tree of Life, the spheres especially associated with the world of fire, and comprises the realm of the ego and the conscious self. As we saw in the previous section, the seventh sphere within us takes the form of our feelings. The eighth sphere takes the form of our thoughts. The ninth sphere is expressed in us by the life force and our perceptions of it. Feelings, thoughts, perceptions of the life force, and the evidence of the five senses concerning the body and its material surroundings: these make up the raw materials from which most human beings construct their conscious selves.

It is worth taking a moment to think about what is implied by the concept of awakening this triad. Most people who have not yet begun any kind of personal spiritual work tend to focus entirely on the world known by the senses—the tenth sphere, in the symbolic language we are using. This is true whether they reject the spiritual side of life completely, or accept some religious ideology that requires nothing from them but belief and obedience to a set of rules. One consequence of this fixation is that they habitually treat the seventh, eighth, and ninth spheres as though they were part of the tenth sphere.

What this means is that they treat their feelings and thoughts about material objects, and the reactions of their life force to those objects, as though they were properties of the objects themselves. Carl Jung called this habit "projection," and pointed out that it is responsible for a very large share of all human misery. In the grip of projection, people convince themselves that this material object will give them happiness or self-respect or love if only they can afford to buy it, that this person hates and fears them when they are the ones who are doing the hating and fearing, and so on down the long, long list of dysfunctional human attitudes. Thus they spend their lives flailing around in a wilderness of self-created phantoms, seeking in the world around them what can only be found in the world within them.

To awaken the third triad and come to grips with the role of the ego in the world we experience is to take back all these projected feelings, thoughts, and flows of life energy from the things and people onto which they have been projected. Set free from these projections, these things and people can simply be what they are, rather than having to carry the burden of our unacknowledged states of life energy, thought, and desire. This makes life much easier for everyone. Since the misunderstandings generated by projection are also a fertile cause of human failure, any significant progress in this stage of the work also makes it much easier to have a successful, productive, and happy life.

The third triad thus cannot be neglected in the work of the student. To feel deeply and honestly, to think clearly and flexibly, to live in a vibrant and healthy manner, and to be aware of the difference between these things and the material objects so many people confuse with them, are essential skills that provide an essential foundation for the higher potentials to come. This is why many esoteric schools begin the instruction of novices with breathing exercises and healing practices, to get the life force flowing smoothly through the material body. Since the ninth sphere, the sphere of the life force in the microcosm, is so often ignored and dismissed as nonexistent in contemporary Western cultures, attention to this aspect of existence is essential to the work of awakening this triad.

In earlier times, by contrast, an ordinary education and a reasonably normal home and family life were sufficient to provide most people with adequate training in the realms of thoughts and feelings. These days this is not always true, and remedial work sometimes needs to be done in one or both of these realms as well, before the student is prepared for the next step.

If we are to embrace our full potential as human beings, we have to be prepared to go beyond these preliminary steps, necessary as they are. To take the next step beyond the four spheres of the conscious self, and to move from the realm of the ego to that of the soul, is to pass beyond ordinary human experience and to begin an encounter with the extraordinary. The teachings I received represented this next step, the awakening of (or to) the second triad, in two symbolic ways.

The first of these draws on a detail of Jewish tradition from ancient times. In the Temple of Solomon, a veil of heavy cloth divided the innermost holy of holies from the main room of the temple building. Symbolically, to pass from the third triad to the second is to part that veil and enter into the holy of holies of the human individual. In Cabalistic writings, accordingly, the division between the third and second triads is called the Veil of the Sanctuary. It's an evocative image, not least because the awakening of the second triad is usually preceded by brief glimpses: symbolically, tremblings of the Veil that allow a little of the light within to spill out.

The second way to speak about the awakening of the second triad draws on psychology, and points to an important aspect of these higher principles. The four lowest spheres of the Tree, as already noted, define the conscious self of most human beings. The next three are accordingly the subconscious, and the three beyond that, the unconscious. The difference between these is of considerable importance. What is subconscious, the realm of the soul, is close enough to the threshold of consciousness that it can become an object of conscious experience, while what is unconscious, the realm of the spirit, is destined to stay forever unconscious.

These two realms correspond in Jungian language to the personal unconscious and the collective unconscious. The conscious self belongs entirely to the lower tetrad; it consists, in John Gilbert's terms, of the body and the ego. In the language of traditional occultism, in turn, the conscious realm belongs to the lower self or personality, the subconscious realm of the reflected triad to the higher self, lower genius, or individuality, and the unconscious realm of the primal triad to the Divine Self, Higher Genius or Holy Guardian Angel.

It may seem surprising at first glance to relate the higher self or soul to the subconscious and the Divine Self or spirit to the unconscious. Remember, though, that this is all from the perspective of ordinary human experience. We may be unconscious of the Divine Self, but it is not unconscious of itself! As we proceed through the transformative journey that Jung called individuation and the older occult traditions call spiritual development, the consciousness of the seeker expands and opens to the heights and depths of reality, so that what was subconscious becomes conscious, and the unconscious—though it remains inaccessible in itself—is experienced more clearly in the energies that it reflects downward into the Lower World.

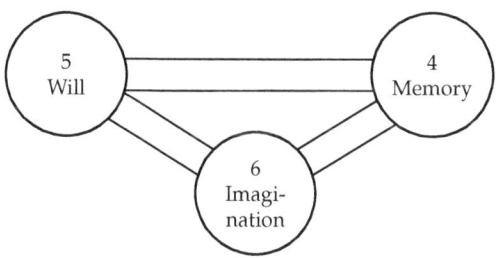

The second triad in the microcosm

The three spheres of the second triad, the realm of the soul, are experienced by us as the higher capacities of the human mind. As explained earlier, the fourth sphere, Love, takes the form of memory; the fifth sphere, Power, takes the form of Will; and the sixth sphere, Harmony, takes the form of Imagination. All three of these are within the reach of consciousness, but among most people they remain subconscious capacities. How many people can remember exactly what they want to remember, when they want it, in as much detail as they choose? How many can summon up the power of will whenever they wish?

How many can awaken the creative imagination any time they desire, and direct it to whatever subject they desire?

Most people, in fact, experience the products of these three human capacities but not the capacities themselves. This is why the teachings assign them to the subconscious sphere. Our memories, our intentions, and the products of our imaginations so often seem to surface out of nowhere: that is, they emerge from the subconscious into consciousness. The goal of this stage of the work is to make the capacities themselves fully conscious, so we pass from a fourfold to a sevenfold world and from fourfold to sevenfold selves. This is the stage where meditation and certain other kinds of esoteric training become essential, so that the capacities of imagination, will, and memory receive adequate training and exercise.

In the process, the student will inevitably make the awkward discovery that these powers of memory, will, and imagination have a dimension that reaches beyond the individual self. This is true even if the sense of self is expanded to include the soul, the part of us that endures from life to life. When it acts freely and consciously, the individual memory is always shading over into what old-fashioned occultists like to call the Memory of Nature, the reflection of past experience in the subtle planes of being. Equally, the stronger and more free our will becomes, the less it is entirely ours, and the more it becomes (and we become) an expression of the will of the Divine acting through its creations.

This is also true of the imagination, but with a twist. The images and insights we perceive through the imagination are not necessarily our creations, for the trained imagination is as much a sense organ as it is a creative power. It perceives the realm that Henry Corbin termed the imaginal world and occultists have long called the astral plane: a realm that is as objectively real, in its own way, as the material world we experience with our ordinary senses.

At the same time, the imagination can also shape that realm. It is a means of action as well as perception, and forms built up by human effort through concentrated and focused imagination can propagate outward and become part of the imaginal world that other people experience. This is why the sixth sphere is shared by both the hexad of the macrocosm and the pentad of the microcosm.

The powers of memory, will, and imagination complete the sevenfold human being. Beyond them lies the Abyss, the gap between the secondary and primary principles and between the Lower World and the Upper World. This is also the line between the subconscious or soul and the unconscious or spirit. Human awareness cannot cross that line. Our capacity to reach upward attains its limit here. This does not mean, however, that we remain forever barred from the influences of the primal triad. It means that our efforts have attained their goal. We have reached upwards as far as we can. Now effort gives way to grace as the Divine reaches down in answer. This answer is the awakening to the first triad, the summit of the spiritual journey that we can take as human beings.

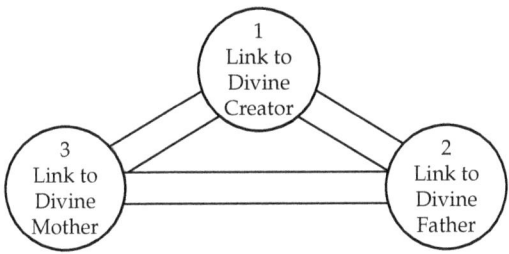

The first triad in the microcosm

Thus the three highest spheres, as they reflect themselves in our microcosm, are not part of us, strictly speaking. They are links to the Divine. In the terminology John Gilbert preferred, the first sphere, Awareness, is the link to the Divine Creator; the second, Intention, is the link to the Divine Father, and the third, Belief, is the link to the Divine Mother. As already noted, other terms and triads can be used just as easily, depending on your religious beliefs. However the first triad is represented in theology and symbol, it remains forever beyond our reach—thus we cannot awaken it, we can only awaken to it. Yet once we awaken to it, the channels of grace by which the Divine blesses the individual and the world open wider.

As mystics have been pointing out since before the dawn of recorded history, this requires a recentering of the self. Before the first stirrings of spiritual awakening, the ordinary personality sees itself as trapped in a world of matter that dominates and limits it, and can only experience its own nature as that nature is projected onto the world around it. The awakening to the third triad causes the ego to discover its own potentials, and it becomes the center of its own world. This is an appropriate and necessary stage, so long as it is recognized as a stage and not the end of the journey.

The awakening to the second triad removes the ego from its self-created pedestal. The seeker discovers that the ego, far from being the essence of the self, is simply a mask taken on by a deeper center of identity, the soul, individuality, or higher self. Occult lore teaches that this is the lowest part of the self that remains outside the cycles of birth and death. To awaken to it is to encounter immortality. This does not mean that you become immortal at this stage. It means that you realize that you have always been immortal, and that your material body and your ego are simply temporary habitations for your own higher principles.

Beyond this, in turn, comes the awakening to the first triad, in which the individuality discovers its own depths. This again is the point at which effort gives way to grace. To reach this stage is to experience union with the Divine. Again, it is not that you attain that union at this stage, it is that you realize that you have never been apart from the Divine. It is at this highest level of human spiritual attainment that all lives become one life, all spirits one spirit, and—in the words of the Hindu mystic Sri Aurobindo—the entire cosmos is simply an eternal child playing an eternal game in an eternal garden.

Thus the completed human being has passed from a fourfold to a sevenfold existence. He or she has roused the subconscious faculties of memory, will, and imagination into full conscious awareness, and at the same time has entered into conscious immortality by awakening the threefold soul that maintains the thread of consciousness intact between death and rebirth. Furthermore, he or she has recognized that birth is not a beginning and death is not an end, and entered into direct relationship with the Divine. All this is a tall order, and according to tradition it takes at least three incarnations of sustained effort to achieve it.

Yet even the first tentative steps toward so mighty a goal bring significant benefits. As mentioned earlier, many people live lives of misery and failure because they never notice how much of their unhappiness is their own creation. The awakening of the third triad can begin to help that—understand the roles that your feelings, your thoughts, and your life force play in shaping your experience, and you can begin working on the mismatches between your outer life and your inner world. Once you begin the awakening of the second triad, the aspects of yourself that awaken—memory, will, and imagination—are potent tools you can use to transform your life for the better. Once you begin awakening to the first triad, finally, the grace of the Divine assists your individual efforts and brings them to completion.

Does this mean becoming superhuman? No, it simply means coming into the full possession of our own humanity. Very few people have even the faintest idea of the immense potentials hidden away within each human individual. We creep like worms when we could stride like titans. Nor is our humanity the summit of possibility. There are entities in the cosmos whose might and wisdom compare to ours as ours compares to that of single-celled algae. What we are, they once were; what they are now, we might someday become—and even they look up as we do, across an infinite Abyss, toward the illimitable Divine.

PART TWO

SYMBOLISM OF THE CABALA

The material covered in the previous sections must be understood in order to make sense of the Tree of Life and apply it in the practical work ahead. The philosophy of the Cabala, however, comprises only a basic framework: the heartwood, so to speak, that supports leaves, fruits, flowers, and the rest of the living reality of the Tree of Life. Much of what makes the Tree so potent an instrument for spiritual practice is provided by the correspondences assigned to each of the ten spheres and the 22 paths.

What are correspondences? In the jargon of operative occultism, this term is used for the words, names, images, and other symbols that cluster around any given archetype and help the human mind grasp something of the archetype's meaning. Which correspondences go with which archetypes has been a routine source of squabbles in the occult community. Such disputes are as pointless as an argument between three Europeans as to whether the animal barking at them ought to be called "*un chien*," "*ein Hund*," or "a dog." Here again, we are discussing tools, not truths; any coherent structure of symbolism that helps you reach the goals of Cabalistic practice is as valid as any other.

In some traditions there are entire books full of correspondences, set out neatly in tables; in others, students are expected to piece together lists of correspondences for themselves. The system I was taught by John Gilbert falls somewhere in the middle of this divide, with the ten spheres being supplied with a rich and relatively complex symbolism and the 22 paths given a sparser set that students can fill out through their own experience. To the symbolism of the ten spheres I received from John I have added a few symbols—some from Pythagorean and Platonic sources, some from other traditions of occult lore, a few from the odd but effective fusion of Golden Dawn magic and Druid Revival nature spirituality I chronicled in my book *The Celtic Golden Dawn*.

For example, I have included the nine muses and their mother, Memory, since these played an important symbolic role in the Renaissance and early modern occult circles that adopted the Cabala. The assignments I have used are traditional and may seem surprising at first—for example, Erato, the muse of erotic poetry, is assigned to the fifth sphere—but meditation on these and the other symbols will reveal their relevance.

The planetary correspondences are mostly traditional but have been modified to fit the Copernican understanding of the solar system. It has taken more than four centuries for the Cabala to catch up to the fact that the stars are not portholes in a sphere outside the orbit of Saturn, and that there is no additional sphere further out that makes the heavens spin around the Earth! The planets Uranus and Neptune fill the resulting gap in the symbolism quite effectively, however. The Tree of Life does not have enough spheres to assign places to dwarf planets such as Ceres, Pluto, and Eris, or to smaller bodies such as the asteroids. Perhaps some future astrologically minded Cabalist will work out a correspondence between these and the paths, but for now they can be left aside.

The colors assigned to each of the spheres come from the Golden Dawn tradition. The Golden Dawn itself had a complicated system of four color scales, which John Gilbert considered cumbersome and impractical, but the basic Queen Scale correspondences work well and were always part of his system.

The symbolism of the spheres of the primal triad is relatively simple, as befits a realm of being we can know only through its effects. To the seven lower spheres of the Tree, the ones that human beings can experience directly, a much more extensive symbolism is assigned. The elemental correspondences and directions are among the things that set John Gilbert's teachings apart from other Cabalistic systems. Equally, the assignment of seven tarot trumps to the seven lower spheres is a distinctive feature of John's teachings, and will be explained when the placement of the tarot trumps on the paths of the Tree of Life has been explored more generally. The questions and conceptions assigned to each of the lower spheres relate to the art of combinations, which will be explained in the section on discursive meditation below.

The seven chakras, as most people know these days, are seven energy centers located along the midline of the body, associated with the endocrine glands and with the major centers of the sympathetic nervous system. Ways of relating the system of chakras to the Tree of Life go back nearly as far as the first Western translations of Indian texts about the chakras, and various approaches have been proposed. The symbolic correspondences given here differ from the structure underlying the practical method given later in this book; this is quite deliberate, and may help serve as a reminder that correspondences are not mutually exclusive. Yet again, they are tools rather than truths; just as the same carpenter can use a hammer for one task and a saw for another, it sometimes works best to use more than one set of relationships to make sense of any given subject or theme.

The musical modes assigned to the seven lower spheres are the seven Renaissance modes, which replaced the older church modes once the clergy lost their stranglehold on music and the hated *modus lascivius* or "lustful mode," the Ionian mode or modern major scale, was no longer forbidden. They are assigned according to their traditional planetary rulerships. The notes are the keynotes of the corresponding mode—for example, F is the keynote of the Lydian mode, because a scale played on the white keys of the piano starting with F is the basic Lydian scale.

Despite the revival of modal music in the late 20th-century folk music scene, very little has been done with the esoteric dimension of the modes; this is a project that musically minded readers might consider pursuing. I have offered one set of suggestions in the section on practice below, making use of the one modal instrument readily accessible to most people in the Western world, the mountain dulcimer. Other options will doubtless occur to students of the Cabala with an adequate background in music.

The temple descriptions for the seven lower spheres are based on the traditions of the ancient city of Harran, the last stronghold of Pagan Platonism in the ancient world. As keepers of the Pythagorean heritage, the Harranians gave their temples a distinctive set of geometrical shapes. These will be used in the practical work of the Cabala, and are discussed in considerably more detail in a later section of this book; they also make fine themes for meditation.

The symbolism of the 22 paths is complex, and the system John taught had its own distinctive way of dealing with them. The principles underlying his system will be covered in the section on the paths later on.

What follows, despite its relative complexity, should be taken as a first sketch or a framework on which you, as a student of the Cabala, can construct your own constellations of symbolism. A notebook setting apart several pages for each of the ten spheres and a single page for each of the paths is a useful investment at this stage of your Cabalistic education. These are used to write down any notes and speculations about the spheres, paths, and correspondences that occur to you as you proceed with your work.

It is important to keep in mind that the symbols that follow, though they belong to one rather idiosyncratic branch of Cabalistic teaching, are by no means wholly arbitrary. Nor are they simply mental clutter to be applied to some sort of recherché trivia game. They are tools which you will apply systematically in the work to come. Just as it takes instruction and practice to learn to use a hammer or a saw, you will need to learn how to use these tools in the inner work of active imagination and discursive meditation, the two pillars that stand before the temple of the spiritual work ahead. Passing between them, you will enter on the path of the third pillar, which is ceremonial invocation. All this will be discussed in ample detail later on.

Correspondences of the spheres

Each of the ten spheres of the Tree has its own distinctive set of symbols assigned to it. In the first three spheres, the Upper World or primal triad, these are relatively simple, since this part of the Tree is beyond the reach of human consciousness. There is an old parable in Zen Buddhism that likens symbols and words concerning reality to fingers pointing at the Moon, and reminds the listener to pay attention to where the finger is pointing, not to the finger in itself. The correspondences of the primal triad should be understood in much this way. They are hints pointing toward realities that are inexpressible by any more direct means. Learn them, but don't become obsessive about them—turn your attention instead to where the finger points.

Correspondences of the first sphere

Number: 1

Title: Awareness

Greek name: the Monad

Hebrew name: Kether, the Crown

Druid name: Celi, the Hidden

Planet: Neptune

Color: White

Law: the Law of Awareness—awareness precedes every conscious creative act, for you can only create what you are aware you can create.

Muse: Mnemosyne, memory, the mother of the muses

Titles: the Ancient of Ancients; the Androgyne; the Creator; the Crown; the Great Deep; the Head which is Not; the Hearth; the Hidden Light; the Present Moment; the Primordial Point; the Ship; Union

Symbols: The point, the circle, the crown

Correspondences of the second sphere

Number: 2

Title: Intention

Greek name: the Dyad

Hebrew name: Chokmah, Wisdom

Druid name: Perydd, the Cause

Planet: Uranus

Color: Silver-gray

Law: the Law of Intention—every act of creation begins with the intention to create.

Muse: Urania, muse of astronomy and astrology

Titles: Anguish; Division; the Formless One; Generation; Movement; Prometheus; the Second Glory

Symbols: The line, the *vesica piscis*

Correspondences of the third sphere

Number: 3

Title: Belief

Greek name: the Triad

Hebrew name: Binah, Understanding

Druid name: Dofydd, the Tamer

Planet: Saturn

Color: Black

Law: the Law of Belief—the act of creation depends on the belief that you can create.

Muse: Polyhymnia, muse of sacred poetry, geometry, and grammar

Titles: the Great Sea; Proportion; Prudence

Symbols: the triangle

Between the first three spheres, the Upper World, and the seven that follow, the Lower World, lies the Abyss. The only symbolism applied to this division is the emptiness, darkness, and silence implied by the traditional label itself. Nor did John Gilbert's Cabala assign any symbols to Knowledge, the phantom presence astride the Abyss, because it denotes the point at which all symbolism breaks down. Below the Abyss, in the Lower World, the symbolism becomes more complex, because these are the spheres to which humanity has the possibility of direct access.

It is important to realize that the division between the Upper and Lower World is not an arbitrary one. John occasionally used to field criticism from people who thought that by stressing the transcendence of the primal triad and the eternal human spirit, he was somehow preventing them from getting access to realms they could otherwise reach! He would chuckle about this sometimes, and point out that the Tree of Life is simply a map, that is, a representation of reality, and not reality itself. A system of Cabala that claims that no realm of existence is beyond the reach of human consciousness does not erase the very real limits to our awareness—it just makes it impossible for its practitioners to take into account the influence of those realms of existence that we cannot access directly.

Once below the Abyss, by contrast, we are within the reach of human awareness. That does not mean that most of us are already aware of the seven spheres of the Lower World. Most human beings are only aware of the tenth sphere, the world reflected in their five material senses and understood by the half-conscious ego processes of feeling, thinking, and the instinctive drives of the life force. Those who have risen above this initial stage have six more worlds to explore, each of them as complex and challenging as the world of everyday life, before they can truly say that they have come into possession of their own sevenfold selves.

Correspondences of the fourth sphere

Number: 4

Title: Love

Greek name: the Tetrad

Hebrew name: Chesed, Mercy

Druid name: Ener, the Namer

Archangel: Cassiel

Planet: Jupiter

Element: Spirit Above

Tarot trump: XXI, the World

Direction: Above

Conception: Purpose

Question: When?

Chakra: Sarasraha, the thousand-petaled crown chakra

Color: Blue

Musical mode: Lydian

Musical note: F

Temple: Triangular

Magical image: an old wise king upon a throne, dressed in blue robes, with a crown and belt of gold. His hair and beard are long and white. He holds a scepter of gold in his right hand, and, in his left, an orb with an equal-armed cross atop it.

Law: the Law of Love—the more love we express in our lives, the more love we draw into our lives. The same is true of every other emotion or mode of experience.

Muse: Euterpe, muse of instrumental music

Titles: Compassion; Custodian of Nature; Majesty; Mercy; the Source of Virtues

Symbols: the four directions, the four elements, the square, the tetrahedron

Correspondences of the fifth sphere

Number: 5

Title: Power

Greek name: the Pentad

Hebrew name: Geburah, Severity

Druid name: Modur, the Mover

Archangel: Camael

Planet: Mars

Element: Spirit Below

Tarot trump: XX, Judgment

Direction: Below

Conception: Power

Question: Where?

Chakra: Ajna, the two-petaled brow chakra.

Color: Red

Musical mode: Phrygian

Musical note: E

Temple: Oblong

Magical image: a warrior queen in a chariot drawn by two roan horses. Her head is bare and her black hair streams out behind her. She wears a crimson cloak and armor of polished steel. In her right hand is a sword, and on her left arm is a round shield painted black with a red pentagram on it.

Law: the Law of Power—we gain power by attaining conscious mastery over fear. The same result proceeds from the mastery of every other emotion or mode of experience.

Muse: Erato, muse of love poetry

Titles: the Demigod; Fear; Freedom; Nemesis; Providence; the Warrior

Symbols: the five senses, the pentagon, the pentagram

Correspondences of the sixth sphere

Number: 6

Title: Harmony

Greek name: the Hexad

Hebrew name: Tiphareth, Beauty

Druid name: Muner, the Lord

Archangel: Michael

Planet: the Sun

Element: Spirit Within

Tarot trump: XIX, the Sun

Direction: Center

Conception: Value

Question: Why?

Chakra: Vishuddhi, the 16-petaled throat chakra

Color: Yellow

Musical mode: Dorian

Musical note: D

Temple: Square

Magical image: there are three magical images for this sphere. The first is a naked child standing and reaching up as though to a parent. The second is a young monarch in golden robes seated on a throne, with a sword in the left hand and a scepter in the right. The third is a sacrificed god, naked except for a loincloth, who is crucified or otherwise suspended above the ground. The gender of these figures is the same as that of the practitioner, as they represent his or her higher self.

Law: the Law of Harmony—by achieving equilibrium between love and power we become able to experience and use both these principles freely. The same is true of every other pair of opposites we experience.

Muse: Melpomene, muse of tragedy, rhetoric, and speech

Titles: the Anvil; the Child; the Door to Heaven and Hell; Equilibrium; the Healer; the King; the Reconciler; the Sphere of Adam; Wholeness of Limbs

Symbols: the cube, the hexagon, the hexagram, the six directions of space (up, down, forward, back, left, and right)

Correspondences of the seventh sphere

Number: 7

Title: Desire

Greek name: the Heptad

Hebrew name: Netzach, Victory

Druid name: Byw, the Living

Archangel: Haniel

Planet: Venus

Element: Fire

Tarot trump: XVIII, the Moon

Direction: South

Conception: Source

Question: How?

Chakra: Anahata, the 12-petaled heart chakra

Color: Green

Musical mode: Ionian (major scale)

Musical note: C

Temple: Triangular, within a square

Magical image: a beautiful naked woman standing in a meadow dotted with flowers. She wears a garland of flowers about her head but nothing else, and her long golden hair is unbound. Her arms are extended downward and out to the sides, as though inviting an embrace.

Law: The Law of Desire—we can attain what we desire when our desire is in accord with the six laws and six spheres already named.

Muse: Terpsichore, muse of dance and education

Titles: Chance; the Crisis; the Forager; the Guardian; the Initiator; the Sphere of Fire; the Stronghold

Symbols: heptagon, heptagram, the seven classical planets, the seven notes of the musical octave

Correspondences of the eighth sphere

Number: 8

Title: Competence

Greek name: the Octad

Hebrew name: Hod, Glory

Druid name: Byth, the Eternal

Archangel: Raphael

Planet: Mercury

Element: Air

Tarot trump: XVII, the Star

Direction: East

Conception: Being

Question: Whether?

Chakra: Manipura, the ten-petaled navel chakra

Color: Orange

Musical mode: Locrian

Musical note: B

Temple: Triangular, within an oblong shape

Magical image: a young man in a short tunic of tawny fabric, with a headband of the same color and sandy hair. He stands firmly on his right foot but his left is rising as though taking a step; his legs are bare and he wears leather sandals. In his right hand he holds a short white staff or baton, the old emblem of a herald.

Law: The Law of Competence—we can attain competence in any realm in which our thoughts, words, and actions are in accord with the seven laws and seven spheres already named.

Muse: Calliope, muse of epic poetry and literature

Titles: Glory; Intelligence; the Sphere of Air; Vibration

Symbols: the octagon, the octagram, the octahedron

Correspondences of the ninth sphere

Number: 9

Title: Foundation

Greek name: the Ennead

Hebrew name: Yesod, the Foundation

Druid name: Ner, the Mighty

Archangel: Gabriel

Planet: the Moon

Element: Water

Tarot trump: XVI, the Tower

Direction: West

Conception: Becoming

Question: What?

Chakra: Svadhishthana, the six-petaled genital chakra

Color: Violet

Musical mode: Aeolian (natural minor scale)

Musical note: A

Temple: Octagonal

Magical image: a beautiful naked man standing with his feet firmly planted on the ground and his arms raised in the posture of Atlas supporting the heavens. His hair is dark and he has a short beard. His muscles are well developed. He radiates a sense of great strength.

Law: the Law of Foundation—where we place our energy and attention determines what we manifest and bring into our life.

Muse: Clio, muse of history

Titles: the Banisher; Enthusiasm; the Finish Line; the Horizon; the Ocean; the Sphere of Water

Symbols: the enneagon, the enneagram, the nine astrological planets

Correspondences of the tenth sphere

Number: 10

Title: Manifestation

Greek name: the Decad

Hebrew name: Malkuth, the Kingdom

Druid name: Naf, the Shaper

Archangel: Auriel

Planet: the Earth

Element: Earth

Tarot trump: XV, the Devil

Direction: North

Conception: Substance

Question: Who?

Chakra: Muladhara, the four-petaled root chakra

Color: Indigo

Musical mode: Mixolydian

Musical note: G

Temple: Hexagonal

Magical image: a young woman seated on a cube of black stone. She wears a plain black dress with a cord belt. Her hair is long, dark, and unbound, her feet are bare, and she sits with her knees together and her hands resting on her thighs. Hanging from a plain cord around her neck, an equal-armed cross of pure but roughly formed gold rests over her heart.

Law: the Law of Manifestation—the world that we experience is a precise and perfect manifestation of our state of consciousness.

Muse: Thalia, muse of comedy, geometry, architecture, and agriculture

Titles: the All; Atlas; the Gate; Necessity; the Receptacle; the Sphere of Earth; the Unwearying; the Virgin

Symbols: the decagon, the decagram, the Tree of Life

The practical application of all these symbols will be covered later, in the third part of this book. For now, take a little while to review the symbols of each of the spheres, and try to get some sense of how they relate to the archetypes and patterns discussed already. Repeat this at intervals, focusing on one sphere at a time, and see how it enriches your understanding of the Tree of Life.

Correspondences of the paths

With the symbolism of the paths we cross into a more personal, and thus also a more problematic, dimension of the Tree's symbolism. Dion Fortune's maxim that the spheres are objective but the paths are subjective is worth keeping in mind here. In her day, it was standard practice for each distinct school of occultism to assign its own set of correspondences to the paths, and to make these among the secrets passed on in ceremonies of initiation. Each of the various assignments seems to have worked as well as any of the others.

What this implies, of course, is that no way of assigning symbols to the paths is more correct or more accurate than any other. It is important to have some set of symbols to represent the paths, in other words, but the choice of a set is up to the individual school or practitioner. This is another reason why the endless, dreary quarrels between partisans of different systems of symbolism on the Tree of Life are so much wasted breath. It is rather as though people started insisting that there was only one true key to open every front door in the country, when it should be clear that the door of every house has its own key.

Perhaps the most bitter of all these battles have been fought over the relationship between the 22 trumps of the tarot deck and the 22 paths of the Tree of Life. There are plenty of competing ways of arranging those connections, and all of them have their proponents. The table below shows just four of the many variations that have been proposed and put to use by Cabalists over the years.

Tarot attributions

Path	Golden Dawn	A.E. Waite	Frater Achad	W.G. Gray
1–2	0, the Fool	IV, Emperor	X, Wheel of F.	V, Hierophant
1–3	I, Magician	III, Empress	XXI, Universe	IX, Hermit
1–6	II, High Priestess	—	XX, Judgment	XVII, Star
1–Daath	—	X, Wheel of F.	—	—
2–3	III, Empress	—	XVII, Star	XX, Judgment
2–Daath	—	VII, Chariot	—	—
2–4	V, Hierophant	I, Magician	XIV, Temperance	IV, Emperor
2–6	IV, Emperor	—	XIX, Sun	XIV, Temperance
3–Daath	—	VIII, Strength	—	—
3–5	VII, Chariot	0, Fool	XVI, Tower	XIII, Death
3–6	VI, Lovers	—	XV, Devil	XII, Hanged Man
Daath–6	—	II, High Priestess	—	—
4–5	VIII, Strength	XX, Judgment	XIII, Death	XI, Justice
4–6	IX, Hermit	IX, Hermit	XVIII, Moon	VIII, Strength
4–7	X, Wheel of F.	V, Hierophant	XI, Justice	III, Empress
5–6	XI, Justice	XIII, Death	IV, Emperor	XVI, Tower
5–8	XII, Hanged Man	XII, Hanged Man	IX, Hermit	XV, Devil
6–7	XIII, Death	XIX, Sun	VII, Strength	VI, Lovers
6–8	XV, Devil	XV, Devil	VI, Lovers	VII, Chariot
6–9	XIV, Temperance	VI, Lovers	XII, Hanged Man	XIX, Sun
7–8	XVI, Tower	XIV, Temperance	V, Hierophant	X, Wheel of F.
7–9	XVII, Star	XVIII, Moon	VII, Chariot	II, High Priestess
7–10	XVIII, Moon	XVII, Star	III, Empress	XXI, World
8–9	XIX, Sun	XI, Justice	II, Priestess	I, Magician
8–10	XX, Judgment	XVI, Tower	I, Magician	0, Fool
9–10	XXI, World	XXI, World	0, Fool	XVIII, Moon

What makes this parade of disagreements even more striking is that all those involved in it—the founders of the Hermetic Order of the Golden Dawn, Arthur Edward Waite, Charles Stansfield Jones (who wrote under the pen name "Frater Achad"), and William G. Gray—were capable occultists, and all of them shared a broadly similar understanding of occult philosophy and the Tree of Life. Yet they all assigned very different correspondences to the paths, and Waite (as noted in an earlier section) also had his own distinctive arrangements of paths on the Tree. Yet each of these systems has turned out to work well in practice, even though they all contradict one another in nearly every particular.

Thus the set of correspondences John Gilbert assigned to the Paths, which I have given below, cannot claim to be the only option, or even the best option. It is one choice among many. It works well, and the various initiatory traditions that John passed on all rely on it, but nothing more exclusive can be said for it.

The paths below the Abyss

Like the other aspects of the Cabalistic teaching I received from John, this set of correspondences takes the distinction between the Upper World and the Lower World more seriously than most other systems. It was an essential theme in his teaching that the primal triad belongs wholly to the Divine and is beyond human comprehension. The paths that unite the spheres of the primal triad to each other and to the spheres below it are therefore paths through which the influences of the Divine descend to us, not paths that we can ascend. It is important to be aware of them, but they are not assigned the same richness of symbolism given to the paths further down, which human beings can traverse.

There are, as it happens, 14 paths and seven spheres below the Abyss, and this number allows all but one of the tarot trumps to be assigned to these paths and spheres. What is more, the last seven trumps of the tarot deck echo those seven spheres to a remarkable degree. The attributions can be set out as follows:

Trump XV, the Devil, is the trump of bondage to the material, and so corresponds to the tenth sphere, Manifestation.

Trump XVI, the Tower, is the trump of liberation from bondage through a release of energy, and so corresponds to the ninth sphere, Foundation.

Trump XVII, the Star, is the trump of awakening consciousness, and so corresponds to the eighth sphere, Competence. (Notice that in many tarot decks, there are eight stars on this trump, and each of them has eight points.)

Trump XVIII, the Moon, is the trump of change and longing, and so corresponds to the seventh sphere, Desire.

Trump XIX, the Sun, is the trump of great success and creative power, and so corresponds to the sixth sphere, Harmony, with its solar symbolism.

Trump XX, Judgment, is the trump of decision and final settlement of affairs, and so corresponds to the fifth sphere, Power.

Trump XXI, finally, is the trump of the universe in balance, and its fourfold structure shows its correspondence to the fourth sphere, Love.

The remaining trumps are assigned to the paths below the Abyss, as follows:

Trump I, the Magician, is the path from the tenth to the ninth sphere.
Trump II, the High Priestess, is the path from the tenth to the eighth sphere.
Trump III, the Empress, is the path from the ninth to the eighth sphere.
Trump IV, the Emperor, is the path from the tenth to the seventh sphere.
Trump V, the Hierophant, is the path from the ninth to the seventh sphere.
Trump VI, the Lovers, is the path from the eighth to the seventh sphere.
Trump VII, the Chariot, is the path from the ninth to the sixth sphere.
Trump VIII, Strength, is the path from the eighth to the sixth sphere.
Trump IX, the Hermit, is the path from the seventh to the sixth sphere.
Trump X, the Wheel of Fortune, is the path from the eighth to the fifth sphere.
Trump XI, Justice, is the path from the sixth to the fifth sphere.
Trump XII, the Hanged Man, is the path from the seventh to the fourth sphere.
Trump XIII, Death, is the path from the sixth to the fourth sphere.
Trump XIV, Temperance, is the path from the fifth to the fourth sphere.

And the remaining trump, 0, the Fool? It has a double meaning in this context. It is the traveler who passes along each of these paths, and therefore is presented at the beginning of the process of initiation; thus its number is zero, because at first the student has not yet encountered any of the paths. Second, it relates to the path that rises straight up from the sixth sphere to the station of Knowledge in the Abyss. It is therefore the path by which the individual reaches up toward the Divine and the grace of the Divine descends to the individual, and its number is zero, because no path can take the traveler across the Abyss. The number of this card is also zero in this latter sense because the path it indicates ends in Knowledge, and the human mind is incapable of having knowledge of the Divine; again, "The Tao that can be described is not the eternal Tao."

John used to insist that the attributions just set out were the true secret tarot attributions taught by the original Hermetic Order of the Golden Dawn. I am quite certain that he believed this to be the case, but as far as I know not a single piece of evidence supports that claim. What seems to be the case instead is that these are the distinctive attributions that John's teacher Dr. Juliet Ashley devised for her branch of the Golden Dawn tradition, for which she claimed to have received a charter from Arthur Edward Waite in 1939. Whatever their origin, these attributions work just as well in practice as the others cited earlier.

With this set of relationships in mind it's easy to sketch out the symbolism of the paths in this system of the Cabala.

No.	Path of ...	Between ...	Trump	Geomancy	Planet	Sign
0	Ignorance	(none)	Fool	Carcer	Saturn	Capricorn
1	Attention	10–9	Magician	Puer	Mars	Aries
2	Memory	10–8	High Priestess	Conjunctio	Ceres	Virgo
3	Imagination	9–8	Empress	Acquisitio	Jupiter	Sagittarius
4	Reason	10–7	Emperor	Fortuna Major	Sun	Leo
5	Intuition	9–7	Hierophant	Albus	Mercury	Gemini
6	Discernment	8–7	Lovers	Puella	Venus	Libra
7	Freedom	9–6	Chariot	Tristitia	Uranus	Aquarius
8	Courage	8–6	Strength	Caput Draconis	North Node	Gemini
9	Instruction	7–6	Hermit	Via	Moon	Cancer
10	Retribution	8–5	Wheel of Fortune	Populus	Moon	Cancer
11	Balance	6–5	Justice	Laetitia	Neptune	Pisces
12	Reversal	7–4	Hanged Man	Rubeus	Pluto	Scorpio
13	Transformation	6–4	Death	Amissio	Vulcan	Taurus
14	Verification	5–4	Temperance	Fortuna Minor	Sun	Leo
15	Seeking	6–Knowledge	Fool	Cauda Draconis	South Node	Sagittarius

Geomancy, which is included in the chart above, is a traditional Western method of geomancy, sometimes called a Western equivalent of the *I Ching*. It uses 16 figures of four single or double dots, which are shown in the diagram below. John was adept at it and used it as a source of symbolism in several of the traditions that he taught.

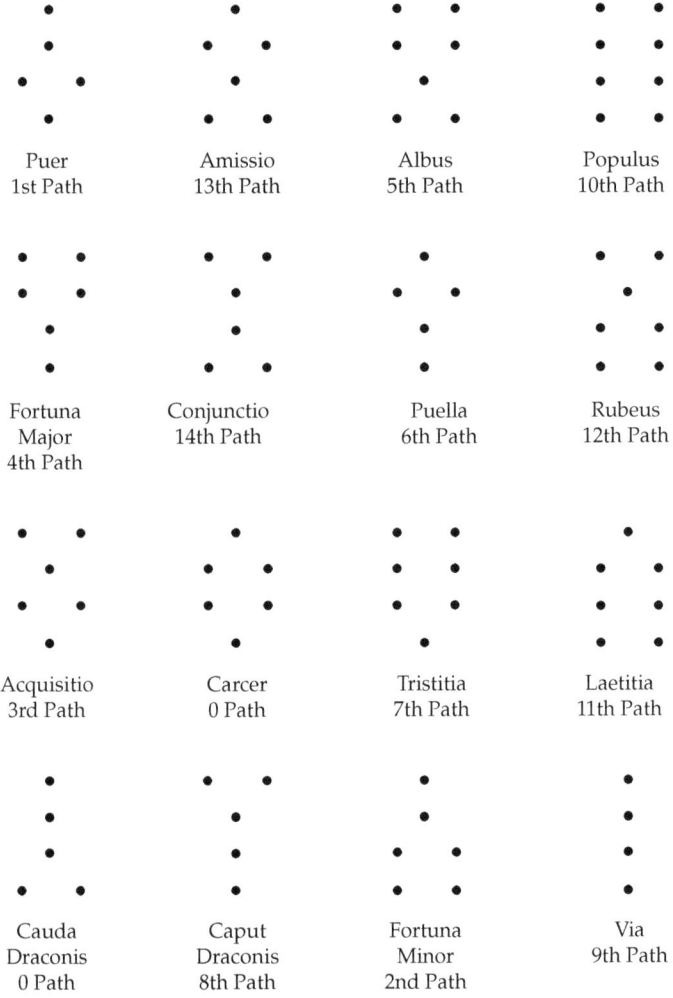

Geomantic figures

John used the standard relationships between the geomantic figures and the signs of the zodiac in his system, though he assigned Caput and Cauda Draconis to the signs in which the north and south nodes of the Moon are exalted. He modified the planetary correspondences, however, to include the two dwarf planets Ceres and Pluto and the esoteric planet Vulcan, which was "discovered" by astronomers in 1859 but apparently does not exist. All three of these have symbolic value, of course; those who prefer not to use dwarf or symbolic planets can replace them with the traditional rulers of the zodiacal signs with which they are associated, Mercury, Mars, and Venus, respectively.

The 14 paths listed above, excluding the Fool on both ends of the sequence, are also represented by the 14 statements of the Emerald Tablet, an alchemical text assigned to the legendary sage Hermes Trismegistus, as follows:

Path 1: "True, without error, certain, and most true."
Path 2: "That which is below is as that which is above, and that which is above is as that which is below, to perform the miracles of the One Thing."
Path 3: "And as all things were from One, by the meditation of One, so from this One Thing come all things by adaptation."
Path 4: "Its father is the Sun, its mother is the Moon, the wind carried it in its belly, the nurse thereof is the Earth."
Path 5: "It is the father of all perfection and the consummation of the whole world."
Path 6: "Its power is integral if it be turned to earth."
Path 7: "Thou shalt separate the earth from the fire, the subtle from the coarse, gently and with much ingenuity."
Path 8: "It ascends from Earth to heaven and descends again to earth, and receives the power of the superiors and the inferiors."
Path 9: "Thus thou hast the glory of the whole world, therefore let all obscurity flee before thee."
Path 10: "This is the strong fortitude of all fortitude, overcoming every subtle and penetrating every solid thing."
Path 11: "Thus the world was created."
Path 12: "Hence are all wonderful adaptations, of which this is the manner."
Path 13: "Therefore am I called Hermes Trismegistus having the three parts of the philosophy of the whole world."
Path 14: "That is finished which I have to say concerning the operation of the Sun."

These correspondences reveal more than may be apparent at a first glance. I was taught that each text refers directly to the trump and path assigned to it. For example, the "Thus" in "Thus the world was created," the 11th statement, refers to Trump XI, Justice, and the Path of Balance. The lesson in this case is that it is through equilibrium, the Royal Secret of certain traditions of initiation, that the world was created. Similarly, the "of which this is the manner" in the 12th statement refers to Trump XII and the Path of Reversal, which teaches that reversal—turning inward from the outer world and reversing the way of creation—is the manner through which wonderful adaptations may be achieved. Careful study of these seemingly simple texts, and repeated meditation on them, are therefore well worth doing.

Finally, the paths were also assigned to chapters of *The Kybalion*, one of the classic texts of American occultism. Written more than a century ago by William Walker Atkinson, *The Kybalion* comprises an introduction and 15 chapters, and summarizes certain core principles of occult philosophy. It is relatively brief and long out of copyright; print copies are readily available, and it may also be downloaded free of charge from Project Gutenberg (www.gutenberg.org) and other online sources. The sections of the text were assigned in simple numerical order—the introduction to the Fool and the "zero-th path," the first chapter to Path 1, and so on throughout the whole volume.

The material given above, plus the colors and musical notes introduced in a later section, makes for a reasonably rich set of correspondences for the paths. In practice, of course, these do not stand alone. You will be enriching each path with a symbolism derived from your own experiences of the paths in active imagination and your own reflections on the paths in discursive meditation. In this way you will develop a personal symbolism, unique to yourself, that will enable you to open up the connections from sphere to sphere and awaken the Tree of Life in yourself.

The paths above the Abyss

Of the paths that cross the Abyss much less was said in John's teaching. These are paths through which the grace of the Divine can descend, but human souls cannot traverse them. Thus they do not have an elaborate symbolism, since the correspondences assigned to the paths further down are meant as tools to assist the seeker to travel them.

CORRESPONDENCES OF THE PATHS 89

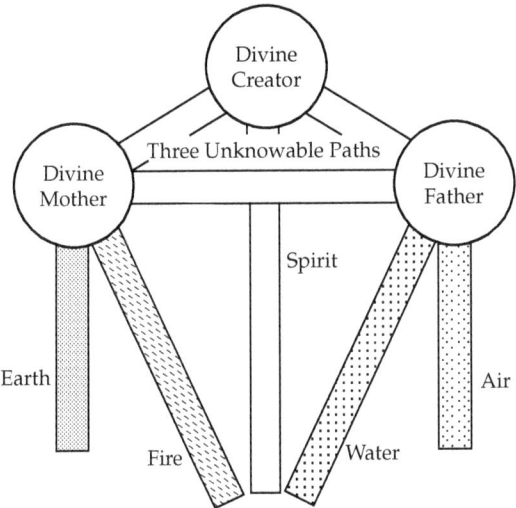

The paths above the Abyss

The only symbolism applied to them is a simple elemental correspondence. The path from Awareness to Harmony corresponds to the element of spirit; the path from Intention to Love, to air; the path from Intention to Harmony, to water; the path from Belief to Harmony, to fire; and the path from Belief to Power, to earth. This symbolism will yield a certain amount of meditation, but those results should only be applied to the ends of the paths that contact one of the seven spheres of the Lower World. To the extent that these five paths reach into the Upper World, they pass out of the reach of human consciousness.

The three paths at the summit of the Tree, uniting Awareness with Intention, Awareness with Belief, and Intention with Belief, exist entirely outside the realm that human minds can comprehend. No symbols were applied to them, only numbers, as given below.

Letters, numbers, and paths

One thing that John Gilbert's Cabala did not include was a set of letters to assign to the 22 paths. The Jewish Cabala, of course, used the Hebrew alphabet for this purpose, and many Christian and occult Cabalists have done the same thing. There are other alternatives, however. William G. Gray evoked a tempest in a variety of occult teapots in the middle years of the 20th century by working out a way to assign the letters of the ordinary English alphabet to the paths of the Tree of Life. Long before his time, though, Eliphas Lévi did the same thing in a more elegant way in his book *Doctrine and Ritual of High Magic*.

Lévi pointed out that the letters I, J, and Y are early modern variants of the Latin letter I—J started out as the way I was written at the beginning of the word, and the lower-case cursive Y was a fast way of writing the doubled letter II at the end of Latin words, where it occurs frequently. In the same way, U, V, and W are all variants of U—we even call the last of these three letters "double U," which is exactly what it was originally. Treat each of these triads as one letter and there are 22 letters in the French or English alphabet. I have found that these attributions work well, as follows:

A—1st Path of Attention, 10–9
B—2nd Path of Memory, 10–8
C—3rd Path of Imagination, 9–8
D—4th Path of Reason, 10–7
E—5th Path of Intuition, 9–7
F—6th Path of Discernment, 8–7
G—7th Path of Freedom, 9–6
H—8th Path of Courage, 8–6
I, J, Y—9th Path of Instruction, 7–6
K—10th Path of Retribution, 8–5
L—11th Path of Balance, 6–5
M—12th Path of Reversal, 7–4
N—13th Path of Transformation, 6–4
O—14th Path of Verification, 5–4
P—15th Path of Seeking or of Spirit, 6–1
Q—16th Path of Fire from 6–3
R—17th Path of Earth from 5–3
S—18th Path of Water from 6–2
T—19th Path of Air from 4–2
U, V, W—20th Path from 3–2
X—21st Path from 3–1
Z—22nd from 2–1

These letters and the path numbers are meant purely as convenient labels, so that students of this system of the Cabala can refer in passing to the 7th Path or the Path of M, instead of having to reference starting and ending points on the Tree of Life.

Letter and number attributions such as these are applied in a different way in older traditions of the Cabala, however. In Greek and Hebrew alike, every letter is also a number, and this gave rise to the custom called isosephy in Greek and gematria in Hebrew: a mystical mathematics in which the value of each word is determined by adding up the number values of the letters that compose it. This habit saw plenty of use in earlier times, as a way of concealing unpopular teachings and of hiding secret teachings from those not yet ready to receive them. Many of the names in the Old and New Testaments alike appear to have been chosen or edited to make them fit numerical schemes, and the same thing is true of later texts influenced by Gnostic traditions.[7]

The version of the Latin alphabet used by English does not have this feature. There are several systems of English numerology; the most common of them, which is given in the table, was among the methods of divination John Gilbert taught. None of these, however, has achieved the kind of general acceptance in spiritual circles that Greek isosephy or Hebrew gematria had within their language communities.

1	2	3	4	5	6	7	8	9
A	B	C	D	E	F	G	H	I
J	K	L	M	N	O	P	Q	R
S	T	U	V	W	X	Y	Z	—

Given enough time, and the sort of subtle editing that has gone into countless scriptures over the centuries, it is entirely possible that a tradition of gematria may emerge in the English language. So far, however, that has not yet happened, and numerology—whatever its value as a divination system—yields equivocal results when used to extract subtle meanings from spiritual writings in English. For now, this branch of Cabalistic tradition may best be seen as a building site left for the work of the architects of the future.

---

[7] The Grail legends are among the examples of this; see Greer 2022a.

The tarot as symbolic synthesis

The attention paid to the tarot trumps in the previous section is anything but accidental. John Gilbert was an expert tarot reader—the best I have ever known—and a gifted teacher of tarot divination, but he also had a keen sense of the deeper dimensions of the tarot. The system of ceremonial initiation he passed on to his students used the tarot as its core symbolic resource.[8] The relations between the trumps and the Tree of Life, in turn, are central to the practical work he taught, and thus to this book. A few words about the tarot are therefore necessary here.

The tarot has been the subject of a great deal of enthusiastic speculation down through the years, not all of it well founded or based on any particular evidence. Despite the claims you may have heard, it did not come from ancient Egypt, nor was it invented by the Romani people or created by a convention of medieval wizards in the city of Fez. Scholars discovered more than a century ago, in fact, that the oldest form of it was invented around 1415 by Marziano da Tortona, the personal secretary of the Duke of Milan, by adding 16 trump cards to the standard Italian playing card deck then in existence.[9]

---

[8] This has been released into the public domain as Greer 2022b.
[9] See, for example, Olsen 1994.

Over the next century or so, different versions of the deck with varying numbers and designs of trump cards became popular in an assortment of northern Italian cities. Finally, one version, the Milanese tarot of 22 trumps, found a new home in the city of Marseille in France and became wildly popular there. This proceeded to give rise to the tarot as we now know it, first as a pack of playing cards and then as a method of fortune-telling. It was in this form that it spread through Europe and came to the attention of the Romani, who adopted it with their usual deftness. Not until the late 18th century, when it had been a fixture in European culture for generations, did the first Cabalists get around to noticing that the 22 trumps of the tarot deck could be assigned to the 22 paths of the Tree of Life.

Granted, this is not as romantic as stories about ancient Egyptian sages. The point that matters is that once Cabalists noticed and adopted the tarot, they reworked it thoroughly, revising the imagery of the trumps as needed to make them fit the symbolism of the Tree of Life, and even changing the order of the cards. Thus it is entirely true that generations of hard work went into making the tarot the elegant Cabalistic instrument it has become. The sole difference from the traditional tale is that the work took place in 19th and early 20th century France, England, and America rather than in Egypt under the pharaohs.

Of the products of that era of creative effort, the one John Gilbert valued most was the deck designed by Arthur Edward Waite and illustrated by Pamela Coleman Smith, usually called the Rider-Waite deck (Rider & Co. was its original publisher). This is the deck that John always used for initiatory purposes, though he used many others for divination. He held that the Rider-Waite was the only deck with the specific symbolic features required by the system of Cabala he received from his teachers.

I am not sure he was entirely correct in this. The impact of the Rider-Waite deck on the tarot tradition in modern times has been so profound that most decks share many of its features, and some decks are essentially Rider-Waite decks redone in slightly different artistic styles. One deck that shares the necessary symbolism is the Builders of the Adytum (BOTA) deck, a lightly modified Rider-Waite deck printed in black on white watercolor paper so that members of the esoteric school that issues it can paint or color their cards themselves. This deck can certainly be used for the purposes of the work given in this book; interestingly, even though BOTA uses the standard Golden Dawn correspondences for the tarot, its deck is in some ways an even closer fit symbolically to John's system than the original Rider-Waite.

THE TAROT AS SYMBOLIC SYNTHESIS

Various other decks may well be close enough to work well with the exercises in this book. One crucial point, however, is that in John's teachings the order of the trumps is always that of the Rider-Waite deck. Thus, the Strength card is always Trump VIII and the Justice card is always Trump XI, not the other way around, as they are in many French and European decks. To work well with the material in this book, a deck should follow the Rider-Waite order.

The fool's pilgrimage

All this implies, of course, that the tarot is not merely a way of telling fortunes, the role that popular culture generally assigns it. As a Cabalistic instrument it has many other uses. One of the most important of these is as a fine source of themes for meditation. Some Western occult schools,

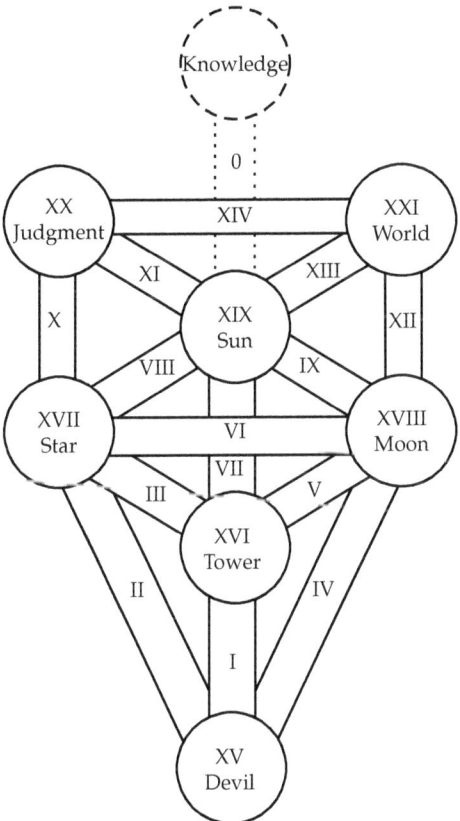

Tarot attributions

in fact, direct their meditative work exclusively toward the imagery and concepts of the tarot, and get excellent results. The practical side of this book is not quite so obsessively tarot-centered as that, though meditation on the trumps certainly has a place in the work ahead. The central role of the tarot in the system taught by John Gilbert is instead as a synthesis of the practical symbolism of the Tree of Life.

In John's teachings, the 22 trumps represent in vivid symbolic images the entire structure of that part of the Tree of Life that the human soul can access. Every sphere and path is present. Notice how, in the diagram above, the trumps fall neatly into three groups of seven: the first group, I–VII, represents the subjective structure of the conscious self and the world that it encounters; the second group, VIII–XIV, represents the

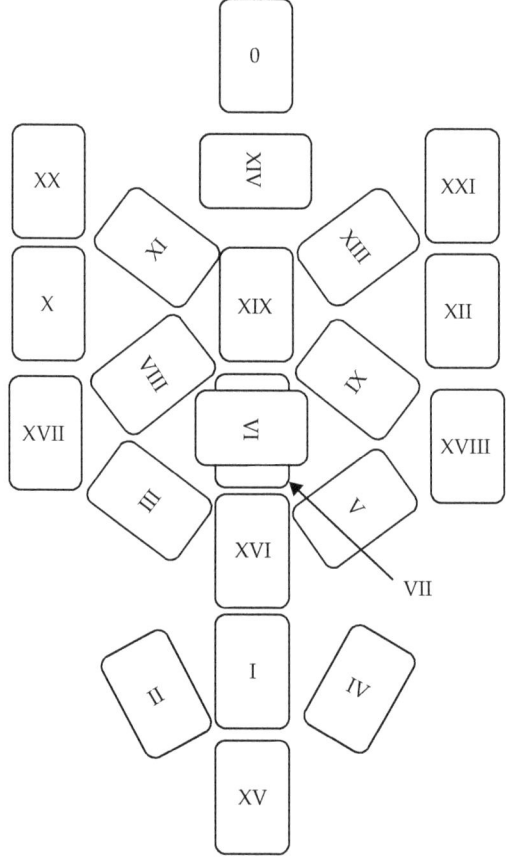

Tarot layout 1

subjective structure of the subconscious self and the world to which it gives access; and the third group, XV–XXI, represents the seven objective spheres that human beings can access in the macrocosm and microcosm alike. Trump 0, finally, has two roles. At the beginning of the sequence of trumps, it represents the ignorant person heedless of the realities of life and death; at the end of the same sequence, it stands for the saint or holy fool who rises up from the point of connection between macrocosm and microcosm, aspiring toward contact with the Divine.

Laying out the cards in this pattern, as shown above, is a useful exercise. It helps in committing the pattern to memory, which is always valuable in the early stages of training, and it also leads the mind to notice meaningful similarities and oppositions among the cards. It also provides more insight into the paths of lightning flash and the arrow, since the paths and spheres emphasized by those symbolic ways of thinking about the Tree of Life correspond to specific tarot trumps which each have their lesson to teach. All this is valuable preparation for the practical work to come.

Another pattern, more traditional, sets out the trumps in three rows of seven, with the Fool by itself above the top row. This is worth doing and studying for the same purposes.

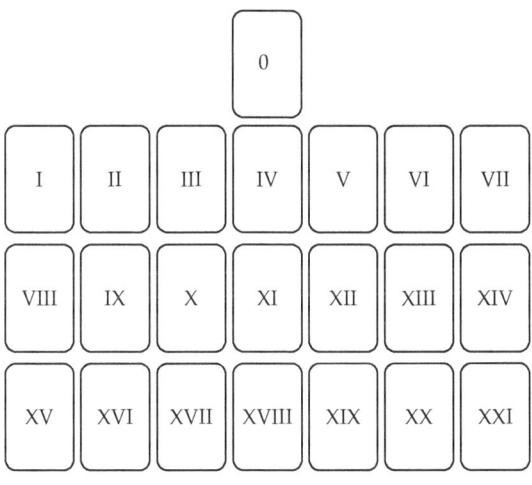

Tarot layout 2

Another layout involves setting out the trumps in the figure-8 pattern shown above the heads of the figures in Trump I, the Magician, and Trump VIII, Strength. This pattern is especially useful because it helps the student see the sequence of trumps as a journey—the Fool's pilgrimage, as John sometimes called it—leading first outward into the objective world and then inward into the subjective world.

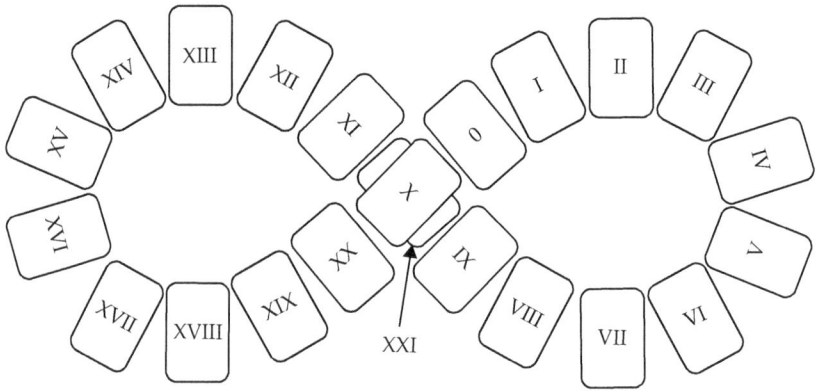

Tarot layout 3

In this diagram the right-hand side represents the objective reality of living in the world known by the senses, and the left-hand side represents the subjective reality of living in the inner world of consciousness, dream, and symbol. Notice how imagery repeats in cards directly above or below each other—for example, the infinity sign above the heads of Trump I, the Magician and Trump VIII, Strength, or the way that the two towers in the distance of Trump XIII, Death, come to the foreground in Trump XVIII, the Moon. This shows how each of the two arcs of the Fool's journey lead into and then back out of the same symbolic landscape.

The pilgrimage of the Fool is best explained through a simple story. It's a story familiar to most of those who take up any kind of occult spirituality, because it is the story of our lives. It begins with a foolish person (Trump 0) who walks off the edge of a cliff, in one sense or another, and ends up baffled, bruised, and in pain. To the Fool comes some encounter with the occult tradition (Trump I), perhaps through a teacher, perhaps through a book or something else. Under the guidance of the Magician, the Fool encounters the four elements of tradition and is initiated by them, awakening the powers of memory, imagination, reason, and intuition (Trumps II–V). Guided by these lessons, the Fool learns how to create the life he or she desires, attracting love (Trump VI), attaining success in a career (Trump VII), overcoming dangers (Trump VIII), and gaining wisdom through acceptance of the human condition (Trump IX).

None of these achievements are permanent, however. The realization that all things in the outer world are transitory (Trump X) and subject to inescapable laws of balance and retribution (Trump XI) shows the Fool the error of a life lived wholly on the objective plane. Understanding this, the Fool plunges headfirst into the inner world (Trump XII) and lets go of all his or her previous successes (Trump XIII). This sets in motion a transformative process (Trump XIV) which ends with the terrible realization that the human soul is held prisoner by its own limitations (Trump XV) and cannot overcome those by its own efforts. It must wait, as though in chains, to be liberated by a force beyond itself.

The moment of liberation (Trump XVI) very often arrives with the force of a thunderbolt. Thereafter, a little at a time, insight begins to dawn (Trump XVII). From that point the Fool must undergo a process of inner maturation (Trump XVIII) until the full light of illumination comes (Trump XIX) and he or she rises up out of the underworld of the subjective realm (Trump XX). Then, having mastered the four elements and found the place of balance in their midst, the Fool can experience the whole process of life as the dance that it is (Trump XXI). And then? The same sequence begins on a higher plane (Trump 0).

This is the way of spiritual development as portrayed by the tarot and fostered by the study and practice of the Cabala. It is not a straight line, or for that matter a zigzag one. Nor does it move in a fixed circle. It cycles from the objective to the subjective and back again, embracing different experiences and new challenges on each arc. Is there a beginning or an end? Not within the limits of the human condition. Humanity is not the be-all and end-all of anything; according to occult tradition, ours is a transitional state, a bridge between the animal and the spiritual, which we each cross at our own speed, once we have finished learning all the lessons of the animal creation and are ready to begin the lessons of the lowest of the spiritual realms. The tarot is one of many tools that can help with that transition. The Cabala is a toolkit with the same purpose—again, one of many.

Learning the attributions

If you wish to make good use of those paired toolkits, you have plenty of work ahead of you. While you proceed through the first steps of the practical work given further on in the third part of this book, learning the art of discursive meditation and exercising it on the symbolism of the ten spheres, it is essential that you learn and commit to memory the basic correspondences of all 22 of the tarot trumps. You should do this using the deck that you intend to work with all through the practices ahead. Again, this should be the Rider-Waite deck, or another deck that shares most if not all of the same symbolism.

As a bare minimum, the symbols included in the following table should be committed to memory. Among the many applications of the trumps is that you can use them as flash cards to check your progress.

Trump	Tree of life	Sphere or path	Astrology	Color	Musical note
I	10–9	Attention	Mars in Aries	Red	C
II	10–8	Memory	Ceres in Virgo	Yellow-green	F
III	9–8	Imagination	Jupiter in Sagittarius	Blue	A flat
IV	10–7	Reason	Sun in Leo	Yellow	E
V	9–7	Intuition	Mercury in Gemini	Orange	D
VI	8–7	Discernment	Venus in Libra	Green	G flat
VII	9–6	Freedom	Uranus in Aquarius	Violet	B flat
VIII	8–6	Courage	N. Node in Gemini	Orange	D
IX	7–6	Instruction	Moon in Cancer	Amber	E flat
X	8–5	Retribution	Moon in Cancer	Amber	E flat

(Continued)

THE TAROT AS SYMBOLIC SYNTHESIS

(Continued)

Trump	Tree of life	Sphere or path	Astrology	Color	Musical note
XI	6–5	Balance	Neptune in Pisces	Magenta	B
XII	7–4	Reversal	Pluto in Scorpio	Blue-green	G
XIII	6–4	Transformation	Vulcan in Taurus	Red-orange	D flat
XIV	5–4	Verification	Sun in Leo	Yellow	E
XV	10	Manifestation	Earth/Saturn	Indigo	A
XVI	9	Foundation	Moon	Violet	B flat
XVII	8	Competence	Mercury	Orange	D
XVIII	7	Desire	Venus	Green	G flat
XIX	6	Harmony	Sun	Yellow	E
XX	5	Power	Mars	Red	C
XXI	4	Love	Jupiter	Blue	A flat
0	6 to Knowledge	Seeking	S. Node in Sagittarius	Blue	A flat

The musical notes assigned to the seven trumps from XV to XXI are not the same as the keynotes assigned to the spheres that correspond to these cards. The notes corresponding to the trumps belong to a different system, one that was brought into Cabalistic practice by Paul Foster Case and reworked by several later writers. Its application will be explained later on. For now, find some instrument, as simple as you like, and play and then hum the note associated with each card as you study it, so the note and the card become associated in your mind.

As you study the tarot trumps and the symbols assigned to them, your goal should be to have their places on the Tree of Life, their titles in this system, and their colors and musical notes come readily to mind. This will make the work ahead easier and more productive.

PART THREE

PRACTICE OF THE CABALA

Each of the great branches of the Cabalistic tree has its own standard methods of practice. In the broad tradition of occult Cabala from which the teachings in this book derive, the core methods are three: discursive meditation, active imagination, and ritual. Each of these requires a few words of basic orientation before we proceed to the instructions.

The great popularity of Asian methods of meditation in the modern Western world has made a good many people forget that the West has its own traditional meditation practices. Discursive meditation is the most important and, in earlier days, the most widely practiced of these. In discursive meditation, instead of silencing the thinking mind, practitioners guide, direct, and discipline their thoughts, guiding them toward the exploration of a theme—a concept, an image, or a short passage from a sacred text or an instructional document. The theme and the insights that emerge from it become the focus of concentration and awareness, providing the same benefits that practitioners gain from other forms of meditation.

At the same time, the process of discursive meditation allows the theme to be "unpacked" in the mind of the meditator, revealing facets of itself not obvious to a more casual glance. Many traditions of Western esoteric spirituality make deliberate use of this "unpacking" process as a way to pass on teachings: the cryptic emblems of alchemy and the equally enigmatic images of the tarot are among the examples, communicating teachings in such a way that only those who are ready for them can understand and apply them.

Alongside discursive meditation, using some of the same skills but applying them in a very different way, is the practice of active imagination. This name comes from Carl Jung, who made it a central part of his own system of inner work, but the practice of active imagination did not originate with Jung, or with psychology. Occult texts often refer to the same practice as "scrying"—an archaic term for "seeing" that also appears in the word "descry." In a Cabalistic context, it is also called "pathworking," since it is very often used to unfold inner experiences related to the 22 paths of the Tree of Life.

Active imagination might also be called "directed daydreaming." In active imagination, practitioners create a frame for imaginative experience and then let images and events rise up spontaneously to fill in the space within the frame. One classic method, much used in the occult Cabala, is to set out on an imagined journey and allow the scenery of the journey to be whatever happens to surface. As Jung pointed out in his writings on active imagination, and as many occultists have discussed in their own terms, the images that surface in such experiences are not merely the results of vagaries of the individual mind. Transpersonal, archetypal, and spiritual contents also rise into consciousness from the subconscious self, and become accessible to the practitioner.

If active imagination is combined with the other disciplines of the occult Cabala, these deeper contents can provide remarkable insights into the subtle dimensions of existence and the needs, potentials, and powers of the individual soul. They can also provide, as some dreams and some daydreams do, a source of motivation and energy, hard to define but easy to recognize in practice. Most of us have seen in others, and some of us have experienced in ourselves, the rush of vitality and enthusiasm that comes to anyone with a strongly and vividly imagined goal. Active imagination is among other things a way of accessing that power at will.

Active imagination functions as the pillar of force in the Tree of Cabalistic practice, and discursive meditation serves accordingly as the pillar of form. The middle pillar between them is ritual. The influential 20th-century Druid teacher Ross Nichols liked to say that "ritual is poetry in the world of acts." It is an insightful definition. Just as the language used in poetry is meant to be taken symbolically rather than literally—when Robert Burns compared one of his many lovers to a red, red rose, he did not mean that comparison to be taken in a botanical sense!—ritual is symbolic action. It brings about a temporary union of the inner and outer worlds, which allows outward acts to have potent inward effects.

Some traditions in the occult Cabala make use of long and complex ritual workings drawn from, or at least strongly influenced by, the literature of medieval magic. A student of one of these systems can expect to spend anything up to two hours at a time performing rituals meant to consecrate working tools, empower talismans, commune with spiritual beings, or the like. Those can be worthwhile exercises and they provide good training for the will and imagination, but there are less labored ways to accomplish that training, and also to achieve the practical benefits at which such rituals generally aim.

The material presented in this book takes one of these less labored approaches. It works with four core ritual workings—the sanctum ritual, the establishment of the Tree of Life in the aura, the bridge of light practice, and the use of the magical images of the spheres as bodies of transformation. These are used in sequence, and combined with meditation and active imagination, to bring about spiritual regeneration in the individual practitioner and positive transformations in his or her environment.

Discursive meditation, active imagination, and ritual are thus the keys to the practical side of the Cabala. In the pages that follow, these practices will be presented in detail and the steps to their mastery set out.

The technical side of Cabalistic practice, however, is not the only aspect that deserves discussion here. There is also the matter of motives and goals. It used to be common in books on the Cabala, and for that matter on the whole range of Western inner spirituality, to insert portentous warnings about right and wrong motives for taking up this kind of practical work. Doing so for less than perfectly pure reasons, according to the usual rhetoric, guarantees a hefty serving of dreadful though usually unspecified consequences.

There are at least two problems with this sort of rhetoric. The first is that people who have not yet taken up a course of intensive spiritual practice rarely have sufficient self-knowledge to know what their real motives are. The second is that, being human, their real motives are inevitably a very mixed bag. All these warnings generally accomplished was to encourage a great deal of half-conscious hypocrisy among novices, who did their level best to suppress their awareness of the less creditable side of their own motives for practice.

Plato had a better idea. In several of his dialogues, especially *The Symposium*, he pointed out that our motives are not set in stone. We desire what seems good to us according to our understanding, and that understanding can change. The education of desire is thus a central theme in Platonist teaching.

A student begins, let us say, convinced that he can be happy if only he can get past a certain problem in his outer life, and never notices that his own attitudes and actions are what keep that problem fixed in place. Instead of flinging him out the door of the school because his motives are mixed, the Platonist teacher gives the student exercises and instructions that lead him to the discovery that he is the source of most of his problems, and can solve the problems by changing the attitudes and habits that cause them. As the student comes to grips with this and begins the hard work of personal change, his life alters accordingly; he is happy because the problem has gone away, but he has also gained the knowledge and skills that he needs to overcome other problems that confront him. Step by step, he walks the road to wisdom, and his motives change with each step as he understands himself and the cosmos more completely.

Every desire, according to Plato's teaching, no matter how confused or destructive, is ultimately a desire for the Divine, hidden under one or more of its veils. Some of those veils can be very thick! Nonetheless, even mixed and murky motives can lead in the right direction, so long as they inspire the discipline and steady effort required to follow the course of instruction given in the pages that follow. This is as much as to say that every road, however rough and winding, eventually leads home.

Stage one: discursive meditation

As noted above, discursive meditation—the kind of meditation central to the work that follows—is not the same as the varieties of meditation that are usually taught and practiced in the modern Western world. Those latter were imported from Asia as part of the great influx of Eastern wisdom to the West in the late 19th and 20th centuries. One thing that nearly all of them had in common was a traditional habit of hostility to the thinking mind. "The mind is the slayer of the Real, slay thou the slayer!" That was how Helena Blavatsky, whose Theosophical Society played a crucial role in importing Eastern teachings to the West, described the central purpose of Asian meditative practice.

There can be a point to this approach, but by and large it is only suited to people who are prepared to turn away from life in the world and settle in monasteries or hermitages, where they no longer need to use the thinking mind. Asian cultures have long made room for this approach. In India, everyone knows the difference between a pandit, who studies the scriptures and can think clearly about them, and a sannyasin, who has renounced thinking along with everything else and seeks only salvation. In the Western world, unfortunately, that sort of clarity is less common, and so practices suited only to sannyasins and the equivalent are passed on to people who have families to support and everyday activities to manage in the hurly-burly of ordinary human society. This has produced too many would-be mystics who can't think clearly or function well in the complexities of daily life.

Discursive meditation, by contrast, is meant for people who are still active in the everyday world, and seek to flourish at all of the levels of the Tree of Life that human beings can attain. It does not work by stopping the thinking process. Instead, it focuses awareness on the thinking process itself. Following a train of thought to its conclusion in this way, with a sustained meditative focus on the process and content of thinking, can become as much of a meditative exercise as reciting a mantra.

A few ground rules for discursive meditation should be kept in mind before we begin. You should plan on practicing every day; many people find that first thing in the morning, before the cares and concerns of the day have a chance to fill your mind, is the best time for meditation practice. If you practice meditation later in the day, you should wait at least half an hour after eating before you meditate, since after a meal your blood and vital energy concentrates in your digestive tract, rather than being available to your brain. Sexual activity of any kind, including masturbation, also redirects the blood and vital energy away from the brain, and the same rule applies here also: wait at least half an hour before beginning your practice. Most intoxicants interfere with meditation, so if you drink or use drugs, wait until after all the effects have cleared, including any hangover or the equivalent, before meditating. The one exception seems to be caffeine, if used in mild to moderate amounts: a cup of tea or ordinary coffee before meditating seems to do no harm, and some people insist that it helps.

Certain practical requirements also need to be in place before you can practice discursive meditation. You will need a place that is quiet and not too brightly lit. It should provide you with privacy during the time you spend meditating; a room with a door you can shut is best, though if you can't arrange that, a quiet corner and a little forbearance on the part of the people you live with will be quite adequate. (It can be a bedroom or a space you use for some other purpose during the rest of the day—you don't need to set a room aside purely for your practices.) You will need a chair with a straight back and an unpadded seat, at a height that allows you to rest your feet flat on the floor while keeping your thighs level with the ground. You will need a clock or watch, placed so that you can see it easily without moving your head.

You will also need a practice journal. Any convenient notebook will do. You will be using the same notebook to record the results of work with active imagination and ritual, however, so get one with a good number of pages. As soon as you have finished each practice session, write down the date, the time, the theme of the meditation, how the practice went, and any ideas or insights that occurred to you while you were meditating. Once you have all these items ready, you are ready to begin learning discursive meditation.

Posture

Asian methods of meditation generally require difficult physical postures that most Western people cannot use comfortably. One of the useful features of discursive meditation is that it does not have this requirement. The Western posture of meditation is a simple, stable way of sitting on a chair. Sit down with your seat far enough forward that your back is not touching the back of the chair.[10] Have your feet flat on the floor, side by side or a little apart. Your legs should be vertical from ankle to knee and horizontal from knee to hip, so that your knees and hips are at right angles. Rest your hands palm down on your thighs, and hold your head straight without tension. Keep your eyes open but relax your eyelids. Look forward and down, as though gazing at something on the floor a few yards ahead of you. Breathe slowly and easily.

Your first lesson in meditation is to take this position, and don't move for five minutes. Don't fidget, shift, wiggle, scratch an itch or anything else. Leave your body completely still for five minutes by the clock. This will not be easy! Do this once a day for a week.

Unless you've already practiced meditation, or explored certain other exercises that have the same effect, this will be much more difficult than you expect. One of the results of our habitual focus on the outer world and our equally habitual neglect of our inner worlds is that our bodies are usually packed full of tensions and discomforts we never notice. Most people constantly fidget and wiggle and shift because they are tense and uncomfortable, but this is so constant a factor in their lives that it never enters into consciousness. The point of this exercise is to make it conscious.

---

[10] If you have a back injury or some other condition that requires back support, on the other hand, you can dispense with this detail and rest your back against the back of the chair.

Keep still for those five minutes, no matter what. As you do this, you will begin the work that meditation is meant to do: you will start becoming aware of your own inner life, instead of remaining forever fixated on the world outside yourself. This is quite literally the most boring, grueling, frustrating thing you will ever do, but it is also the most powerful tool for personal liberation you will ever experience. Once you realize just how important it is, and how great the benefits are, doing it every day will stop being a chore or a burden; as Dion Fortune says in one of her books, skipping a day's meditation will feel as uncomfortable as skipping a meal.[11]

This practice, and all those that follow, should be preceded by the opening visualization and followed by the closing self-massage given below.

Opening visualization

Most traditions of inner work include some way of clearing the mind of the practitioner and cleansing the place of practice of unwanted influences before meditation. Those readers who know their way around Japanese *anime* will recall the *kuji-in*, the nine mysterious hand postures used by ninja and practitioners of other Japanese esoteric traditions. Those are quite real, of course; each interlacing of the fingers is associated with a Buddhist deity, a mantra, and an image held in the mind. All these serve to focus and direct the consciousness of the practitioner, and they are often used as a preparation for meditation of various kinds.

The teachings I received from John Gilbert included several such practices, though none of these have yet found their way into *anime*! One of them, the Sphere of Protection ritual, has already been featured in a number of my books, among them *The Druid Magic Handbook*, *The Dolmen Arch*, and *The Way of the Golden Section*. It is an effective preparation for meditation, among its many other uses, and if you already practice it you can certainly do that before your meditation practice. Equally, the Lesser Ritual of the Pentagram—a basic ritual in the Golden Dawn tradition—has long been used for the same purpose and can be used if you prefer.

---

[11] Fortune 1987, p. 135.

STAGE ONE: DISCURSIVE MEDITATION 113

For those readers who have not yet taken up any such practice, on the other hand, one of John's simpler methods of preparing the practitioner and the space is equally suitable. This is among the things John learned from his teacher Dr. Juliet Ashley. Confusingly enough, she called it the Sphere of Protection, though its structure is very different from the ritual of that name. In this book we will call it the opening visualization. Perform it as follows.

First, take the posture described above.

Second, say aloud: "Let a strong Sphere of Protection be established around me."

Third, imagine a current of sparkling green energy rising up from the center of the earth to your solar plexus, the region just below your ribcage. This represents the telluric current. Say aloud: "I lift the spiritual energy of the Divine from Mother Earth below me to place myself inside a Sphere of Protection."

Fourth, imagine a current of intense, brilliant white energy descending from the heavens above you to your solar plexus, where it blends with the green energy. This white energy represents the solar current. Say aloud: "I call down the spiritual energy of the Divine from the heavens above me to strengthen the Sphere of Protection around me."

Fifth, imagine the two currents kindling a brilliant golden light which expands outward from your solar plexus, forming a sphere of light around you three or four feet out from your body. This golden light represents the lunar current, the secret current produced by the proper union of the solar and telluric currents. Say aloud: "I call upon the spiritual energy of the Divine Within me to reinforce this Sphere of Protection around me."

Take a moment to see and feel yourself within the golden sphere of light. Feel yourself protected and focused. Then proceed with your practice.

Closing self-massage

When you finish your practice, it's helpful to do something to bring your attention back to ordinary concerns so you can go on with your day. This set of simple self-massage movements will do that very effectively, and also free up the flow of the life force throughout the body. It is borrowed from *Do-In* (導引, pronounced "dough-inn"), one of the most ancient of the Asian healing arts, and was adopted from that source into certain esoteric schools in France in the last century. The set of massage movements I recommend is very simple and takes just a few minutes. Do it sitting in your chair right after you finish your meditation practice.

One crucial detail is almost always forgotten by beginners, however, so I will insert it here and then repeat it. *Between each set of movements, pause, breathe deeply, and relax.* As you relax, imagine all unnecessary tension draining out of you. That moment of stillness between movements is at least as important as the massage itself.

First, rub your hands together vigorously, palm to palm. Then rub the back of each hand and fingers with the other hand. Do this until the skin is warm.

Pause, breathe, and relax.

Second, hold your arms out loosely in front of you and shake your hands, letting them flop freely. Do this for a minute or so.

Pause, breathe, and relax.

Third, wrap the fingers of one hand around the thumb of the other, as though taking hold of a handle. Pull gently, and let your thumb slide out against the pressure of the fingers. Do this to every finger on both hands in turn.

Pause, breathe, and relax.

Fourth, rub your face, making little circles with your fingertips. Start up at the hairline (or where your hairline used to be, if you're balding) and work down the face, trying not to miss any spot. Press harder or softer depending on how it feels—if it hurts, you're pressing too hard.

Pause, breathe, and relax.

Fifth, form your hands into loose fists and tap them gently and rhythmically all over your scalp, from your hairline back and around all the way to the nape of your neck and from one side to the other. Again, if it hurts you're doing it too hard.

Pause, breathe, and relax.

Sixth, still sitting, cross one leg across the other knee, so it's easy for you to get to your foot. Tap the sole of your foot from the heel up to the toes with a loose fist. Most people can do this a good deal harder here than on the scalp! Then, using both hands, rub the top and sole of the foot until the skin is warm. (You can do this in stocking feet if you prefer—it's just as effective.)

Put your foot down flat. Pause, breathe, and relax.

Seventh, repeat the process with your other foot.

Put that foot down flat. Pause, breathe, and relax.

That completes the process. Do this after each daily practice of meditation.

Relaxation

The second week's work is devoted to relaxation. Most people these days realize that it's possible to be too tense. The opposite of one bad idea is generally another bad idea, and it's also possible to be too relaxed. Until quite recently, very few people in Western societies suffered from this problem—instead, nearly everybody in Western societies was far too tense. Teachers of spiritual exercises accordingly focused on relaxation practices, and now it's not at all uncommon to meet people who are so relaxed they are limp and floppy. This is no more useful than excessive tension. The goal here as elsewhere is to find the balanced midpoint between the extremes: between too much tension and too much relaxation lies the state of poise.

The posture you have learned, which is fixed and slightly unnatural, will help keep you from becoming too relaxed. Keeping the spine straight, the head held up, the legs parallel, and the body still requires a slight but necessary tension in an assortment of muscles. Now it is time to move from one pillar to the other, symbolically speaking, and see to it that you do not become too tense. This is done by relaxing your muscles while retaining the posture you've established. You remain motionless, without shifting or wiggling or stretching. All you do is let go of the tensions you do not need to keep the posture.

Start at the crown of the head. Consciously relax any muscular tensions you find there. If you encounter a tension that does not want to release, imagine that it is relaxing and go on. (You will find that over time, imagination will become reality.) Spend a few moments relaxing the top of your head, and then move further down your head. Consciously relax any tensions you find there, or imagine the tensions dissolving if they will not relax at once. Go all the way down your whole body this way, a little at a time. As you reach every part of your body, consciously relax what you can, and imagine the rest letting go. This should take you at least five minutes, and quite possibly more. As you do this, maintain the seated posture without moving. Focus on your body, without paying attention to anything but the tension and relaxation of your muscles.

Many people find that the first few times they do this, they ache from head to foot afterwards. Some find that some part of their body hurts more than others. This is normal. All that pain and discomfort in your body was there all along. You simply learned not to notice it. As you practice this simple relaxation drill, day by day, the excess tension will gradually drain away, leaving you less burdened by unnecessary stress and pain. You may also find that some of your muscles feel as though they have had a workout. Of course, they have—you have been holding your body in an unfamiliar position, which requires you to use some of your muscles. With a few days of practice that will become easy.

Do this every day for a week, beginning with the opening visualization and finishing with the closing self-massage. Then proceed to the third step of preparation for meditation.

Breathing

Different patterns of breathing can have powerful effects on your state of consciousness, and many esoteric traditions from around the world have methods for using this in their practices. Some of those methods require close supervision by an experienced teacher, who has been through the process and knows the signs of trouble to watch for. Breathwork of certain kinds can stimulate the vagus nerve, a nerve that connects the vital organs with the brain, and so can have significant effects on your nervous system and your endocrine glands. This means that if you do certain kinds of intensive breathwork without skilled supervision, you can give yourself serious health problems.

Fortunately not all forms of breathwork have this drawback. There are methods of breathwork that are perfectly safe to practice on your own. One of them, the fourfold breath, has become the standard method for meditative practice in many occult schools. It is very simple. Breathe in through your nose, slowly and deeply, to the count of 4. Hold the breath in to the count of 4. Breathe out through your nose, slowly and fully, to the count of 4. Hold the breath out to the count of 4. Repeat over and over to the same steady rhythm.

How fast or slow to make the rhythm of counting is up to you. It is best to make it as slow as you can while still remaining comfortable. If you gasp or run out of air, you are counting too slowly! Similarly, make it a reasonably deep breath but don't strain to breathe in as much as possible. Keep the movement of your breath steady, gentle, and flowing. No two people will have exactly the same rhythm, nor will you have the same rhythm every time you practice. Don't use a metronome or any other mechanical aid. Give yourself the chance each time to find a pace that works for you.

One point to keep in mind as you learn the fourfold breath is that you shouldn't hold your breath by closing your throat. Hold it instead by keeping the muscles of your chest and abdomen in their positions, either expanded or relaxed. If you're used to closing your throat to hold your breath, it can take some practice to stop doing so. How do you tell if you're closing your throat? Draw in a deep breath, hold it for a little while, and then breathe out. If you hear or feel a little "pop" inside your throat, you've closed it. To keep from doing that, keep trying to breathe in a trickle of air while you hold your breath in, and keep trying to breathe out a trickle of air when you're holding your breath out. You'll get the hang of it quickly.

For the next week, five minutes of the fourfold breath will be your practice. Take the meditation, perform the opening visualization, hold yourself still, and let the tension drain away from the crown of your head to the soles of your feet. Take a minute or two to do this, then begin the fourfold breath. Keep doing the breathing for five minutes by the clock. Then perform the closing self-massage to finish.

Meditation

Posture, relaxation, and breathing are the preliminaries to discursive meditation. With the preliminaries out of the way, you can proceed to meditation itself. To make sense of the instructions that follow, keep in mind that the word "meditation" literally means "thinking." This is why the word "premeditated" refers to a crime that the perpetrator thought about before committing, not one for which he prepared by chanting a mantra!

As you practice discursive meditation, you will be thinking, deliberately, seriously, and intentionally. The subject for each day's meditation is called the *theme* of the meditation. Themes for meditation can come from almost any imaginable source. During the time you spend working on this book, of course, your themes will come from the Cabala, and specifically from the structures and symbolism of the Tree of Life and the cards of the tarot deck. You will choose a theme before you start each meditation session, and focus on that theme and nothing else during that session.

Begin in the following way. Take the posture of meditation and perform the opening visualization. Relax excess tensions from your body, beginning with the top of your head and descending from there, and then spend five minutes by the clock practicing the fourfold breath. At this point, if you wish, you can say a brief prayer to whatever form of the Divine you revere, asking for guidance and inspiration in your meditation.

Then the real work begins. Call to mind the theme you have chosen. For your very first meditation in this sequence, the theme is the concept of "tree." What is a tree? What makes something a tree and not a shrub or a bush? Genealogists talk of family trees, and computer scientists of decision trees—what do these metaphoric trees have in common with actual trees? What role have trees played in your life, and what roles do they play in the life of humanity? Many other questions like this may come to mind. All of them, finally, feed into the question that matters most: why does the Cabala describe the structure of macrocosm and microcosm as a tree? Sort through these various questions, choose one that interests you, and think about it.

As you do so, your thoughts will wander off the theme. Bring them back. They'll wander off again. Bring them back again. You'll have as much trouble keeping your mind on the theme as the practitioners of other styles of meditation have keeping thoughts at bay, and you'll develop the same skills of catching your mind wandering and bringing it back to the subject of the meditation. Spend ten minutes pursuing that one question. Even if it seems as though you are getting nowhere with it, keep your mind circling around it and exploring it.

Sometimes, especially at first, you will spend an entire practice session doing nothing but catching your thoughts as they stray and bringing them back to the theme. At other times, there will be intervals of clear thinking between bursts of irrelevant mental chatter, and in those intervals another kind of work will take place. You will learn something about the theme, and you'll also be working on the capacity for focused reflective thought, an essential human skill that is very poorly developed by most of us. Keep working on the theme for ten minutes by the clock. When you are finished, do the closing self-massage, write up your experiences in your practice journal, and then go on with the rest of your day.

Themes for practice

This is the method of meditation you will use for the work in this book. A few helpful hints may be useful before we proceed. The first is that your results will be better if you take each theme in very small bites. That's why you should focus on just one train of thought having to do with trees in your first practice session, and then go on to another the next day, and still another the day after that. Once you have meditated on all the thoughts and questions that trees bring to mind, go on and do the same thing to the concept of life. What is life? What makes something alive? Where does life come from, and where does it go? Many other questions follow from the concept of life, and once again all of them feed into the question that matters most: why does the Cabala describe the basic structure of existence as a tree of *life*, rather than some other kind of tree?

The concepts "tree" and "life" are your first two themes for meditation. Give each of them several sessions of meditation at least, with ten minutes of actual meditation (apart from the opening visualization, relaxation, breathing, and closing self-massage) as a minimum for each session. Then go on to the ten spheres of the Tree of Life. Start with the first sphere, Awareness. Start with the concept of awareness itself, devoting at least one session of meditation to that, and then go on to meditate on all the other concepts and correspondences associated with the first sphere, taking them one at a time. You can give each of them as many sessions as you wish. If ten minutes of meditation becomes easy for you, start doing 15. 20 minutes a day is a good maximum at this stage of the work.

When you have finished with the first sphere, go on to the second, and proceed from there step by step down the tree. Take your time. There is nothing to be gained by hurrying through the process—quite the contrary, the more time you put into meditating on the basics, the better the results will be later on. Do this while learning the sanctum ceremony, which is covered in the next section of this book, and you will be well prepared for the stages of practice that follow. There will be plenty of material for further meditations as you proceed!

Much of what results from this will seem completely useless to you, especially at first. Keep at it anyway. You are learning to ask the questions that most people never ask because they seem too simple, or too pointless, or too silly. Those questions very often matter more than the ones that seem important at first glance. As Charles Fort, that indefatigable researcher of the impossible, wrote: "It is by thinking things that schoolboys know better than to think that discoveries are made."[12]

Give yourself the freedom to ask questions and explore concepts that seem absurd or meaningless at first glance. One of the benefits of doing this is that you will start to notice how many of the questions and concepts that are treated as serious and important in modern life are more absurd than anything you can come up with yourself. This will make it easier for you to think your own thoughts and make your own choices in life, instead of copying the thoughts and choices of others—and this, in turn, is among the secret gifts of meditation.

Helps to meditation

The work of discursive meditation can be made a little more productive by adding two further elements to the work. The first is a way to generate new perspectives on the themes you work with; the second is a way to put the experience of wandering thoughts to work for you.

The first of these, the art of combinations, was created by the Catalan mystic Ramón Lull back in the late 13th century. Lull encountered early forms of the Cabala and was inspired by his studies to create a remarkable system of inner work, the Lullian Art. All through the Middle Ages and Renaissance, his insights were developed in various ways, some more complicated and others less. The art of combinations I learned from an offshoot of the Druid tradition some years ago is one of the simplest forms, and works very well as an aid to discursive meditation.

The method is quite simple. You need to learn, and commit to memory, the seven basic conceptions and seven simple questions introduced in the symbolism of the spheres earlier in this book. As a reminder, the conceptions are being, becoming, source, substance, power, purpose, and value, and the questions are whether, what, how, who, where, when, and why. If you combine each question with each conception, you end up with 49 inquiries, each of which can be applied to a theme in meditation.

As an example, let's take the first conception, being, and add the questions. The results are "whether it is," "what it is," "how (in what manner or form) it is," "whose it is," "where it is," "when it is," and

---

[12] Fort 1933, p. 210.

"why it is." If you can answer these seven inquiries about something you know quite a bit about that thing—and any one of these inquiries, applied to a theme, can yield enough fodder for one session of meditation. Next, you can go on to the second conception, becoming, and generate a similar set of inquiries: "whether it becomes," "what it becomes," "how it becomes," "whose (or who) it becomes," "where it becomes," "when it becomes," and "why it becomes." Then proceed to the third, and so on.

Two simple pointers will make this easier to work. First, a certain amount of flexibility in wording the combinations makes generating inquiries easier: thus "being + whether" works out to "whether it is." In the same way, "power + what" can be "what powers it," and "value + who" can be "who values it." Second, not every inquiry is applicable to every theme: it's a rare theme, in fact, that can be explored with the full set of 49 inquiries. Treat the art of combinations as a way of coming up with ideas for meditation, not a straitjacket into which every theme has to be stuffed by force.

Alongside the method of combinations is a habit you can take up whenever your mind strays away from the theme. Instead of breaking off the straying thought and going straight back to the theme, follow your train of thought backward step by step to where you left the theme, and then go on from there. Suppose you set out to meditate on the tarot trump corresponding to the sixth sphere—Trump XIX, the Sun—and all at once you realize that you're thinking about Afghanistan instead. Yes, this sort of thing happens to all of us! Instead of leaping back to the tarot card, figure out how your thoughts wandered all the way to Afghanistan. What occupied your thoughts before Afghanistan? You were thinking of guerrilla warfare. And before that? You were thinking of gorillas. And before that? You were thinking of bananas. And before bananas? It occurred to you that in the tarot deck you own, the sun in Trump XIX is exactly the color of a ripe banana, bringing you back to the theme.

Tracing your thoughts back to the theme benefits you in two ways. First of all, it teaches you to pay closer attention to your thoughts, which is a valuable skill in discursive meditation. Second, it teaches your thinking mind to run back to the theme just as enthusiastically as it runs away from it. With time and practice, your mind will get in the habit of keeping itself entertained by making little forays to each side of the theme and then returning to the main route of your meditation, and quite often these little forays will bring back images and ideas that will enrich your understanding of the theme itself.

As your work with meditation continues, explore both these helps to your practice and use them whenever it seems appropriate. You should be able to use both of them easily before you finish your first sequence of meditations descending the Tree of Life and proceed to the next phase of the work, in which active imagination starts to play a role.

Stage two: the sanctum ceremonies

The ritual work presented in this book is a relatively simple form of a much richer and more complex system. People vary in their attitudes toward ritual; for some it is a chore, for others it is a performing art made even more enticing than other arts by the fact that the performer and the audience are the same person. Those readers who want to expand the ritual dimension of this practice are welcome to do so, and almost any opening and closing ceremony can be used for this purpose. Those that are descended from John Gilbert's work, which I have published in several books, are especially well suited to this purpose.[13]

For those who prefer a simpler approach, at least at first, the following ritual will be found entirely adequate for the work. Certain suggestions for expansion, derived from the more complete system, have been included later in this section for those who are interested in exploring them.

The place where you will be doing your ritual work is called a sanctum, from a Latin word meaning "set apart" or "sacred." You can make this the same place where you practice your daily meditation and

---

[13] See Greer 2021 and Greer 2022b for rituals particularly well suited to this.

other Cabalistic work. In order to perform the basic sanctum ceremonies, you will need a few items:

- A place where you can have privacy for half an hour to an hour at a time. You do not have to set aside a room specifically for this; as with your meditation practice, a corner of a bedroom is quite adequate.
- An altar with an altar cloth. This may be any small table or folding tray, or the top of a bookshelf, covered with a cloth of any convenient type.
- A chair. The same chair you use for your meditations is suitable.

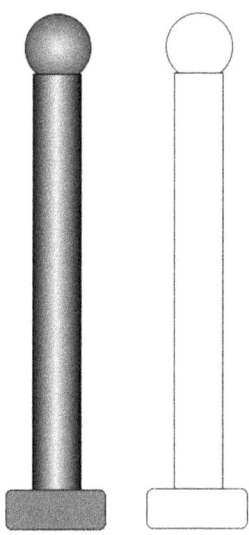

Two Pillars

- Two pillars, one black and one white. They should be between 6 and 12 inches tall and an inch or so in diameter; you can make them of any convenient substance, depending on your resources. (A pair of cardboard cylinders from the center of rolls of paper towels, one covered with black paper and the other with white, will do quite adequately if that is what you can manage.) Before and after the ceremony, they are set somewhere near the altar but not on it. During the ceremony, at the point indicated below, they are set upon the altar, the black one on the left side and the white one on the right side.

- Emblems of the four symbolic elements. These are small objects placed on the altar. A folding fan, a votive candle in a holder, a cup or glass of water, and a small dish of salt are quite adequate. If you wish something more formal, however, instructions for preparing and consecrating the four working tools of the elements—the book of air, the wand of fire, the cup of water, and the pentacle of earth—are given later on in this section.

If possible, your sanctum should be large enough that you can set up the altar more or less in the middle and walk around it in a circle. If you can't arrange for this, simply put the altar on one side of the space and the chair on the other side. If you have at least enough room to stand between them and turn around in a circle, this is sufficient.

The first ritual practice to learn, which you should begin as soon as you start learning discursive meditation, is the opening and closing ceremony. This uses the opening visualization presented earlier, but places it in a ceremonial context. Practice this at least twice a week until you can do it from memory. Only when you no longer need to fumble with a book or a "cheat sheet" can you combine imagination, will, and memory to make a ritual working function as it should and accomplish what it can.

The reference to the inner teachers in the opening and closing ceremonies relates to a very widespread tradition among Cabalists and occultists generally that the great initiates and adepts of the past, while they are no longer incarnate in physical bodies, are still active in the inner side of things as teachers and guides to today's students. By calling them in this way you are inviting their guidance and help. This assistance will almost certainly not be obvious, at least at first; it very often takes the form of little intuitive glimpses and helpful coincidences that direct you away from blind alleys and toward productive directions of study and practice. Subtle as it so often is, the help of the inner teachers is a real factor and is worth inviting.

The references to the Divine in the opening and closing ceremonies are phrased according to John Gilbert's usual habits. They may be adjusted to fit your own religious beliefs. By all means invoke the deity or deities to whom you pray, using whatever names and other symbolism is appropriate.

With all this in mind, we can proceed to the sanctum ceremonies themselves.

Opening ceremony

Before you begin, have the four symbols of the elements on the altar, and the black and white pillars ready to be placed on the altar. Be sure that you know where east, south, west and north are. (The kind of simple pocket compass used by hikers can help with this.) Sit in the chair facing the altar, and take a few moments to clear and center your mind. Then rise and go to the altar. Say: "I prepare to open this sanctum in due form. I invoke the presence and protection of my guardian angel." (If you are a Pagan, or for some other reason are uncomfortable with the words "guardian angel," use the phrase "guardian genius" instead— this is what the ancient Romans called the beneficent spirit that protects each individual.) Imagine the guardian angel or guardian genius as a tall, winged, luminous figure in the east, facing you. Be aware of its protective influence.

Once you have done this, place the black and white pillars on the altar, the black pillar on the left side and the white pillar on the right side, both toward the back. Then say: "Let a strong Sphere of Protection be established around this sanctum."

Imagine a current of sparkling green energy, representing the telluric current, rising up from the center of the earth. Imagine it forming a sphere of green light just above the altar. Say aloud: "I lift the spiritual energy of the Divine from Mother Earth below me to place this sanctum within a Sphere of Protection."

Imagine a current of intense, brilliant white energy, representing the solar current, descending from the heavens above you. It comes down to the space above the altar, where it blends with the green energy. Say aloud: "I call down the spiritual energy of the Divine from the heavens above me to strengthen the Sphere of Protection within this sanctum."

Imagine the two currents kindling a brilliant golden light representing the lunar current. This expands outward from the altar, forming a sphere of light around the entire space where you are doing the working. Say aloud: "I call upon the spiritual energy of the Divine Within me to reinforce this Sphere of Protection within my sanctum and around me."

Say: "I now clear and cleanse this sanctum according to the ancient ways." Take the fan (or other emblem of air) to the east, and raise it up in front of you. Imagine the wind blowing toward you from the east, and imagine it swirling around the fan. Now walk clockwise around the sanctum (or, in a small sanctum, turn clockwise where you stand) with the fan, and say the following words as you do so: "I purify this sanctum and all within it with the element of air, and I invoke the spirits and powers of air. May they bless this sanctum and further its work."

When you have finished the circle, put the fan back on the altar. Pick up the incense or other symbol of fire, take it to the south, and hold it up before you. Imagine heat streaming toward you from the south, and imagine it flowing around the incense. Walk or turn clockwise around the sanctum with the incense, and say the following words as you do so: "I purify this sanctum and all within it with the element of fire, and I invoke the spirits and powers of fire. May they bless this sanctum and further its work."

When you have finished the circle, put the incense back on the altar. Pick up the cup or other emblem of water, take it to the west, and hold it up before you. Imagine cold spray drifting toward you from the west, as though you stood near a waterfall, and imagine the spray gathering around the cup. Now walk or turn clockwise around the sanctum with the cup, and say the following words as you do so: "I purify this sanctum and all within it with the element of water, and I invoke the spirits and powers of water. May they bless this sanctum and further its work."

When you have finished the circle, put the cup back on the altar. Pick up the salt or other emblem of earth, take it to the north, and hold it up before you. Imagine the rich dark scent of freshly turned soil coming toward you from the north, and imagine it gathering around the salt. Now walk or turn clockwise around the sanctum with the salt, and say the following words as you do so: "I purify this sanctum and all within it with the element of Earth, and I invoke the spirits and powers of Earth. May they bless this sanctum and further its work."

When you have finished, put the salt back on the altar, and take your seat. Say: "I now call on my inner teachers to be ever vigilant and give me such instruction as I require while this sanctum is open." Pause to welcome the inner teachers. Then say: "I ask the Divine to be with me while this sanctum is open and at all times." Pause to invoke the Divine and listen for a response. If you wish, say a prayer at this point.

When you are ready to go on, say: "I now declare this sanctum open in due form."

At this point, while you are still learning the ritual, simply sit in the chair and notice the quality of the space around you. When you are finished, proceed to the closing ceremony.

Closing ceremony

Before you start the closing, sit in the chair facing the altar, and take a few moments to clear your mind. Then rise and go to the altar, standing on the west side, facing east. Say: "I prepare to close this sanctum in due form and return to my duties in the outer world. I now clear and cleanse the sanctum according to the ancient ways."

Now clear and cleanse the sanctum with the symbols of the four elements, using exactly the same actions and words you used in the opening. When you have finished, take your seat. Say: "I thank the Divine for its presence and protection while this sanctum was open and at all times." Pause to make contact with the Divine; if you wish, say a prayer here. Then say: "I thank the inner teachers for the instruction I have received and ask for their continued guidance." Pause to say farewell to them.

Rise and approach the altar. Then say the following: "I now release the strong Sphere of Protection I placed about this sanctum, and send its influence to benefit those who need strong protection at this time."

Imagine the protective energies going elsewhere to protect others. Then remove the white and black pillars from the altar and set them somewhere else. When this is done, say: "I now declare this sanctum closed in due form." This concludes the ceremony.

The four working tools

These two ceremonies for opening and closing are the only ritual requirements for the work of this book. If you wish, however, you may prepare and consecrate four symbolic working tools to represent the elements in these ceremonies and in ritual work more generally. One of the basic principles of occult philosophy is that symbolic action in the material world has effects, often quite powerful ones, on the inner worlds of consciousness. If you choose to follow the instructions below and provide yourself with a book of air, a wand of fire, a cup of water, and a pentacle of earth, you will find that this helps balance and activate the four functions—thought, intuition, feeling, and sensation—that the four elements represent. One rule should always be followed with these working tools: once made and consecrated, these should never be used for any purpose outside of ritual.

The ceremonies for consecrating the working tools are simple and elegant. They derive much of their structure and symbolism from the writings of Eliphas Lévi, who first connected the tarot and the Tree of Life. The four prayers of the elements are much older, dating from the ancient world, though Lévi helped return them to common use in Western esoteric circles; in the form of prayers offered by the four kinds of elemental spirits—the sylphs of air, the salamanders[14] of fire, the undines of water, and the gnomes of earth—they express the longing of the elements themselves for the Divine. You should of course modify all references to the Divine in the following rituals to fit your own religious needs, and you may replace the word "angels" with "spirits" or "devas" if you find these more appropriate.

The working tools may be prepared and consecrated in any order that is convenient to you. I have given them in their seasonal order—spring is the season of air, summer the season of fire, autumn the season of water, and winter the season of earth—but you need not follow this order unless you wish.

Preparing and consecrating the book of air

The working tool of elemental air is the book. Some readers may be surprised to see a book given here as the symbol of the element of air, in place of the dagger or the wand. This is one of the traditions John Gilbert received from his teacher Dr. Juliet Ashley. Over the years, there has been a great deal of pointless bickering about the elemental symbols assigned to air and fire; some writers assigned the wand to fire and the dagger to air, and some did it the other way around. Juliet Ashley decided to settle the whole matter in advance by using a more straightforward symbol of the element of air. The book of air, her invention for this purpose, has proven to work well in practice.

Any convenient blank book, as plain or fancy as you like, may be used for this purpose. Mine has handmade paper handstitched to the binding, and is bound in tooled leather with an ornate metal clasp, but

---

[14] This word meant a type of spirit long before it was borrowed by biologists for a type of amphibian.

you can use something much simpler if you prefer. The pages may be left blank, or you may use the book as a place to write down the insights and discoveries you encounter as you pursue your Cabalistic work; it should not, however, be the same book you use for your practice journal, as you will need to replace that regularly. Once you have your book, it should be consecrated using the following ritual.

* * *

Prepare to perform an opening ceremony as described above. Have a fan, incense, water, and a dish of salt on the altar, along with the book, and have the pillars close by. Then perform the opening ceremony.

Say: "This sanctum is open in due form for a ceremony of consecration for my book of air. May the Divine bless and strengthen me so that I may properly accomplish this consecration." (You may of course use the name of the deity or deities you revere in place of "the Divine.")

Next, purify the book in the following way.

Go to the altar. Lift up the fan in one hand and the book in the other, and face east. Say: "Book of air, I purify you with air to remove all inappropriate energies from you, so that you may become a fit vessel for the energies of air of air." Use the fan to move air across the book, turning the book so that the wind from the fan touches both sides of it.

Put down the fan, pick up the incense, and face south. Say: "Book ofair, I purify you with fire to remove all inappropriate energies from you, so that you may become a fit vessel for the energies of fire of air." Move the book over the incense so that the incense smoke touches both sides of it.

Put down the incense, pick up the water, and face west. Say: "Book of air, I purify you with water to remove all inappropriate energies from you, so that you may become a fit vessel for the energies of water of air." Dip your fingers into the water and sprinkle a little of it on both sides of the book.

Put down the water, pick up the salt, and face north. Say: "Book of air, I purify you with earth to remove all inappropriate energies from you, so that you may become a fitting vessel for the energies of earth of air." Take a pinch of salt between thumb and finger and sprinkle it across the book.

Face east. Raise the book in one hand as high as you can easily reach. Say: "O limitless Divine, I ask for your help and blessing in this work.

May you consecrate this book that it may be unto me now and always as a sign of light and a sacrament of will." (Again, modify the phrasing as needed to fit your own religious beliefs.)

Still facing east, lower the book to the level of your head. Say: "Angels who work in the element of air, wise and powerful ones, I ask for your help and blessing in this work. May you consecrate this book that it may be unto me now and always as a sign of light and a sacrament of will."

Lower the book to the level of your solar plexus. Say: "Elementals of air, you who dwell in the substance of the air, I ask for your help and blessing in this work. May you consecrate this book that it may be unto me now and always as a sign of light and a sacrament of will."

Say: "I declare that my book has been consecrated in due form." Raise the book and say:

"And with this book I thank and bless the element of air. May the powers of air join with me in the Prayer of the Sylphs."

> Spirit of life! Spirit of wisdom! Whose breath giveth forth and withdraweth the form of all things; thou, before whom the life of beings is as a shadow which changeth, and a vapor which passeth; thou, who mountest upon the clouds, and who walkest upon the wings of the wind. Thou, who breathest forth thy breath, and endless space is peopled: thou, who drawest in thy breath, and all that cometh from thee, returneth unto thee!
>
> Ceaseless motion in eternal stability, be thou eternally blessed! We praise thee and we bless thee in the changeless empire of created light, of shades, of reflections, and of images; and we aspire without cessation unto thy immutable and imperishable brilliance.
>
> Let the ray of thy intelligence and the warmth of thy love penetrate even unto us! Then that which is volatile shall be fixed; the shadow shall be a body; the spirit of air shall be a soul; the dream shall be a thought. And no more shall we be swept away by the tempest, but we shall hold the bridles of the winged steeds of dawn, and we shall direct the course of the evening breeze to fly before thee!
>
> O spirit of spirits! O eternal soul of souls! O imperishable breath of life! O creative sigh! O mouth which breathest forth and withdrawest the life of all beings, in the flux and reflux of thine eternal word, which is the divine ocean of movement and of truth.

Say: "I thank and bless all beings who have participated in this working and all who have assisted me and will assist me in this work." Then be seated and meditate on the ritual you have just performed. When you are ready, perform the closing ceremony.

Preparing and consecrating the wand of fire

The working tool of elemental fire is the wand. The wand of fire should be made of wood, and it can be any convenient length—from 6 to 12 inches long is convenient for most people. You may make it yourself from a stick found in the woods or from a length of doweling, or you can purchase a suitable wand if you can find one that appeals to you. Its color and design, and any decoration that might be on it, are up to you. Once you have the wand, it should be consecrated using the following ritual.

* * *

Prepare to perform an opening ceremony as described above. Have a fan, incense, water, and dish of salt on the altar, along with the wand, and have the pillars close by. Then perform the opening ceremony.

Say, "This sanctum is open in due form for a ceremony of consecration for my wand of fire. May the Divine bless and strengthen me so that I may properly accomplish this consecration." (You may of course use the name of the deity or deities you revere in place of "the Divine.")

Purify the wand in the following way.

Go to the altar. Lift up the fan in one hand and the wand in the other, and face east. Say: "Wand of fire, I purify you with air to remove all inappropriate energies from you, so that you may become a fit vessel for the energies of air of fire." Use the fan to move air across the wand, turning the wand so that the wind from the fan touches all sides of it.

Put down the fan, pick up the incense, and face south. Say: "Wand of fire, I purify you with fire to remove all inappropriate energies from you, so that you may become a fit vessel for the energies of fire of fire." Move the wand over the incense so that the incense smoke touches all sides of it.

Put down the incense, pick up the water, and face west. Say: "Wand of fire, I purify you with water to remove all inappropriate energies from you, so that you may become a fit vessel for the energies of water of fire." Dip your fingers into the water and sprinkle a little of it on the wand.

Put down the water, pick up the salt, and face north. Say: "Wand of fire, I purify you with earth to remove all inappropriate energies from you, so that you may become a fitting vessel for the energies of earth of fire." Take a pinch of salt between thumb and finger and sprinkle it across the wand.

Face south. Raise the wand in one hand as high as you can easily reach. Say: "O limitless Divine, I ask for your help and blessing in this work. May you consecrate this wand that it may be unto me now and always as a sign of light and a sacrament of will." (Again, modify the phrasing as needed to fit your own religious beliefs.)

Still facing south, lower the wand to the level of your head. Say: "Angels who work in the element of fire, wise and powerful ones, I ask for your help and blessing in this work. May you consecrate this wand that it may be unto me now and always as a sign of light and a sacrament of will."

Lower the pentacle to the level of your solar plexus. Say: "Elementals of fire, you who dwell in the substance of the fire, I ask for your help and blessing in this work. May you consecrate this wand that it may be unto me now and always as a sign of light and a sacrament of will."

Say: "I declare that my wand has been consecrated in due form." Hold up the wand and say:

"And with this wand I thank and bless the element of fire. May the powers of fire join with me in the Prayer of the Salamanders."

> Immortal, eternal, unspeakable and uncreated father of all, borne upon the chariot of worlds which ever roll in ceaseless motion. Ruler over the ethereal vastness where the throne of thy power is raised, from the summit of which thine eyes behold all and thy pure and holy ears hear all—help us, thy children, whom thou hast loved since the birth of the ages of time!
>
> Thy majesty, golden, vast, and eternal, shineth above the heaven of stars. Above them art thou exalted. O thou flashing fire, there thou illuminatest all things with thine insupportable glory, whence flow the ceaseless streams of splendor which nourish thine infinite spirit. This infinite spirit nourisheth all and maketh that inexhaustible treasure of generation which ever encompasseth thee, replete with the innumerable forms wherewith thou hast filled it from the beginning.
>
> From this spirit arise those most holy kings who are around thy throne and who compose thy court. O universal father, one and

alone! Father alike of immortals and mortals. Thou hast specially created powers similar unto thy thought eternal and unto thy venerable essence. Thou hast established them above the angels who announce thy will to the world.

Lastly, thou hast created us as a third order in our elemental empire. There our continual exercise is to praise and to adore thy desires: there we ceaselessly burn with eternal aspirations unto thee, O father! O mother of mothers! Archetype eternal of maternity and love! Child, the flower of all children! Form of all forms! Soul, spirit, harmony and numeral of all things.

Say: "I thank and bless all beings who have participated in this working and all who have assisted me and will assist me in this work." Then be seated and meditate on the ritual you have just performed. When you are ready, perform the closing ceremony.

Preparing and consecrating the cup of water

The working tool of elemental water is the cup. Any convenient cup, chalice, or goblet may be used for your cup of water; you may make it if you have the necessary skills, though it's more common for a cup of water to be purchased. Many people find that a pottery cup is very well suited to the work, but you may use glass or metal if you prefer, and the design and decoration of the cup is entirely up to you. Once you have the cup, it should be consecrated using the following ritual.

* * *

Prepare to perform an opening ceremony as described above. Have a fan, incense, water, and dish of salt on the altar, along with the cup, and have the pillars close by. Then perform the opening ceremony.

Say: "This sanctum is open in due form for a ceremony of consecration for my cup of water. May the Divine bless and strengthen me so that I may properly accomplish this consecration." (You may of course use the name of the deity or deities you revere in place of "the Divine.")

Purify the cup in the following way.

Go to the altar. Lift up the fan in one hand and the cup in the other, and face east. Say: "Cup of water, I purify you with air to remove all inappropriate energies from you, so that you may become a fit vessel for the energies of air of water." Use the fan to move air across the cup, turning the cup so that the wind from the fan touches all sides of it.

Put down the fan, pick up the incense, and face south. Say: "Cup of water, I purify you with fire to remove all inappropriate energies from you, so that you may become a fit vessel for the energies of fire of water." Move the cup over the incense so that the incense smoke touches all sides of it.

Put down the incense, pick up the water, and face west. Say: "Cup of water, I purify you with water to remove all inappropriate energies from you, so that you may become a fit vessel for the energies of water of water." Dip your fingers into the water and sprinkle a little of it on the cup.

Put down the water, pick up the salt, and face north. Say: "Cup of water, I purify you with earth to remove all inappropriate energies from you, so that you may become a fitting vessel for the energies of earth of water." Take a pinch of salt between thumb and finger and sprinkle it across the cup.

Face west. Raise the cup in one hand as high as you can easily reach. Say: "O limitless Divine, I ask for your help and blessing in this work. May you consecrate this cup that it may be unto me now and always as a sign of light and a sacrament of will." (Again, modify the phrasing as needed to fit your own religious beliefs.)

Still facing west, lower the wand to the level of your head. Say: "Lords of Form who work in the element of water, wise and powerful devas, I ask for your help and blessing in this work. May you consecrate this cup that it may be unto me now and always as a sign of light and a sacrament of will."

Lower the pentacle to the level of your solar plexus. Say: "Elementals of water, you who dwell in the substance of the water, I ask for your help and blessing in this work. May you consecrate this cup that it may be unto me now and always as a sign of light and a sacrament of will."

Say: "I declare that my cup has been consecrated in due form." Hold up the cup and say:

"And with this cup I thank and bless the element of water. May the powers of water join with me in the Prayer of the Undines."

> Terrible king of the sea, thou who holdest the keys of the cataracts of heaven, and who enclosest the subterranean waters in the cavernous hollows of earth, king of the deluge and of the rains

of spring. Thou who openest the sources of the rivers and of the fountains; thou who commandest moisture which is as the blood of the earth, to become the sap of the plants, we adore thee and we invoke thee. Speak thou unto us, thy mobile and changeful creatures, in the great tempests, and we shall tremble before thee. Speak to us also in the murmur of the limpid waters, and we shall desire thy love.

O vastness wherein all the rivers of being seek to lose themselves, which renew themselves ever in thee! O Thou ocean of infinite perfection! O height which reflectest thyself in the depth! O depth which exhalest into the height! Lead us into the true life, through intelligence, through love! Lead us unto immortality through sacrifice, that we may be found worthy to offer one day unto thee, the water, the blood and the tears for the remission of sins.

Say: "I thank and bless all beings who have participated in this working and all who have assisted me and will assist me in this work." Then be seated and meditate on the ritual you have just performed. When you are ready, perform the closing ceremony.

Preparing and consecrating the pentacle of earth

The working tool of elemental earth is the pentacle. This is a disk, usually made of wood, of any convenient size—most people find that a pentacle between 4 and 8 inches across is most functional. You may make it or purchase it, and it may be decorated in whatever way you prefer. Despite the name, it need not have a pentagram on it; many Christian occultists put a cross or a crucifix on theirs, for example. The decorations may be painted or carved, or applied in any other way you prefer; mine, which I made myself with hand tools, has pieces of colored paper glued on the surface, and a layer of spray varnish over all to protect them. Once you have the pentacle, it should be consecrated using the following ritual.

* * *

Prepare to perform an opening ceremony as described above. Have a fan, incense, water, and dish of salt on the altar, along with the pentacle, and have the pillars close by. Then perform the opening ceremony.

Say, "This sanctum is open in due form for a ceremony of consecration for my pentacle of earth. May the Divine bless and strengthen me so that I may properly accomplish this consecration." (You may of course use the name of the deity or deities you revere in place of "the Divine.")

Purify the pentacle in the following way:

Go to the altar. Lift up the fan in one hand and the pentacle in the other, and face east. Say: "Pentacle of earth, I purify you with air to remove all inappropriate energies from you, so that you may become a fit vessel for the energies of air of earth." Use the fan to move air across the pentacle, turning the pentacle so that the wind from the fan touches both sides of it.

Put down the fan, pick up the incense, and face south. Say: "Pentacle of earth, I purify you with fire to remove all inappropriate energies from you, so that you may become a fit vessel for the energies of fire of earth." Move the pentacle over the incense so that the incense smoke touches both sides of it.

Put down the incense, pick up the water, and face west. Say: "Pentacle of earth, I purify you with water to remove all inappropriate energies from you, so that you may become a fit vessel for the energies of water of earth." Dip your fingers into the water and sprinkle a little of it on both sides of the pentacle.

Put down the water, pick up the salt, and face north. Say: "Pentacle of earth, I purify you with earth to remove all inappropriate energies from you, so that you may become a fitting vessel for the energies of earth of earth." Take a pinch of salt between thumb and finger and sprinkle it across the pentacle.

Face north. Raise the pentacle in one hand as high as you can easily reach. Say: "O limitless Divine, I ask for your help and blessing in this work. May you consecrate this pentacle that it may be unto me now and always as a sign of light and a sacrament of will." (Again, modify the phrasing as needed to fit your own religious beliefs.)

Still facing north, lower the pentacle to the level of your head. Say: "Angels who work in the element of earth, wise and powerful ones, I ask for your help and blessing in this work. May you consecrate this pentacle that it may be unto me now and always as a sign of light and a sacrament of will."

Lower the pentacle to the level of your solar plexus. Say: "Elementals of earth, you who dwell in the substance of the earth, I ask for your help and blessing in this work. May you consecrate this pentacle that it may be unto me now and always as a sign of light and a sacrament of will."

Say: "I declare that my pentacle has been consecrated in due form." Trace the earth sign toward the north using the pentacle and say:

"And with this pentacle I thank and bless the element of earth. May the powers of earth join with me in the Prayer of the Gnomes."

> O invisible king who, taking the earth for foundation, didst hollow its depths to fill them with thy almighty power. Thou whose name shaketh the arches of the world, thou who causest the seven metals to flow in the veins of the rocks, king of the seven lights, rewarder of the subterranean workers, lead us into the desirable air and into the realm of splendor. We watch and we labor unceasingly, we seek and we hope, by the 12 stones of the holy city, by the buried talismans, by the axis of the lodestone which passes through the center of the earth—O Lord, O Lord, O Lord! Have pity upon those who suffer. Expand our hearts, unbind and upraise our minds, enlarge our natures.
>
> O stability and motion! O darkness veiled in brilliance! O day clothed in night! O master who never dost withhold the wages of thy workers! O silver whiteness—O golden splendor! O crown of living and harmonious diamond! Thou who wearest the heavens on thy finger like a ring of sapphire! Thou who hidest beneath the earth in the kingdom of gems, the marvelous seed of the stars! Live, reign, and be thou the eternal dispenser of the treasures whereof thou hast made us the wardens.

Say: "I thank and bless all beings who have participated in this working and all who have assisted me and will assist me in this work." Then be seated and meditate on the ritual you have just performed. When you are ready, perform the closing ceremony.

Ceremonies of the equinoxes and solstices

One further extension of the ritual side of this work is a set of rituals for celebrating the equinoxes and solstices, the traditional holy days of many of the traditions of Western esoteric spirituality. According to occult teachings, at each of these four stations of the year the play of interactions between the subtle influences of the sun and the earth shifts significantly. Attuning to these times using ritual and meditation helps balance the subtle bodies of the human microcosm and bring them into balance with their equivalents in the macrocosm.

The rituals given below are quite simple to perform and require only the skills and equipment needed for the opening and closing ceremonies. They nonetheless have considerable depth and the symbols mentioned in each of them make good themes for meditation. One detail that some esoterically literate readers may find surprising is the seasonal correspondences of the four royal stars referenced in the ceremony: these were once attributed to other seasons, but the precession of the equinoxes has moved them nearly a quarter of the way around the ecliptic from their ancient positions. It seems reasonable to acknowledge that in a book written with an eye toward the century ahead.

Readers who are interested in weaving these four ceremonies into a broader system of elemental training may want to consult my book *The Way of the Four Elements*.[15] This contains its own sequence of practices including study, ritual, active imagination, psychic development, and magical workings, alongside the working tool consecration ceremonies just presented and the equinox and solstice rituals that follow. The ritual practices given in this book can be substituted for those of the Golden Section Fellowship, the system presented in that book (and the others in the same series), if you prefer.

Spring equinox ceremony

This ritual should be performed within 48 hours at most of the moment of the equinox, which you can find online or in any almanac. It is performed as follows.

Begin with the opening ceremony, then face the altar and speak aloud the following words:

> The Spring Equinox has arrived, and the Sun and Earth renew the bonds that unite them. In this time of balanced powers, I invoke the blessings of the powers of nature upon myself, my community, and the Earth.
>
> In the world of nature, the winter has ended and the Sun has completed half his long journey toward the north. The streams

---

[15] Greer 2024.

are full of water from the melting snow and the spring rains; sap rises in the trees and flowers begin to bloom. Birds return from their winter dwellings far to the south as life wakes from its time of sleep.

The ancients knew this season as the seedtime of the year, not only for the farmer and the herder but also for those who stand at the gates between the Seen and the Unseen. They recognized at this time the power of the thought held in the mind's clarity and the word spoken upon the wind's breath; they called down wisdom from the Sun and called up power from the Earth to illuminate their minds.

Therefore the work of this season begins from the quarter of air.

Face east. Visualize the presence of the elements of air and water in their quarters, and feel the polarity between them. Say: "East; west. air; water. The realm of the mind; the realm of the heart. May they enter into the great harmony."

Visualize the presence of the elements of fire and earth in their quarters, and feel the polarity between them. Say: "South; north. fire; earth. The realm of the spirit; the realm of the body. May they enter into the great harmony."

Visualize the presence of all four elements in their quarters, and feel the complex fourfold relationship among them. Say: "The realm of the winds; the realm of the flames; the realm of the waves; the realm of the stones. May they enter into the great harmony."

Still facing east, say: "By the hawk of May in the heights of morning, I invoke the air and the powers of the air! May their blessings be with all beings during the season to come." While saying this, imagine a blazing star at the zenith, almost infinitely far above the sanctum; this is Fomalhaut, the Royal Star governing the ceremony.

Face south, and say: "By the white stag of the summer greenwood, I invoke the fire and the powers of the fire! May their blessings be with all beings during the season to come." While saying this, imagine a ray of light descending from the star at infinite height to the golden sphere of the Sun, blazing at zenith above the sanctum, high above but much closer than the star.

Face west, and say: "By the salmon of wisdom who dwells in the sacred pool, I invoke the water and the powers of the water! May their blessings be with all beings during the season to come." While saying this, imagine the ray of light descending further from the blazing Sun to the sphere of the full Moon standing at the zenith above the sanctum, high above but much closer than the Sun.

Face north, and say: "By the great bear who guards the starry heavens, I invoke the earth and the powers of the earth! May their blessings be with all beings during the season to come." While saying this, imagine the ray of light descending from the shining Moon all the way to the Sphere of Protection you established around the sanctum. The entire Sphere is seen to be filled with rainbow-colored light, which radiates outward in all directions.

Face the altar. Say: "In this season of spring may the Sun send forth his rays of blessing; may the Earth receive that blessing and bring forth her abundance." Be seated and enter into meditation, taking the season of spring as your theme. Perform the closing ceremony to finish.

Summer solstice ceremony

This ritual should be performed within 48 hours at most of the moment of the solstice, which you can find online or in any almanac. It is performed as follows.

Begin with the opening ceremony, then face the altar and speak aloud the following words:

> The Summer solstice has arrived, and the Sun and Earth manifest the polarities of being. In this time of balanced powers, I invoke the blessings of the powers of nature upon myself, my community, and the Earth.
>
> In the world of nature, spring's promise has given way to summer's fulfillment and the Sun now stands at his highest point in the sky, preparing for his long journey into darkness. The land is mantled in green as every growing thing bends its strength toward the harvest. Life rejoices in the golden afternoon of the year even as it makes its preparations for the cold months to come.
>
> The ancients knew this season as the year's bright summit, and waited in their temples of stone for the fiery sign of midsummer sunrise, the seal of harmony that unites the turning worlds. They recognized at this time the power of destiny born from the innermost self and the kindling flame of the awakening spirit; they turned their faces to the Sun and set their feet upon the Earth to accomplish the work of their wills.
>
> Therefore the work of this season begins from the quarter of fire.

Face south. Visualize the presence of the elements of earth and fire in their quarters, and feel the polarity between them. Say: "South; north. fire; earth. The realm of the spirit; the realm of the body. May they enter into the great harmony."

Visualize the presence of the elements of water and air in their quarters, and feel the polarity between them. Say: "East; west. air; water. The realm of the mind; the realm of the heart: may they enter into the great harmony."

Visualize the presence of all four elements in their quarters, and feel the complex fourfold relationship among them. Say: "the realm of the flames; the realm of the waves; the realm of the stones; the realm of the winds. May they enter into the great harmony."

Face east. Say: "By the hawk of May in the heights of morning, I invoke the air and the powers of the air! May their blessings be with all beings during the season to come." While saying this, imagine a blazing star at the zenith, almost infinitely far above the sanctum; this is Aldebaran, the Royal Star governing the ceremony.

Face south. Say: "By the white stag of the summer greenwood, I invoke the fire and the powers of the fire! May their blessings be with all beings during the season to come." While saying this, imagine a ray of light descending from the star at infinite height to the golden sphere of the Sun, blazing at zenith above the sanctum, high above but much closer than the star.

Face west. Say: "By the salmon of wisdom who dwells in the sacred pool, I invoke the water and the powers of the water! May their blessings be with all beings during the season to come." While saying this, imagine the ray of light descending further from the blazing Sun to the sphere of the full Moon standing at the zenith above the sanctum, high above but much closer than the Sun.

Face north. Say: "By the great bear who guards the starry heavens, I invoke the earth and the powers of the earth! May their blessings be with all beings during the season to come." While saying this, imagine the ray of light descending from the shining Moon all the way to the Sphere of Protection you established around the sanctum. The entire Sphere is seen to be filled with rainbow-colored light, which radiates outward in all directions.

Face the altar and say: "In this season of summer may the Sun make manifest the power of Light. May the Earth reflect that manifestation in the power of Life." Be seated and enter into meditation, taking the season of summer as your theme. Perform the closing ceremony to finish.

Autumn equinox ceremony

This ritual should be performed within 48 hours at most of the moment of the equinox, which you can find online or in any almanac. It is performed as follows.

Begin with the opening ceremony, then face the altar and speak aloud the following words:

> The Autumn Equinox has arrived, and the Sun and Earth renew the bonds that unite them. In this time of balanced powers, I invoke the blessings of the powers of nature upon myself, my community, and the Earth.
>
> In the world of nature, summer has given way and the Sun sinks from the heights of heaven into the south. The leaves of the trees blaze with orange and red as the fields turn harvest gold. The cries of the geese sound overhead as they begin their long journey toward their winter homes. Squirrels leap from branch to branch as they prepare for the long cold months to come; the sound of clashing antlers rings through the woods as stags test their strength before the watchful eyes of does.
>
> The ancients knew this season as the harvest time of the year, not only for those who gathered in the sheaves and led the cattle down from summer pastures but also for the wise whose harvest is the lore of past ages and the whispers of the Unseen. They recognized at this time the power of the desire cherished in the heart's silence and the bonds that reach from person to person like the sea uniting shore with shore; they called down power from the Sun and called up wisdom from the Earth to illuminate their hearts.
>
> Therefore the work of this season begins from the quarter of water.

Face west. Say the following words, visualizing the presence of the elements of air and water in their quarters, and feeling the polarity between them: "West; east. water; air. The realm of the Heart; the realm of the Mind. May they enter into the great harmony."

Say the following words, visualizing the presence of the elements of fire and earth in their quarters, and feeling the polarity between them: "North; south. earth; fire. The realm of the body; the realm of the spirit. May they enter into the great harmony."

Visualize the presence of all four elements in their quarters, and feel the complex fourfold relationship among them. Say: "the realm of the waves; the realm of the stones; the realm of the winds; the realm of the flames. May they enter into the great harmony."

Face east and say: "By the hawk of May in the heights of morning, I invoke the air and the powers of the air! May their blessings be with all beings during the season to come." As you say this, imagine a blazing star at the zenith, almost infinitely far above the sanctum; this is Regulus, the Royal Star governing the ceremony.

Face south and say: "By the white stag of the summer greenwood, I invoke the fire and the powers of the fire! May their blessings be with all beings during the season to come." As you say this, imagine a ray of light descending from the star to the golden sphere of the Sun, blazing at zenith above the sanctum, high above but much closer than the star.

Face west and say: "By the salmon of wisdom who dwells in the sacred pool, I invoke the water and the powers of the water! May their blessings be with all beings during the season to come." As you say this, imagine the ray of light descending further to the sphere of the full Moon standing at the zenith above the sanctum, high above but much closer than the Sun.

Face north and say: "By the great bear who guards the starry heavens, I invoke the earth and the powers of the earth! May their blessings be with all beings during the season to come." As you say this, imagine the ray of light descending from the shining Moon all the way to the Sphere of Protection you established around the sanctum. The entire Sphere is seen to be filled with rainbow-colored light, which radiates outward in all directions.

Face the altar, and say: "In this season of autumn may the Sun send forth his rays of blessing; may the Earth receive that blessing and bring forth her abundance." Be seated and enter into meditation, taking the season of spring as your theme. Perform the closing ceremony to finish.

Winter solstice ceremony

This ritual should be performed within 48 hours at most of the moment of the solstice, which you can find online or in any almanac. It is performed as follows.

Begin with the opening ceremony, then face the altar and speak aloud the following words:

> "The Winter solstice has arrived, and the Sun and Earth manifest the polarities of being. In this time of balanced powers, I invoke the blessings of the powers of nature upon myself, my community, and the Earth.
>
> "In the world of nature, the harvest is over and the Sun has descended to the place of his death and rebirth. Cold blows the wind, and colder still lie the snow and the bare earth and the bare black branches of the trees beneath the bright stars; ice rimes the edges of the streams and breath bursts white from the lips. Only those creatures that cannot sleep the winter away pace through the silence of the cold days and wait for the coming of spring.
>
> "The ancients knew this season as the end and beginning of the year, and waited in their temples for the first light of the newborn sun, the promise of the new year yet to come. They recognized at this time the power of patience and the wisdom of the world beneath the turning stars, the lessons woven by countless seasons into bone and sinew and sense; they gazed with renewed wonder on the pale Sun and the cold Earth as they awaited the common destiny of all material things.
>
> "Therefore the work of this season begins in the quarter of earth."

Face north. While saying the following words, visualize the presence of the elements of earth and fire in their quarters, and feel the polarity between them. Say: "North; south. earth; fire. The realm of the Body; the realm of the Spirit. May they enter into the great harmony."

Visualize the presence of the elements of water and air in their quarters, and feel the polarity between them. Say: "West; east. water; air. The realm of the heart; the realm of the mind. May they enter into the great harmony."

Visualize the presence of all four elements in their quarters, and feel the complex fourfold relationship among them. Say: "the realm of the stones; the realm of the winds; the realm of the flames; the realm of the waves. May they enter into the great harmony."

Face east and say: "By the hawk of May in the heights of morning, I invoke the air and the powers of the air! May their blessings be with the living Earth during the season to come." While you say this, imagine a blazing star at the zenith, almost infinitely far above the sanctum; this is Antares, the Royal Star governing the ceremony.

Face south and say: "By the white stag of the summer greenwood, I invoke the fire and the powers of the fire! May their blessings be with the living Earth during the season to come." While you say this, imagine a ray of light descending from the star at infinite height to the golden sphere of the Sun, blazing at zenith above the sanctum, high above but much closer than the star.

Face west and say: "By the salmon of wisdom who dwells in the sacred pool, I invoke the water and the powers of the water! May their blessings be with the living Earth during the season to come." While you say this, imagine the ray of light descending further from the blazing Sun to the sphere of the full Moon standing at the zenith above the sanctum, high above but much closer than the Sun.

Face north and say: "By the great bear who guards the starry heavens, I invoke the earth and the powers of the earth! May their blessings be with the living Earth during the season to come. While you say this, imagine the ray of light descending from the shining Moon all the way to the Sphere of Protection you established around the sanctum. The entire Sphere is seen to be filled with rainbow-colored light, which radiates outward in all directions."

Face the altar and say: "In this season of winter may the Sun make manifest the mystery of Light. May the Earth reflect that manifestation in the mystery of Life." Be seated and enter into meditation, taking the season of winter as your theme. Perform the closing ceremony to finish.

Stage three: active imagination and dreamwork

Once you have completed the initial set of discursive meditations on the Tree of Life described earlier, and have learned the opening and closing sanctum ceremonies and committed them to memory, the next step is to integrate active imagination and the placing of the Tree of Life in your body into your practices. The active imagination work given in this section should be practiced while you are learning how to formulate the Tree of Life in and around your body, as explained in the following section of this book. The further applications of active imagination in pathworkings and sphere workings will come later, after you have learned the complete bridge of light working and explored the Tree of Life more thoroughly in meditation.

In all of this it is essential to grasp that active imagination and the rest of the work you will learn are supplements to meditation, not substitutes for it! Daily discursive meditation is the foundation stone on which you will build your inner temple of Cabalistic practice. Everything else rests on that firm foundation.

That said, active imagination is a powerful tool and should be taken up as soon as you have completed the preliminary meditations described earlier. As you learn how to use it, it will bring you into contact with the realm of inner experience that many occultists call the astral plane and historian of religion Henry Corbin called the imaginal world. Corbin's choice of a term—imaginal, not imaginary—was deliberate and precise. He recognized, as occultists have known for countless millennia, that what is experienced by the imagination is not "imaginary" in the debased modern sense of the world.

It is because the imaginal world is an objective reality in its own right that similar images show up in dreams, myths, and folklore around the planet and throughout human history. This is also why dreams and other forms of inner experience can sometimes pass on bits of accurate information that could have been gotten by no ordinary means.

Here again, of course, the practices we are discussing contradict some of the most deeply held dogmas of contemporary Western culture. According to those dogmas, consciousness is an odd phenomenon that happens inside human brains, and only there. According to those dogmas, similarly, each of our minds is cut off from all others, except when some kind of indirect contact can be made through material means—speech, writing, gesture, or what have you. This conviction comes out of the modern world's most rigidly enforced belief, the claim that everything that is real is material, that there is nothing in the universe but matter and energy in various states and combinations.

It's an odd belief system to have, all things considered. Perceptions of the life force, of the kind discussed in an earlier section of this book, contradict it completely, and all those who take the time to direct unbiased attention to their own inner lives will soon realize just how inaccurate a belief the dogma of mental separateness really is. One lesson that life is constantly trying to teach us is that each of the four worlds of the Cabala is a continuum: just as the world of matter is a unity woven together by constant interactions among seemingly separate things, the world of ordinary consciousness, the world of higher consciousness that remains subconscious in most of us, and the world of spirit that is wholly unconscious to us, are all unities. Each of these worlds has its own laws, and all but the last has its limits, but all are part of a single mighty whole. That is to say, the universe is a uni-verse—"that which turns as one," as the word originally meant—not a collection of isolated fragments floating in the void.

There are many ways to become conscious of the imaginal world. Dreams are perhaps the best known, not least because psychologists since the time of Sigmund Freud have seen dreams as the royal road to the subconscious mind. Many people have trouble learning to remember their dreams, however, and in today's increasingly stressful world the worries and confusions of the day very often spill over so extensively into our dreams that getting past them to more interesting things can be difficult. For these reasons active imagination is generally a more useful tool. I have, however, included a basic guide to Cabalistic dreamwork at the end of this section for those who are interested in exploring it.

There are many ways to induce active imagination. The method described here has proven its value in occult circles for well over a century now. It also has the advantage of using the same posture and the same opening and closing procedures as the method of discursive meditation you have just learned. The one additional item it requires is a set of the 22 trumps of the tarot deck. The tarot has been discussed earlier in this book, and you have been instructed in how to prepare to use the cards, by providing yourself with an appropriate deck (Rider-Waite or some close equivalent) and memorizing the basic symbols for each trump. This is the stage at which that necessary drudgery begins to pay off.

Beginning active imagination

Set aside a practice session apart from your usual meditation time for active imagination. The one thing you will need in addition to the normal requirements of meditation is one of the tarot trumps. It should be placed in a location where you can see it clearly without moving your head or disrupting your practice; many people find that some kind of simple stand or frame that will hold it upright directly ahead of you, when you are in your meditation chair, works well. Begin with Trump I, the Magician. In this first phase of active imagination, you will devote one session to each of the tarot trumps in order, starting with the Magician. Work with Trump 0, the Fool, last of all, after Trump XXI, the World.

Before you begin, review the correspondences for the trump you intend to work with. If you like, this can also be a good time to reread the chapter of the Kybalion assigned to that trump. If you have a musical instrument, play the musical note assigned to the trump several times, and sing, hum, or whistle it until you remember it clearly.

When you are ready to begin, put the trump in its stand so that you will be able to see it in your practice. Take the familiar meditation posture and go through all the usual preliminaries for meditation.

At the point when you would normally go on to consider the theme of a meditation, however, imagine yourself surrounded by the color assigned to the trump, and hear in your mind the trump's musical note.

Then turn your attention to the tarot trump. Study it carefully for a few minutes. Then imagine that it grows, becoming not a card but a portal. The edges of the card have become like the frame of an open door, and you are looking through it at the figure, the objects, and the landscape shown in the card.

In the case of the Magician, imagine that you are seeing the Magician himself standing at his table, pointing up with one hand and down with the other. He and the table are in a garden of roses and lilies, with a rose arbor overhead. Try to see it, not as an illustration, but as though you were looking at a real person standing in a real garden.

People vary in their capacity to imagine things. Some can picture them as vividly as the images their senses bring to them. Others experience no mental imagery at all. Most of us fall between those extremes. While vivid imagery is helpful in active imagination and several other aspects of the practical work of this book, it is not required. Nor is visual imagery the only kind that can be used; some people, who have trouble getting clear visual images, can "tactilize" shapes and textures as though touching them, and this is as useful as visualization. To judge your current ability to imagine, pay attention to your memories and daydreams and notice what role imagery plays in those. That will be the starting point from which you can build.

Spend some time making the image as clear as you can, as though it were a door standing before you. Don't limit yourself to an abstract image or purely visual imagery. See every detail of the Magician and the garden in your mind's eye. Catch the scent of the roses and the lilies in the garden, hear the wind rustling the leaves, feel the heft and texture of the table and the objects on them. Then, slowly and clearly, imagine yourself rising from your chair, walking to the doorway, and passing through it. The doorway remains open behind you, and if you look back you can see your physical body sitting in the chair.

Look around at the realm beyond the door, and allow yourself to notice as many details as you can. Some of these may be unexpected! Then speak to the Magician. Introduce yourself if you like, and explain that you want to learn about the first path of the Tree of Life. See what response you get. The Magician may speak to you briefly or at length, and he may lead you to other places in his garden to show you things.

Ask him any questions you wish, and pay close attention to his answers. Every detail of the landscape around you and every word spoken to you has something to teach.

It is important to let things happen in active imagination, rather than making them happen. If you treat the things you encounter as though they were real, for the duration of the scrying, they will usually respond accordingly, and display the same unexpected independence that is shown by the figures and things in your dreams. Let this happen. You can always leave the practice if it becomes uncomfortable. In the meantime, what you experience will provide you with themes for meditation, and very often new glimpses into the inner meanings of the tarot trumps, or anything else you choose as a focus for this practice.

Once you are ready to end the practice, thank the Magician and, if you have gone on a journey, return to the place where you started, the garden scene shown in the tarot card. Then return through the doorway, imagine yourself sitting back in the chair where your physical body has been all the while, and then slowly and carefully imagine the portal turning back into the flat image on a tarot card. As it makes this transformation, concentrate on the thought that no unwanted energies or beings can come into your daily life from the realm of the figure you've been scrying.

Use a few cycles of the fourfold breath to end the practice, and then finish as you would with a session of meditation. Be sure to write up the experience in your practice journal as soon as possible, while the details are still fresh in your mind. You will need those details for the next phase of the work, so write them down as completely as you can.

You may find yourself a little disoriented at first after scrying, especially the first few times you do it. If so, eating some food will close your visionary senses down and bring you solidly back into your body. Routine activities such as washing the dishes can also help reorient your awareness back to the realm of ordinary experience.

Active imagination and meditation

At the conclusion of your first session of active imagination, you have gathered a series of more or less cryptic images and experiences related in some way to the Magician. It is at this point that discursive meditation comes back into the picture. Every one of those images and experiences should be taken as a theme for meditation. Each session of active imagination is like a letter you have received from the inner worlds; meditation is how you open the envelope and read the contents.

Plan on spending at least three daily sessions of meditation, and preferably more, on the results of every session of active imagination. In this stage of the work, you will be devoting one session of active imagination to each of the 22 trumps of the tarot deck. Everything you experience will help you expand the symbolism of the paths and spheres of the Tree of Life, so take your time and understand each symbol as clearly as you can.

For example, let's say that in your session with the Magician, the figure in the card took you further back into the garden to a meadow surrounded by trees. In the middle of the meadow was a cube of white stone, on top of which a flame danced and flickered. The Magician then told you to watch in silence for a little while. As you watched, a unicorn came into the meadow from one side and a stag came from the other. Both approached the flame. The Magician then told you that the unicorn was from the heavens and the stag was from the earth.

The cube and flame in the meadow, the unicorn, the stag, and the Magician's words are all themes for meditation. Give each one its own session of daily meditation. In working with each of them, try to relate them to the imagery shown on the card itself—the flame above the cube of stone, for example, to the table in the card with the four elemental symbols on it, and the Magician's comments about the heavens and the earth to his own gesture in the card, with one hand pointing to the sky and one to the ground. Of course, it is also helpful to relate the symbols encountered in active imagination to each other—for example, the flame above the cube can also be related to the unicorn and the stag, and to the heavens and the earth.

This is not to say that everything in a scrying is necessarily a fount of wisdom. One problem faced by many people when they start working with active imagination, especially if they have little previous experience with meditation, is that stray notions and irrelevancies end up being brought into the experience as a result of wandering thoughts. This is why it is helpful to spend some time meditating before you take up active imagination, and also why memorizing the basic symbolism of each of the trumps is important, since that encourages your mind to focus on those symbols and concepts that are relevant to the trump.

Especially at first, your experiences in active imagination might best be compared to a radio signal in which the message is mixed with static, containing a mix of useful material and random imagery dragged in by your mind. As you meditate on each of the things you experienced, always be aware of both possibilities. Among the touchstones you can use to sort out the message from the static are the color and the other symbolism attributed to the trump you used as your portal. When you encounter these, this is a good indication that the material that contains them is likely to be useful, while colors and symbols belonging to other trumps is a sign that you picked up plenty of static.

Thus it is important to take your time and sort through what you have encountered in your work with active imagination. If a single session of meditation doesn't seem adequate to finish unpacking everything that is implied by something you encountered, give it another. You gain nothing by rushing through this stage of the work. One symbol that you open up fully to understanding through meditation will take you further than dozens that you've skimmed over lightly and then forgotten.

It is also important to keep a sense of proportion while exploring the results of your work with active imagination. This can be a powerful took for expanding your awareness and attuning yourself to the subtle dimensions of existence, but it can also open the way to many different kinds of foolishness, some of them amusing, some a good deal less so. People have made spectacular blunders by blindly trusting information received from scrying and similar practices in a simple-minded literal way, and in extreme cases—which are rare, but not rare enough—the results have included madness and death.

The best way to avoid these pitfalls is to remember that the journeys of active imagination take place in a world of their own, the imaginal world that Henry Corbin named and described. What you experience in them may or may not have anything to do with the hard facts of the material plane. Remember also that the beings you encounter in active imagination may not know the truth about things of the material plane and, even if they know it, may lie to you for reasons of their own. It's as foolish to take what they say at its face value as it would be to offer the same trust to the first stranger you happen to encounter on the street.

The modern Druid teacher Philip Carr-Gomm has suggested that anyone who seeks contact with the subtler realms of existence, before worrying about developing strange psychic senses, needs to start by cultivating three more basic senses: common sense, a sense of proportion, and a sense of humor. This is excellent advice in any context, and especially when working with active imagination.

Cabalistic dreamwork

Active imagination, as already noted, is far from the only way to make contact with the imaginal world. All of us spend several hours every night in that world during the dreaming stages of sleep. One of the interesting discoveries of sleep researchers over the last half century or so is that everyone dreams, whether they remember their dreams or not. The telltale brain waves and rapid eye movements (REM) that signal the dream state show up at regular intervals all through sleep.

You dream every night, then. The first step in putting your dreaming time to work as part of Cabalistic practice is learning to remember your dreams. This requires a certain amount of work and patience, because during childhood most of us were taught to ignore our dreams. Getting past that childhood programming often takes time.

The crucial first step is to start recording any scrap of dream you remember when you first wake. For most people, the best way to do this is to have a notepad and a pen next to your bed, with a lamp or a flashlight close by for use during the hours of darkness. Any time you awaken from a dream, no matter what the hour, write down at least a few words about it before you do anything else. The more you can write down, the better, but very often even a brief note will be enough to keep the memory from being lost.

If you have trouble remembering your dreams, one simple trick that works for most people is to try to remember what you were thinking about when you first woke up. Teach yourself to do this as soon as you can after waking. Very often you'll find that this brings up a dream image, and from that image at least some of the dream can be recovered. Here again, write down as much as you can recall as quickly as possible while the memory is still fresh.

Later in the day, copy the dream from the notepad into a notebook. Many people find that doing this brings back additional details, and sometimes entire episodes of the dream will surface from memory. Write these down as well. Note down the date when you dreamed each dream, and consider giving it a simple title—"Down the Stairs" for a dream in which going down stairs was an important action, or what have you.

Some people also find that now and again, often for no reason they can identify, they will suddenly remember part of a dream. Here again, if that happens to you and you can possibly do so, write down as many details as you remember as soon as you can. The simple act of writing down your dreams will encourage your subconscious mind to help you remember more of them.

There is also a simple practice to be done while falling asleep each night. Imagine a ray of light shining on the point where the top of your spine joins the base of your skull. As you imagine this, think, "This helps me remember my dreams." Then let yourself go to sleep. If you wake up during the night, you can repeat this process.

Once you remember dreams at least a few nights each week, and have at least a dozen dreams written down, you can move on to the next step, which is to begin to interpret your dreams. Here again, discursive meditation is your most important tool. Take a few minutes, before you begin meditating on a dream, to break it down into its components— the beings, objects, and events that you remember from it. Each of these is a theme for meditation.

In exploring dream imagery in discursive meditation, keep in mind that your dreams are powerfully influenced by the contents of your mind and memories. They may not follow the same pattern as anyone else's dreams. (This is why dream dictionaries and similar guides are so rarely useful.) Don't rely on anyone else's interpretation of your dreams, and don't try to make the meanings conform to anyone else's scheme! Instead, as you meditate on your dream imagery, let yourself draw freely on your own experiences and reflections. If you dream of a cheeseburger, for example, let yourself think of cheeseburgers you have eaten, and see if that stirs up any insights.

You can also apply the tools of active imagination to your dreams. To do this, use the same process described above. Instead of turning a tarot trump into a portal, however, imagine a doorway, and then imagine your dream on the other side of it. Go through the doorway into the dream, and interact with the beings and things you encounter there in the same way you would with the imagery of a tarot card.

Here again, as a rule, it is important to let things happen rather than making them happen. The one great exception is when you have remembered a nightmare and choose to explore it through active imagination. In this case it can be a good idea to take control of the dream imagery—to defeat the monster, escape the danger, or do whatever else you need to do to overcome the fearful aspect of the dream. Even then, change only what you must. Defeat the monster, don't transform it into a bunny! Leave it its monstrousness, and get it to explain to you why it is monstrous and what it means.

Whenever you use active imagination to explore a dream, in fact, consider asking the beings in the dream what they represent and why they appeared to you. Sometimes, if you do this, the dream will quite literally interpret itself. In other cases, what the dream entities say will give you clues that can be explored and unpacked in discursive meditation. Yes, you will be meditating on every detail from these active imagination sessions too.

The next stage in Cabalistic dreamwork is to begin teaching your dreaming mind to explore Cabalistic themes. You may find that this happens spontaneously—it is not uncommon, for example, for imagery from a session of active imagination to show up in dreams not long after, or for meditations to spill over into dreams. Whether or not this happens by itself, you can begin the process by concentrating on a tarot trump before you go to bed each night.

This does not require the preliminaries of meditation. Immediately before you lie down, simply sit in a chair or on the side of your bed, hold the trump in both hands, clear your mind as best you can and look at it without thinking of anything for five minutes. Then, when you settle down to sleep and visualize the beam of light shining on the place where the spine joins the skull, call the trump back to mind, and imagine yourself going into it as though passing through a portal. Do this in a relaxed way, without intensive concentration. Then let yourself go to sleep.

When you wake, write down any dreams you remember. Later, explore the dream or dreams from that night and see if you can find any symbols in the dream that correspond to the tarot trump you used as a focus for concentration. Discursive meditation is again a useful tool here. It may take repeated tries before your dreams start reflecting the symbolism of the trumps, but once they do so, you can use your dreams as a way of exploring the paths and spheres of the Tree of Life.

There is a great deal more to dreamwork than this, of course. Books considerably larger than this one have been written about dreamwork, and if you find this aspect of Cabalistic practice worth pursuing you can learn a great deal from resources of this kind.[16] The essential principle in any work with dreams is to let your dreams teach you, rather than trying to tell them what to mean or how to behave.

A word should doubtless be added here about lucid dreaming. This is the state in which a dreamer realizes that he or she is dreaming, and can control the events of a dream while in it. Some people attain this state fairly easily, others achieve it only rarely, and still others never have the experience at all. There are various ways to become lucid in the dream state, and these are covered in detail in a great many easily available books.

If you are interested in exploring lucid dreaming as part of your Cabalistic work, by all means do so. Your local public library or bookstore can provide you with the guidance you need. It is not necessary to become lucid in your dreams to practice Cabalistic dreamwork, however. The ordinary kind of dreaming can be just as effective a portal to the imaginal realm—and it is a portal that most people can pass through with a little effort and patience.

---

[16] I have had particularly good experiences with Williams 1985.

Stage four: the Tree of Life in the body

Placing the centers of the Tree of Life in and around the body of the individual practitioner has been an important practice in the occult traditions of the Cabala for a very long time. The knowledge lectures of the Hermetic Order of the Golden Dawn taught initiates of the Portal grade to visualize the spheres of the Tree in and around themselves.[17] Cabalist and Golden Dawn initiate Israel Regardie took that exercise, reworked it in the light of early 20th-century publications about Eastern spiritual exercises, and created the middle pillar exercise, one of the most widely practiced Cabalistic practices in today's world.

The Cabalistic teachings I received from John Gilbert included a different practice, which I have given below. It is probably also descended from the Golden Dawn Portal grade exercise, but followed a different trajectory of development from there. It is performed sitting down, in a meditative state, wherethe middle pillar exercise is done standing. Unlike the middle pillar exercise, John's practice allows a precise correlation to be made between the Tree of Life and the seven chakras.

---

[17] Regardie 2015, pp. 110–112.

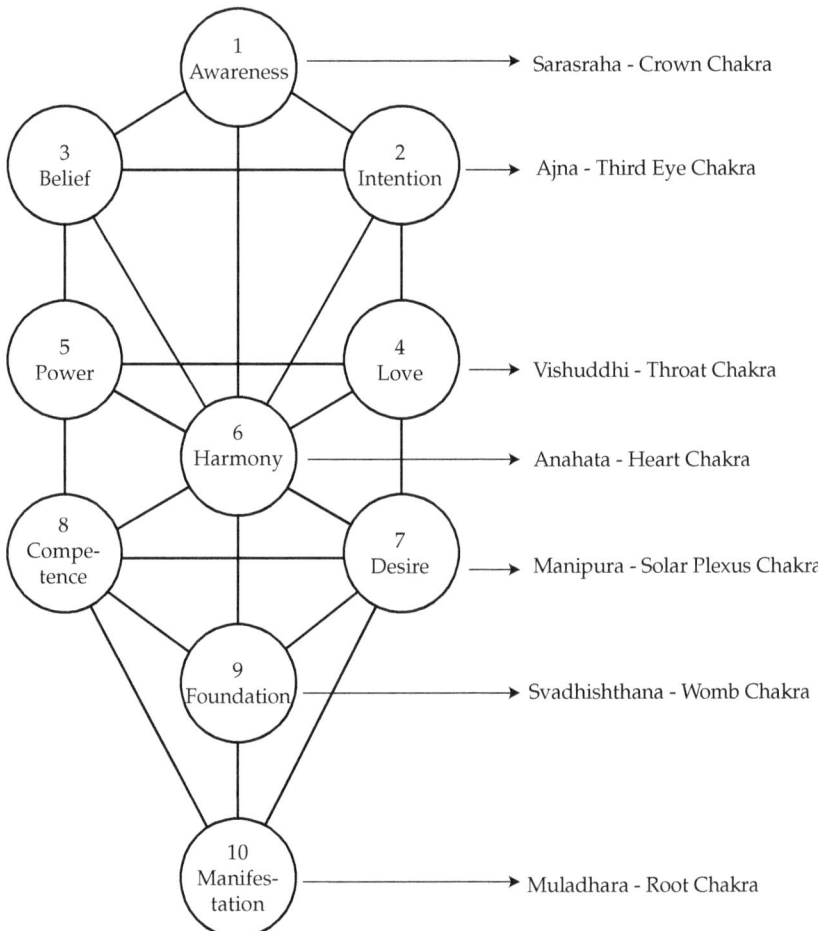

The tree and the chakras

It is important to remember here that every symbol has many meanings and can be applied in many ways. In terms of their general symbolism, the seven chakras relate to the seven lower spheres of the Tree of Life, as reflections of divine energies in the Lower World of ordinary human experience. In terms of their position in the human subtle bodies, they can be more precisely equated with the Tree of Life in a different manner, as shown in the diagram. Paying attention to the variable nature of symbolism helps avoid the kind of dogmatic rigidity that gets in the way of effective practice.

Placing the centers of the Tree of Life in your subtle body is done in four steps, beginning with the primal triad. Begin it as soon as you have finished the basic meditations given in the first section of practice, and work with it while you are practicing active imagination using the tarot trumps, as given in the previous section of this book. It should be practiced at least once a week; once a day would not be too often.

The tree in the body: first step

Start by opening your sanctum using the ritual you have been taught. Then sit in the chair facing the altar, take the posture of meditation and go through the usual preliminaries of relaxation and breathing. (Leave out the preliminary visualization, since you've already established the protective sphere in the sanctum opening.) When you have reached the point where you would normally begin the meditation, imagine that a sphere of brilliant white light a few inches across appears a short distance above your head. Concentrate on it for a time, seeing it in your mind's eye and sensing the light streaming down upon you from above.

Now imagine a second sphere of light, the same size as the first, appearing below and to your left of the first sphere. It is directly above the point of your left shoulder and a little higher than the level of your

Tree in the body 1

left ear; it does not touch your skull. Concentrate on it for a time, being aware of the first sphere as well.

Now imagine a third sphere of light, the same size as the first two, appearing below and to your right of the first sphere. It is directly above the point of your right shoulder and on the same horizontal level as the second sphere. Concentrate on it for a time, being aware of the first two spheres the whole time.

Practice formulating these three spheres for several sessions until you can do it easily, and then go on to the next part of this step. Imagine a line of silver-white light descending at an angle from the center of the first sphere to the center of the second. A second line extends across from the center of the second to the center of the third, passing through your head. A third line then slants up from the center of the third sphere back to the center of the first. Through the triangle formed by these three lines, a current of creative energy flows—from the first sphere to the second, then to the third, and back to the first.

These spheres, of course, represent the first three spheres of the Tree of Life: Awareness, Intention, and Belief. They also represent your link with the three expressions of the Divine you have chosen to invoke in your Cabalistic work. In the phrasing John Gilbert liked to use, the link with the Divine Creator is directly above you, the link with the Divine Father is above and to your left, and the link with the Divine Mother is above and to your right. Of course, you should use whatever names and symbols you prefer when invoking the Divine.

If this seems backward to you, remember that when you look at the Tree of Life in a diagram on the page, it is as though you are looking at another person facing you—their left is your right, and their right is your left. Another way to think about the same thing is to imagine yourself backing up against the Tree of Life. In effect, you are facing the same way it is. This same orientation will be used all the way down the Tree.

Practice visualizing the primal triad above you until you can do it easily without having to consult this book or a cheat sheet, and maintain the visualization steadily for several minutes at a time. Once you are comfortable doing this, proceed to the work of the second step.

The tree in the body: second step

The work of this step begins with the practice you have already learned. Open your sanctum in the usual manner, take the meditation posture, and go through the usual preliminaries. Then visualize the three spheres of the primal triad above and to each side of your head, one after another, and formulate the three paths connecting them. Once you have done this, direct your attention to the point of your left shoulder. Imagine a sphere of pure white light, the same size as the others you have already imagined, with the point of your shoulder at its center. Concentrate on it for a time.

Tree in the body 2

Then shift your attention to the point of your right shoulder. Imagine an identical sphere of pure white light there, and concentrate on it for a time. Next, shift your attention to the area of your heart. Imagine another sphere of light there, the same size as the others. This one should be entirely inside your material body. Again, concentrate on it for a time.

These spheres represent the reflected triad in your energy body, the three spheres of Love, Power, and Harmony. They symbolize the three powers of your subconscious higher self, memory, will, and imagination. They are also the points of contact through which the three expressions of the Divine above you descend into manifestation within you. It is through these points that Divine Love blesses you, Divine Power protects you, and Divine Harmony heals you. Practice formulating the primal triad and then these three spheres for several sessions until you can do it easily.

Then go on to the next part of this step. Imagine another line of silver-white light emerging from the heart of the fourth sphere and going horizontally across to the fifth sphere. From there, a line of the same light angles downward to the sixth sphere at the heart, and from there, a third line angles back up to the center of the fourth sphere. Through these lines, a current of creative energy flows, from the fourth sphere to the fifth, down to the sixth, and then back up to the fourth, reflecting the current that unites the primal triad. Practice formulating the primal triad, the three spheres of the reflected triad, and the paths connecting these three spheres until you can do this easily.

Then go on to the final part of this step, in which you formulate the paths that connect the primal triad and the reflected triad. All these paths are the same silver-white color as before. From the first sphere of Awareness, a path descends straight to the sixth sphere of Harmony. From the second sphere of Intention, two paths descend, one to Harmony and one to the fourth sphere of Love. From the third sphere of Belief, similarly, two paths descend, one to Harmony and one to the fifth sphere of Power. Through all five of these lines, currents of creative energy flow from the realm of the Divine into the realm of your higher self.

This completes the second step of the practice, and finishes the formulation of the hexad of the microcosm. When you can do this easily, and maintain the visualization for several minutes at a time, proceed to the work of the third step. Please don't get ahead of yourself. Master the first two practices before continuing further.

The tree in the body: third step

This step is similar to the second step. In it, you will be formulating the third triad and the final sphere of Manifestation. Begin as before by opening your sanctum and entering into a meditative state. Then imagine the three spheres of the primal triad above and to either side of your head, one at a time, and then connect the spheres with the three paths that unite them. Go on to imagine the three spheres of the reflected triad, one at a time, and connect them with the three paths that unite them. Next, formulate the five descending paths of grace that unite the two higher triads.

Once this is done, imagine a sphere of pure white light with its center between your left elbow and the point of your left hip. Concentrate on it for a time. Next, imagine a similar sphere with its center between your right elbow and the point of your right hip. Concentrate on it for a time.

Then imagine a third sphere inside your abdomen with its center an inch or so below your navel, midway through your body. Concentrate on it for a time. Finally, imagine a fourth sphere with its center just forward of the tip of your tailbone. Practice the sequence this far for several sessions until you can do it easily.

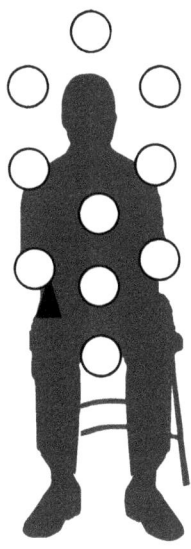

Tree in the body 3

The next part of this step is to formulate the three paths that link the spheres of the third triad. Do this in the same way you did the paths linking the spheres of the second triad, except that the energy flows in the other direction—from Competence to Desire, from Desire to Foundation, and from Foundation back up to Competence. (The point of this difference will become clear later.) Practice the entire sequence up to this point until you can do it easily.

Next comes the three paths uniting the lowest sphere to the spheres of the third triad. Learn to establish these three paths. Energy flows down the path from Desire and Competence to Manifestation, but it flows up the path from Manifestation to Foundation. Practice the entire sequence this far until you can do it easily.

Finally, formulate the five paths connecting the reflected triad with the third triad. On the path from Love to Desire and from Power to Competence, the energy flows downward. On the three paths from

Foundation, Competence, and Desire to Harmony, however, the energy flows upwards. Once you are able to do this in addition to all the earlier steps, you have completed the work of this step and the entire Tree of Life is established in and around you. Practice this until you can do it easily without having to consult this book or a "cheat sheet," and then go on to the fourth and final step of this practice.

The tree in the body: fourth step

This step adds no new spheres or paths, as the Tree of Life is complete. Instead, you begin adding certain elements of the symbolism you have already learned to the spheres you have already established. First, instead of seeing the spheres as pure white light, make them the colors appropriate to the spheres themselves: respectively, white, silver-gray, black, blue, red, yellow, green, orange, violet, and indigo. Practice this a few times until it becomes easy.

Next, as you formulate each sphere, think about it in terms of the symbolism you have already studied. In the first series of meditations, you gained a certain sense of the nature and character of each of the ten spheres of the Tree of Life. Sense that nature and character in each of the spheres you formulate in and around you. Many students find that it helps to focus on one set of symbolism at a time: for example, you might spend one session concentrating on the planetary energies in each sphere, from Neptune at the top to the Earth at the bottom; another time, you might focus on one or more of the titles, or the symbols, or the Muses. All this will help you experience the pattern of imagery you have been building up as a true reflection of the Tree of Life, and this is turn will yield benefits in the further stages of practice.

Then add a set of simple invocations or affirmations to the spheres. Once you have formulated each sphere and established its nature and character in the image, silently repeat the invocation or affirmation you have chosen. These can be any texts you find appropriate. For example, you might use the following:

> For Awareness: "I ask for inspiration from the Divine Creator."
> For Intention: "I ask for wisdom from the Divine Father."
> For Belief: "I ask for protection from the Divine Mother."
> For Love: "May I awaken my capacity for love."
> For Power: "May I awaken my capacity for power."

> For Harmony: "May I awaken my capacity for harmony."
> For Desire: "May my desires be guided by love."
> For Competence: "May my competences be guided by will."
> For Foundation: "May my life be guided by harmony."
> For Manifestation: "May my body be a temple of the Divine."

Alternatively, you may prefer this one:

> For Awareness: "My awareness is turned toward the Infinite."
> For Intention: "My intentions are in balance with the cosmos."
> For Belief: "My beliefs are open to new information."
> For Love: "My memory is a well of wisdom."
> For Power: "My will is directed by understanding."
> For Harmony: "My imagination is a mirror of the cosmic harmony."
> For Desire: "My desires seek the best for all beings."
> For Competence: "My competence serves my ideals."
> For Foundation: "My life is lived to the fullest."
> For Manifestation: "My body is blessed with health and strength."

Or, if you are a Christian, you may prefer this, which draws on the traditional division of the Lord's Prayer into seven petitions:

> For Awareness: "In the name of the Father,"
> For Intention: "And of the Son,"
> For Belief: "And of the Holy Spirit."
> For Love: "Our Father, who art in heaven, hallowed be thy name."
> For Power: "Thy kingdom come."
> For Harmony: "Thy will be done on earth as it is in heaven."
> For Desire: "Give us this day our daily bread."
> For Competence: "Forgive us our trespasses as we forgive those who trespass against us."
> For Foundation: "Lead us not into temptation."
> For Manifestation: "But deliver us from evil."
> (The usual words "For thine is the kingdom, the power, and the glory forever, Amen" may be recited at this point if you wish.)

Alternatively, you may certainly create your own. Choose some such set of invocations or affirmations. Commit them to memory and use them as part of your practice. When you can do the whole sequence of establishing the Tree of Life in and around your body easily, and hold the imagery and ideas in mind for several minutes after you have finished, you have completed the work of this stage. Once you have also completed the active imagination work discussed in the previous section, you are ready to go on to the next stage of the work.

Stage five: the bridge of light

In the previous stages you have learned discursive meditation, ritual, active imagination, and the establishment of the spheres of the Tree of Life in your body. During this next stage, continue your daily meditation, focusing on the patterns formed by the spheres of the Tree—the worlds, the pillars, the triads, and so on. If you finish with those before the rest of the work of this stage is complete, go on to meditate again on the symbolism of the ten spheres, beginning with the first sphere and proceeding down from there one symbol at a time.

While you are doing this, begin working on the following set of visualizations, which proceed from the formulation of the spheres in and around your body. All the preliminaries are the same: open your sanctum using the ritual, go through the usual steps to prepare for meditation, and then establish the spheres one at a time as you did in the fourth step in the previous section. Then proceed to the following steps.

The bridge of light: step one

Begin, once you have finished all the preliminary steps, by breathing in slowly and steadily. While you do this, imagine a current of brilliant white light descending from infinite space above you to the sphere of Awareness above your head. From there it takes a zigzag path: from Awareness to Intention, from Intention to Belief, from Belief to Love, from Love to Power, and from Power to Harmony. Do all this in one in-breath. Pause, allowing the current of light to fill the center of Harmony at your heart. Then, breathing out, imagine the light flowing out of the center of Harmony to fill your entire body.

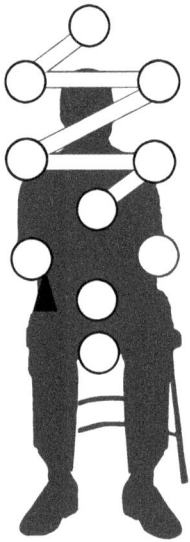

Bridge of light 1

The descending light follows the paths of the Tree of Life, with one dramatic exception. There is no path diagonally across the Abyss from Belief to Love, but the flow of light descends that way nonetheless. This is a reminder of the important fact that the divine powers above the Abyss are not subject to the rules that apply further down the Tree.

Do this sequence of bringing light down from above three times in as many breaths. Then simply attend to the state of your body and mind for a little while, before closing in the usual way. Make this your regular practice until you can do it easily, and then go on to the second step.

The bridge of light: step two

The first step, which you have already learned, calls on the descending influence of the Lightning Flash from Awareness to Harmony, activating what we have called the way of creation. In the second step, you will awaken the rising influence of human spiritual evolution from Manifestation to Harmony, activating what we have called the way of initiation.

To do this, do all the previous steps as described above: open your sanctum, prepare for meditation, formulate the ten spheres of the Tree of Life in and around your body, and call down the Lightning Flash from far above you to the center of Harmony.

When you pause before breathing out, however, instead of focusing on Harmony, imagine a current of brilliant green energy rising up from the center of the earth, far beneath your feet. Imagine it entering the tenth sphere, Manifestation, at the base of your body. From there it follows a zigzag course of its own; straight up to Foundation, then diagonally up to Competence, horizontally across to Desire, and then up at an angle to Harmony, as shown in the diagram. As you breathe out, imagine the green energy filling your body.

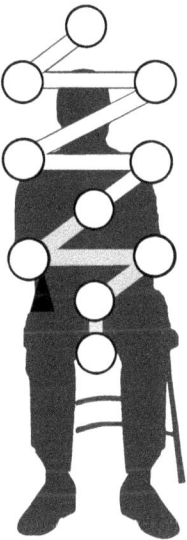

Bridge of light 2

On a philosophical level, what you are doing here is uniting the descending force of the Divine that brings the worlds into being with the ascending force of your own soul and all other souls, striving upwards toward the Divine from the material realm. On a practical level, what you are doing is drawing on the two great currents of subtle force that are available in our reality, the solar current descending from the heavens and the telluric current rising from the center of the earth, and uniting them in yourself. Both these levels are relevant to the work, and should be kept in mind.

Do this sequence of bringing light down from above and up from below three times in as many breaths. Then simply attend to the state of your body and mind for a little while, before closing in the usual way. Make this your regular practice until you can do it easily. Proceed to the next step only when you can bring the white light down to Harmony on half of an in-breath, and the green light up from Manifestation on the second half of the same in-breath; this takes practice, as you will need to be familiar enough with the exercise that you can do each phase of it relatively quickly and smoothly.

The bridge of light: step three

Once you can bring both the currents from above and below to Harmony on a single in-breath, you are ready to proceed. Do the entire process described above, opening your sanctum, preparing for meditation, formulating the spheres of the Tree of Life in and around you, calling down the white light from above you, and calling up the green light from beneath you. At the completion of this part of the practice you will have drawn in a deep breath and the center of Harmony at your heart will be full of both the white and the green energy.

Now, pause before breathing out, and as you pause imagine the white and green energy fusing together into golden energy, warm and bright. As in the visualization you do before meditating or the formulation of the protective sphere, this represents the lunar current, the secret current which is formed from the fusion of the solar and telluric currents. It is a current of healing, blessing, and empowerment. Feel and see the Harmony center at your heart radiating the golden light of this current. Then, as you breathe out, imagine the golden light filling your entire body. Do this sequence of bringing light down from above and up from below, and then blending it into golden radiance, three times in as many breaths. Then simply attend to the state of your body and mind for a little while, before closing in the usual way.

Once you have practiced this for a while, and can do it without too much trouble, you can add an additional bit of imagery to strengthen the effect. To do this, once you pause before breathing out and concentrate on the white and green energies blending into gold, imagine more white and green energies flowing in from above and below, respectively, joining in the blending process. With practice, this will build a subtle sense of pressure within and around the Harmony center. When you allow the golden energy to flow out to fill your body, you will feel the pressure decrease to normal.

Make all of this your regular practice until you can do it easily and feel the pressure build and release, and then go on to the fourth step.

The bridge of light: step four

At this point you have learned the basic Bridge of Light technique and can begin to apply it practically. In the teachings I studied with John Gilbert, the Bridge of Light was one of the most important practices for healing and blessing. He usually taught it, in fact, as part of the work of the Modern Order of Essenes, the healing order he had inherited from his teacher Rev. Matthew Shaw. The first stage in the healing work was self-healing; you may already have noticed that the flow of golden energy into your body at the peak of step three above has healing effects on your body, mind, and spirit. To proceed to the fourth step is to begin to heal and bless others using the same technique.

An important ethical principle needs to be brought up here. You have no right to force healing and blessing on anyone. You can offer these things, but they have the right to refuse. There are people who do not want to be blessed and healed. You can see this in the way they work, sometimes very hard, to maintain their patterns of unhappiness and poor health. You have no right to deprive them of these things, no matter how much you may want to do so and no matter how much happier you think they would be without them.

Thus it is crucial, before you perform healing or blessing work for anyone else, to ask for and receive their consent. You do not have to go into detail about what you intend to do. You can simply tell them that you want to do some healing or blessing work for them, or even that you want to pray for them to receive healing or blessing. If they consent, you can go ahead and do the work for them. If they do not consent, you need to accept that.

There are certain exceptions to this rule. If the person is someone for whom you have the right to give consent for medical treatment—for example, a child of yours, or a person unable to give consent for whom you have a medical power of attorney—you have the same right to consent for spiritual healing and blessing on their behalf. It is always appropriate to heal and bless animals and plants; according to occult tradition, one of the reasons why human souls have incarnated here on the material plane is to heal and bless the world of nature. Similarly, blessings for those who have died are always appropriate.

It is also worth remembering that you should not expect sudden results from this work, especially at first. Spiritual healing, especially, is not child's play. It is a subtle, difficult, and demanding kind of work, and much practice is often needed to become good at it. For this reason it is important not to make a fuss about what you are doing. Simply ask the person you want to help if you can do spiritual healing work for them, or pray for their health, and leave it at that. If their condition improves unexpectedly, pay attention to that fact but do not boast about it.

Provided that you have consent, or you intend to heal or bless someone or something that falls under one of the exceptions given above, perform all the preliminaries you have already learned. Open your sanctum in due form, and go through all the preparations for meditation. Before you go on to start formulating the spheres in and around your body, speak aloud the intention you have chosen for the working; for example, "My intention is to help my friend Joan recover from her head cold" or "My intention is to bless the plants in the park across the street." Then go on with the rest of the work.

It is when you reach the point where the golden light is formed that things become different. Instead of simply radiating the light through your body, send it outside yourself to the person or thing that you intend to heal or bless. Do this with each out-breath, and imagine the light flowing across the difference that separates you from the recipient of the healing or blessing. See and feel it flow into the recipient and spread healing or blessing with it.

To begin with, do this three times per session, just as you did in the previous step. With practice, you can begin increasing the number of breaths. Do not rush this. It is more important to maintain steady concentration on the imagery than it is to push the number of repetitions. You will find that with practice you can feel the energy reach its destination and do its work. When you can do this reliably for three breaths, add a fourth; when this is easy, add a fifth. Seven breaths is as much as you should attempt to do at this point in your work.

What if you have no specific intention in mind? In that case, you can direct the golden energy out in all directions to bless the entire cosmos and everything in it. This is worth doing as a regular practice, because it raises the spiritual quality of your surroundings and the whole world. You will find that the more you bless, the more you will be blessed; the more you heal, the more you will be healed. In the phrasing John Gilbert liked to use, you raise the vibration of the whole creation every time you use this technique.

Practice the bridge of light as a means of spiritual healing and blessing while you complete your meditations on the patterns of the Tree of Life. Keep on performing this work now and again even after you go on to the next stage of the work, the practice of sphere workings.

Stage six: sphere workings

Up to this point, except for the final step of the stage you have just completed, your work has focused on your own microcosm. This is appropriate, for the same reason that it is a good idea to learn how to bless and heal yourself before you offer help to others: your capacity to help them will be much greater if you have taken care of your own needs first. Now, however, if you have done all the preparatory work of the first five stages, you are prepared to go on and begin working in a sequence of mesocosms.

What is a mesocosm? As the word implies, it is a cosmos on a scale that fits in between the microcosm and the macrocosm. It is a symbolic representation of the universe; it is also a symbolic representation of yourself. The creation and use of mesocosms is the most important of all the secrets of occultism, and like most of these secrets, it is hidden in plain sight. All the arts of operative occultism create mesocosms, and use them to explore, understand, and shape the microcosm, the macrocosm, or both.

Consider a diviner who casts and interprets a tarot reading for another person. The tarot deck is a mesocosm—that is, it is a symbolic cosmos that consists of 78 cards. Each of the cards represents some factor in the microcosm of the diviner's client, and each card also represents some factor in the macrocosm in which the diviner and her client both live. From the seemingly random play of the cards, the diviner catches the subtle influences of synchronicity that connect the client's microcosm to the macrocosm and vice versa. In this way, the cards can reveal to her the shape of the client's future and suggest possibilities for action that a merely rational approach will not disclose.

Equally, consider a mage—a practitioner of magic—who seeks to gain strength of will and uses magical ritual to further that goal. He drapes the altar in the center of his working space with a red cloth and places five red candles on it. He puts a red tabard over his white ritual robe. An iron blade is his working tool and the incense he burns is made of herbs that resonate with the energies of the sphere of Power. When Mars stands on the eastern horizon, unafflicted by hostile astrological aspects, our mage begins his ceremony, calling on the influences of the sphere of Power using names and symbols traditionally assigned to it. All these things are meant to create a mesocosm in which will is the single most potent factor. Over the days and weeks that follow the ceremony, the mage finds that his will has become significantly stronger and more focused, and he is able to brush aside obstacles that frustrated or frightened him before.

The sphere workings given in this book can work like this second example, as we will see. Their principal functions, however, are to bring the different forces and factors in your own microcosm into balance, and to prepare the way for the more intensive and tightly focused pathworkings that will follow. In this phase of the work, you will use the techniques you have already learned to construct eight imaginal temples, one for each of the seven spheres of the Lower World and one for the enigmatic not-sphere Knowledge which bestrides the Abyss. Through repeated practice, these will become vivid realities for you, seen, sensed, and felt around you when you enter them.

You will be building these imaginal temples one at a time, beginning with the temple of Manifestation at the base of the Tree of Life and rising up from there. During the time you spend building each temple, meditate on the symbolism of the corresponding sphere. Don't hesitate to return to the themes of previous meditations and explore them in more detail. You will find that a second pass through these themes will reveal far more than your first explorations did. As a general rule, the more work you do meditating on a symbol, the more it will reveal to you.

Constructing the temples

The method you will use to construct each of the imaginal temples of the spheres follows on from the work you have already done. As before, open a temple in the usual way, prepare for meditation, formulate the spheres of the Tree of Life in and around your body, and draw in the solar and telluric currents from above and below as you have been taught. As you breathe out, however, the golden energy you have created from the two currents flows out to form a temple around you, changing color as needed in the process. With each out-breath, build up the temple in your imagination. As you do this, imagine that you are sitting in the temple facing the image at its center. Start with four breaths, and add an additional breath once you can do so while maintaining steady concentration. Ten breaths is as much as you should aim for at this phase of the work.

Once you have finished, remain still for a while, continuing to imagine the temple around you. Feel the presence of whichever sphere of the Tree of Life that the temple represents. Review as much of the symbolism of that Sphere as you remember. When you are ready, perform the closing ritual. Do nothing when you close the working to banish or disperse the temple, so that its pattern will be ready for you to reenter the next time you do the same practice.

Work on one temple at a time, performing the practice just described at least four times to establish the temple solidly in your imagination and on the inner planes. You may do as many more repetitions as you feel would benefit the process. By the time you finish this stage of the work you will have formulated the seven temples below the Abyss and the mysterious eighth temple of Knowledge, so that you can enter them in your imagination any time you choose. In the process, by creating this series of imaginal mesocosms, you will have activated all seven of the spheres of the Lower World within yourself, and helped to balance your own mind and body accordingly.

The temples are described below. Read through the description and study the diagram several times before you begin working on any of the temples, and review the text regularly so that you do not forget any of the details. Anything that is not specified—for example, the exact shape of the pillars, the presence or absence of carvings on the walls, or decorative details on the magical images—may be imagined in whatever way you choose.

One traditional practice you can put to use in decorating your inner temples is a simple form of the art of memory. This is a system of mnemonics developed in ancient times, and put to occult use during the Renaissance.[18] The founders and practitioners of the system in ancient times discovered that visual images stay in the memory longer than words or concepts, and took to creating imaginary places stocked with mental images to remind them of things they wanted to remember.

To combine the art of memory with the work you do in your inner temples, simply imagine pictures, carvings, or statues around the walls of each temple corresponding to the symbolism of the sphere the temple represents. For example, you might put an image or a symbol of the planet Earth on one wall of the temple of Manifestation, to remind you that the tenth sphere corresponds to Earth in astrology. Start with a small number of images so that you can remember them easily, without a reminder, whenever you formulate the temple. You can always add more later. When you are in any of your imaginal temples, make a point of noticing each of the memory images you have placed in it, so that the habit of remembering the images and what they suggest becomes automatic.

Manifestation

The temple of Manifestation has a hexagonal floor plan, and its walls are black. Four massive pillars support a dome over the center, where stands a statue of baked clay representing the magical image of the tenth sphere: a young woman seated on a cube of stone. She wears a plain dress with a cord belt. Her hair is long, dark, and unbound, her feet are bare, and she sits with her knees together and her hands resting on her thighs. Hanging from a plain cord around her neck, an equal-armed cross of pure but roughly formed gold rests over her heart.

A banner bearing the image of Trump XV stands to the right of the statue. The floor is paved with alternating squares of white and black, representing the alternation of joy and sorrow in earthly life. Three portals, as shown in the diagram, lead to other spheres; each is painted to represent its corresponding tarot trump.

---

[18] Yates 1966 is a good introduction to the system.

STAGE SIX: SPHERE WORKINGS 181

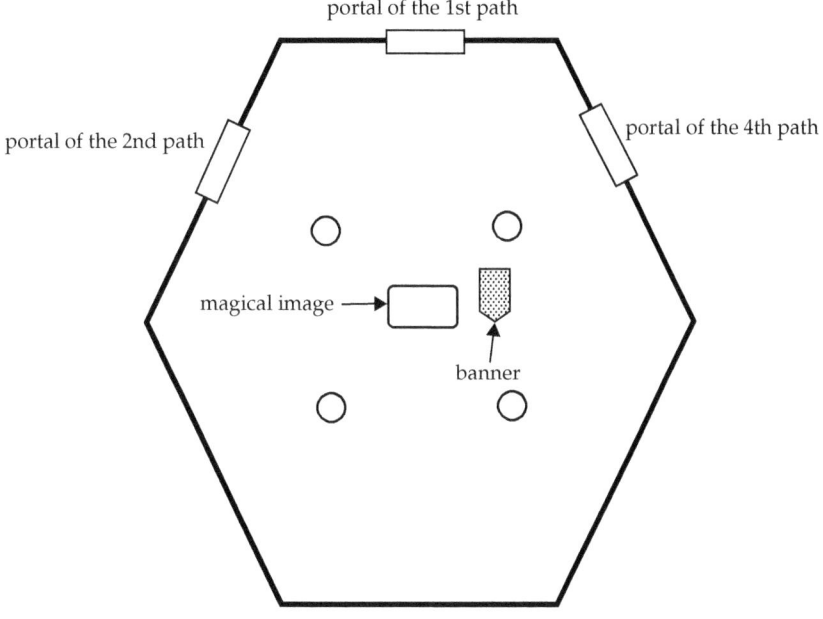

Temple of manifestation

Foundation

The temple of Foundation has an octagonal floor plan. Its walls are of silver and white crystal. In the center stands a great statue of white stone representing the magical image of the ninth sphere: a beautiful naked man standing with his feet firmly planted on the ground and his arms raised in the posture of Atlas supporting the heavens. His hair is dark and he has a short beard. His muscles are well developed. He radiates a sense of great strength, and his arms and hands bear the weight of the temple roof.

A banner bearing the image of Trump XVI stands to the right of the statue. The floor is paved with intricate mosaic work in violet and white. Four portals, as shown in the diagram, lead to other spheres; each is painted to represent its corresponding tarot trump.

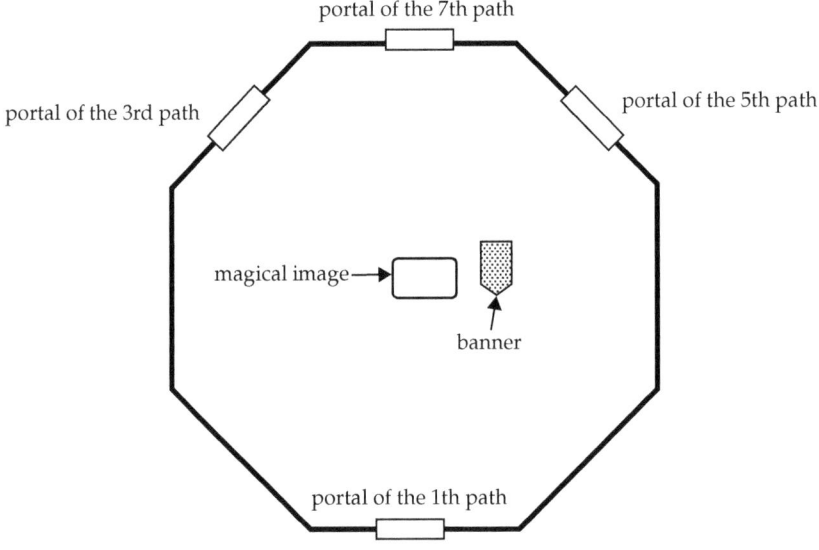

Temple of foundation

Competence

The temple of Competence has an oblong floor plan, and its walls are of tawny stone. Three pillars of the same stone, placed in a triangle, hold up the central dome. In the center is a statue of fired clay pottery representing the magical image of the eighth sphere: a young man in a short tunic of tawny fabric, with a headband of the same color and sandy hair. He stands firmly on his right foot but his left heel is rising as though take a step. His legs are bare and he wears leather sandals. In his right hand he holds a short white staff or baton, the old emblem of a herald. This image has been painted with glaze in lifelike colors.

A banner bearing the image of Trump XVII stands to the right of the statue. The floor is a mosaic of many colors, showing animals, birds, and fish of all kinds. Five portals, as shown in the diagram, lead to other spheres; each is painted to represent its corresponding tarot trump.

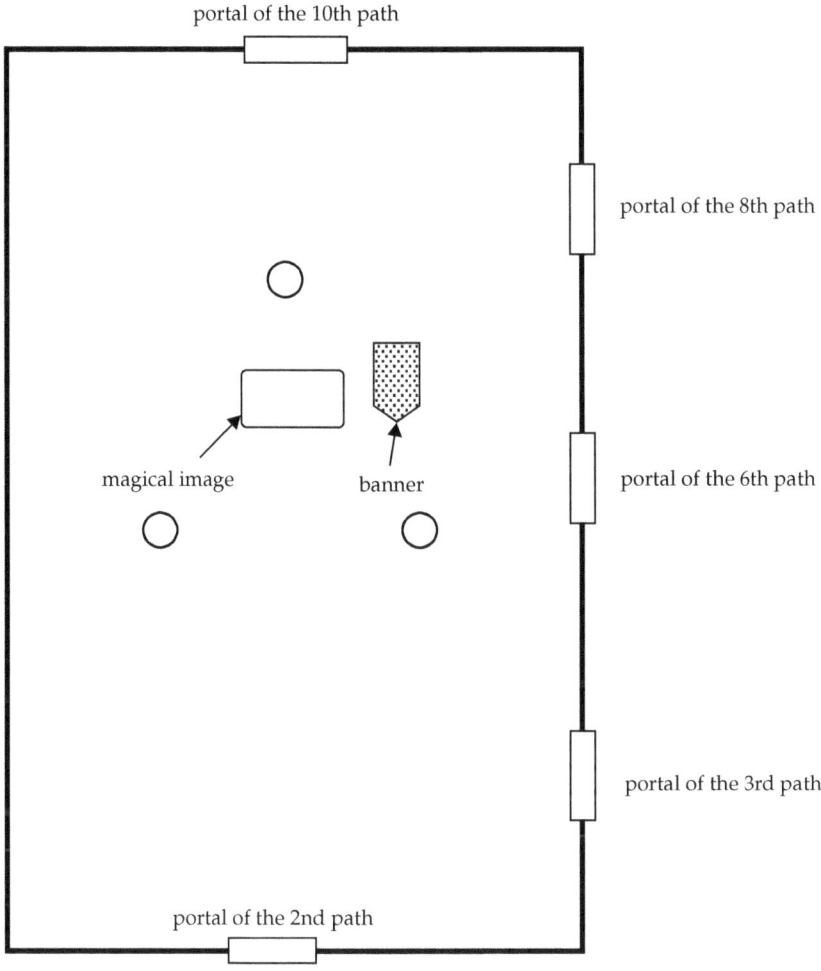

Temple of competence

Desire

The temple of Desire has a square floor plan and its walls are of blue turquoise and copper. Three copper pillars, placed in a triangle, hold up the central dome. Beneath the dome is a bronze statue representing the magical image of the seventh sphere: a beautiful naked woman standing in a meadow dotted with flowers. She wears a garland of flowers about her head but nothing else, and her long hair is unbound.

Her arms are extended downward and out to the sides, as though inviting an embrace.

A banner bearing the image of Trump XVIII stands to the right of the statue. The floor is a mosaic of various shades of green, representing leaves of all kinds. Five portals, as shown in the diagram, lead to other spheres; each is painted to represent its corresponding tarot trump.

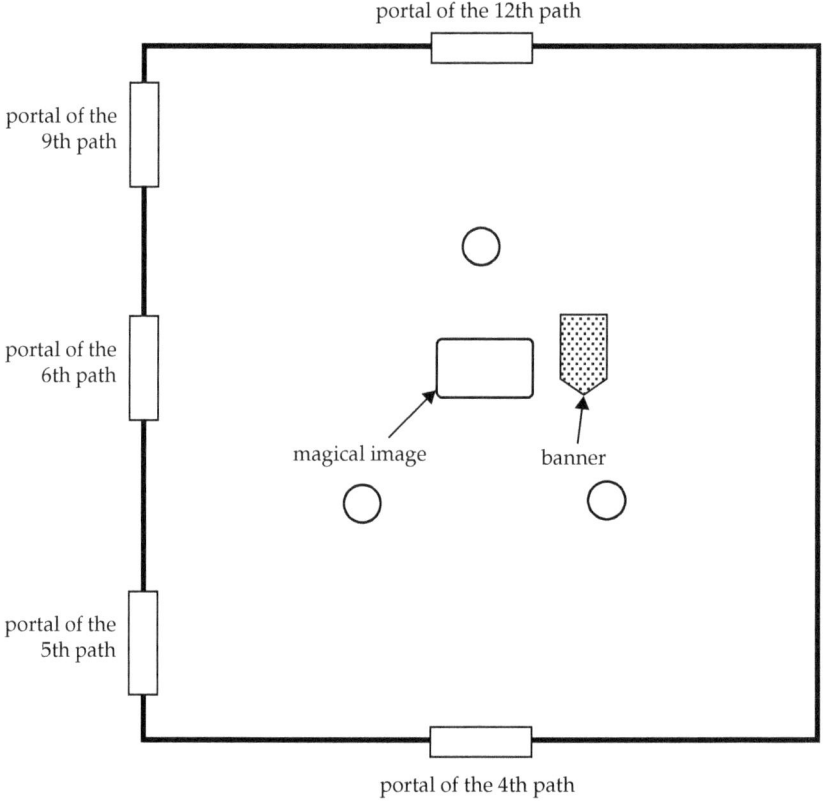

Temple of desire

Harmony

The temple of Harmony is square in floor plan, and it is made of golden stone and ornamented with gold. It has a dome which rests squarely on the four walls. In the center, beneath the dome, is a group of golden statues representing the magical images of the sixth sphere.

There are three of these. The first is a naked child standing and reaching up as though to a parent. The second is a young monarch in ornate robes seated on a throne, with a sword in the left hand and a scepter in the right. The third is a sacrificed god, naked except for a loincloth, who is crucified or otherwise suspended above the ground. The gender of these figures is the same as that of the practitioner, as they represent his or her higher self. The child is in front, the enthroned monarch just behind, and the sacrificed deity is above and behind all.

A banner bearing the image of Trump XIX stands to the right of the statues. The floor is made of polished squares of pure white marble. Six portals, as shown in the diagram, lead to other spheres; each is painted to represent its corresponding tarot trump.

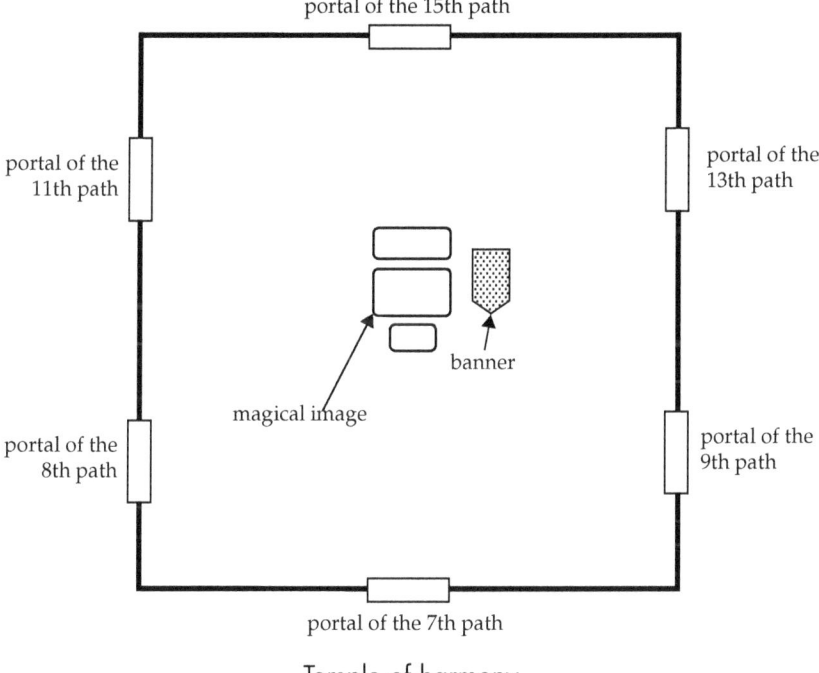

Temple of harmony

Power

The temple of Power is oblong in floor plan, and its walls and ceiling are of red stone. It has no dome. A little past the center toward the far end is a group of statues made of iron, showing the magical image of the fifth sphere: a warrior queen in a chariot drawn by two horses. Her head is bare and her black hair streams out behind her. She wears a cloak and armor of polished steel. In her right hand is a sword, and on her left arm is a round shield with a pentagram on it.

A banner bearing the image of Trump XX stands to the right of the statues. The floor is of black marble polished to a mirror finish. Three portals, as shown in the diagram, lead to other spheres; each is painted to represent its corresponding tarot trump.

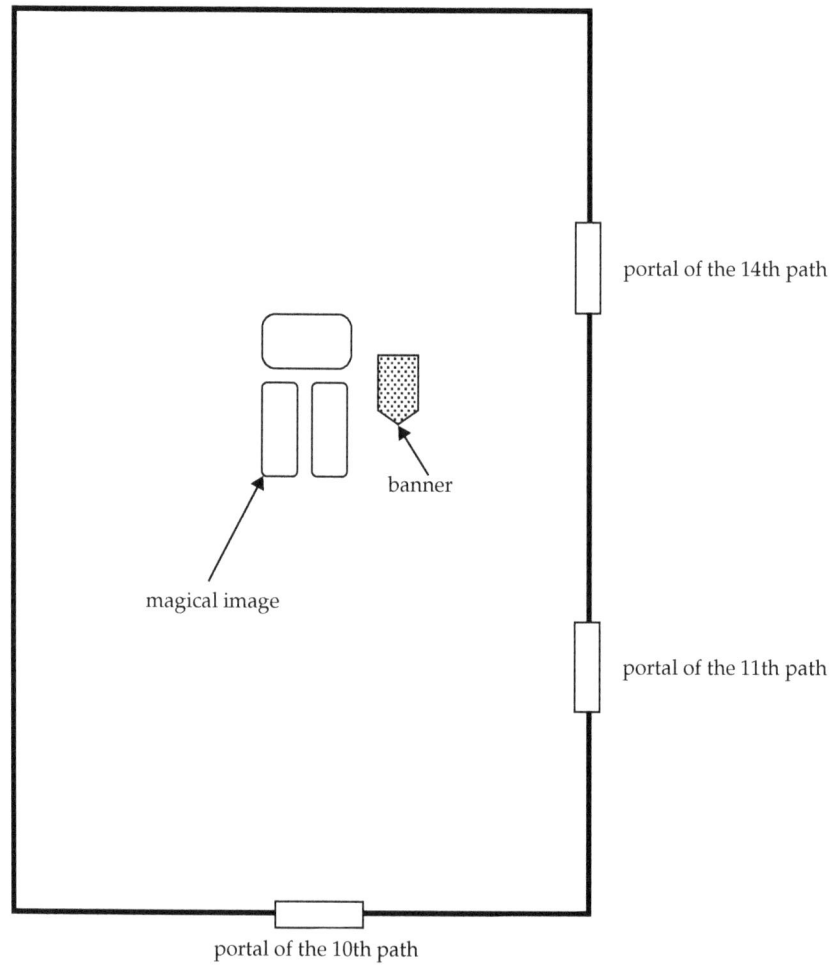

Temple of power

Love

The temple of Love is triangular in floor plan, with the entrance in the middle of one of the sides, and it rises up like a pyramid to a point high above. It is made all of green stone, and the floor is tiled in triangular slabs of the same stone. In the center stands a statue of polished tin representing the magical image of the fourth sphere: an old wise king upon a throne, dressed in ample robes and wearing an ornate crown. His hair and beard are long and his face shows the marks of great age. He holds a scepter in his right hand, and, in his left, an orb with an equal-armed cross atop it.

A banner bearing the image of Trump XXI stands to the right of the statue. Three portals, as shown in the diagram, lead to other spheres; each is painted to represent its corresponding tarot trump.

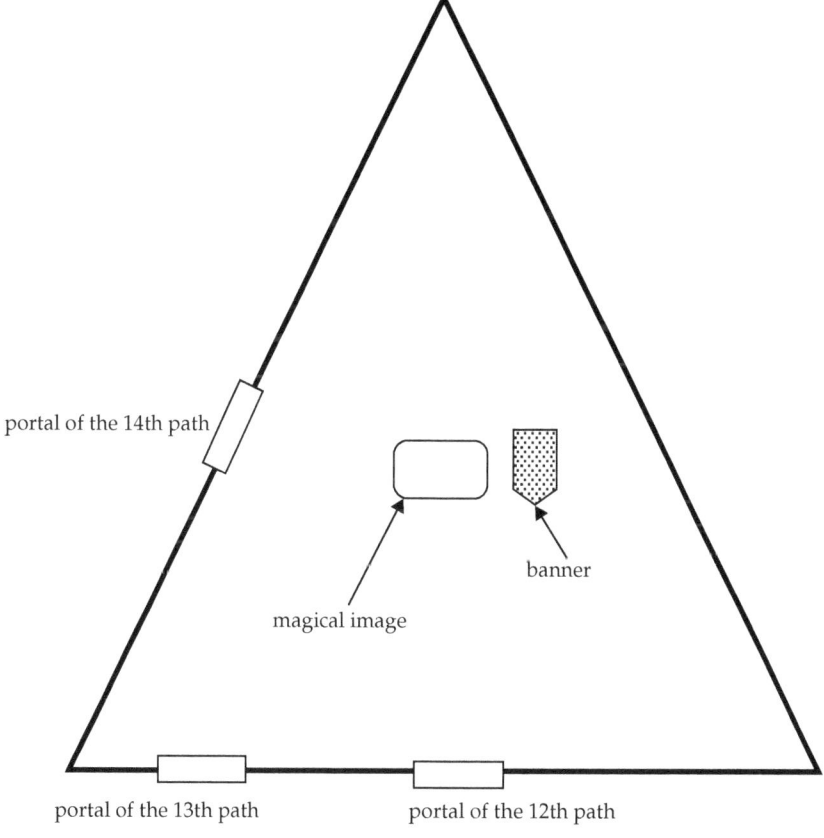

Temple of love

Knowledge

The temple of Knowledge is circular and its floor, its walls, and its domed ceiling are all made of cloudy gray stone. There is nothing in it—no magical image, no banner, nor anything else. The portal through which you enter is the only entrance or exit, and it is painted with its corresponding tarot trump.

The musical dimension

Music in each of the seven traditional modes can also be used to help you attune yourself to the seven imaginal temples just described. Each mode, as you have learned, corresponds to one of the seven spheres of the Lower World, and so playing or listening to music in the corresponding mode is an effective way to place your consciousness in harmony with the influences of the spheres.

If you already know enough about music to understand the modes, simply pick tunes that appeal to you in each mode and play or listen to them before you begin your practice in each temple. If music theory is still a mystery to you, but you want to learn the modes well enough to use them in this work, the simplest way to do this is to purchase a mountain dulcimer or lap dulcimer. This is not the kind of dulcimer that looks like a naked piano, and is played by hitting the strings with wooden hammers; it is an odd and pleasant little instrument invented in America's Appalachian region, usually shaped like a stretched figure 8, with four unevenly spaced strings and a fretboard with unevenly spaced frets.

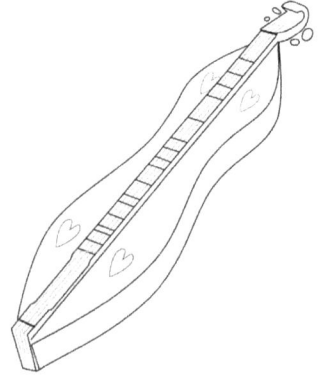

Mountain dulcimer

STAGE SIX: SPHERE WORKINGS 189

Mountain dulcimers are inexpensive to buy and easy to play; during the 20th century, they were adopted enthusiastically in folk music circles all over the English-speaking world as a result, and can be obtained quite readily. If you get one, along with a book or video for beginners, a month or two of regular practice well get you to the point of being able to play well enough for the purposes of the work of this section.

The secret of the dulcimer is that with one exception, you can tune it to any mode just by retuning the two melody strings (the pair of high strings closest to your body when you put the dulcimer on your lap). If you tune the melody strings to the same note as the middle string, that gives you the Ionian mode, the familiar major scale, which corresponds to the seventh sphere. Tune the melody strings one note lower than the middle string and you have the Dorian mode, corresponding to the sixth sphere, and so on. The table below tells you which tunings produce each of the seven modes. When it says "2nd" under "Tune melody strings," that tells you to fret the melody strings at the 2nd fret and tune them while keeping them fretted; "open" tells you to tune them without fretting them.

Sphere	Mode	Degrees	Scale begins:	Tune melody strings ...
Manifestation	Mixolydian	1–5–8	nut	open, to 7th fret on bass string
Foundation	Aeolian	1–5–7	1st fret	open, to 6th fret on bass string
Competence	Locrian	1–(5)–6	2nd fret	2nd, to 2nd (or 9th) fret on bass string*
Desire	Ionian	1–5–5	3rd fret	open, to same note as middle string
Harmony	Dorian	1–5–4	4th fret	open, to 3rd fret on bass string
Power	Phrygian	1–5–3	5th fret	2nd, to same note as middle string
Love	Lydian	1–5–2	6th fret	open, to 1st (or 8th) fret on bass string

*To make the proper Locrian mode, you also have to retune the middle string; once you have tuned the melody strings, fret them at the 6th fret and tune them to one octave below this.

You can find plenty of tunes in dulcimer songbooks and online sources for most of these modes. Phrygian and Locrian are less common, but they can be found. On the other hand, it's always appropriate simply to tune the dulcimer to the mode you want and strum across all the strings, using your fingers or a pick, while improvising whatever sequence of notes appeal to you on the melody strings with your fingers or a noter (a little piece of wooden dowel). Played this way, the bass and middle strings produce a drone while the melody is in the appropriate mode. This style of playing is the oldest and most traditional way of using a mountain dulcimer; it is easy to learn and can produce lovely music, and it is entirely suitable for the work of this section. Play for at least five minutes, and as much more as you wish, before beginning your workings.

Practical applications

Your first task in working with the inner temples of the spheres below the Abyss is to learn how to formulate them quickly and completely. You will find that with practice, the temples will become robust realities for you, and each time you enter one it will be easier to call up the imagery and feel the presence of the sphere that it represents. This builds a foundation for the work still to come, and it also has immediate benefits. By creating representations of the seven spheres of the Lower World and charging them with your imagination and intention, you help the seven forces represented by these spheres to manifest in your body, mind, and spirit in a more balanced fashion. The practice also gently stimulates the seven spinal chakras, bringing improved health and the awakening of psychic perceptions.

The work with the first four temples can also play a very significant role in the awakening of the third triad discussed in an earlier chapter. By formulating these four temples in the imaginal realm, you make the process of letting go of projections easier, because you have an inner template for the difference between the world of material objects and the worlds of life, thought, and feeling that are so often muddled up with it.

This can sometimes be a rough experience. It is very common for people to use projection to keep from noticing things about themselves they do not way to admit, by pretending that this or that quality they have actually belongs to some other person or thing. You may discover, for example, that your irritation with certain people for their selfish behavior is how you avoid noticing a well-developed selfish streak in yourself, or something of the same kind. Jung liked to point out that whatever bothers you most in other people is usually a habit of your own that you haven't admitted to yourself; by and large, this is right.

If you find yourself having to deal with an awkward situation like this, remember that it's not just you! Somewhere in the world there may be someone sufficiently saintly and wise to have no projections at all, but I have never met such a paragon and it is unlikely that you will ever meet one either. Accept it, deal with it as best you can, and go on. Perfection is not a useful goal in this work; simply do your best, and let awareness—the universal solvent of the alchemists—dissolve your projections and bad habits a little at a time.

Once you have completed the work of this stage, you can also use the temples of the spheres as the basis for sphere workings: meditative workings that concentrate your energies on consciousness on one of the seven lower spheres, or on the non-sphere Knowledge. You can do this any time you need to strengthen the qualities or capacities of one of the spheres in yourself. Any time one of the other spheres has become overstimulated, you can also do a sphere working of another sphere that will balance it and release any surplus energy and attention that has become fixated in the overstimulated sphere.

Sphere workings of this kind are best kept simple. Open your sanctum, formulate the Tree of Life, and call power down from the heavens and up from the earth to formulate and energize one of the temples. Spend some minutes making the imagery of the temple around you as clear, exact, and solidly felt as you can make it. Then simply remain in the temple for a time before closing.

If you wish, you can meditate on the quality or capacity of the sphere that you wish to develop in yourself, but be sure to keep the meditation as abstract and impersonal as possible. For example, if you are doing a sphere working of the eighth sphere in order to help yourself develop an agile mind so that you can learn difficult subjects easily, do not let your meditation stray into what you want to learn, much less the problems you have had learning things in the past! Focus instead on learning in the abstract. What is it, and how does it relate to the sphere of Competence? How does an agile mind help with learning? Which of the symbols of the sphere reflect the mental agility you seek? Doing this will keep your past problems and the emotions connected with them from making the working less effective than it would otherwise be.

The following notes will help you decide which sphere working to practice in different situations. Each of the spheres can be used for purposes other than the ones listed. Your own meditations are your best guide here; as you meditate on the Tree of Life, let yourself consider which factors in your life express the energies of each sphere, and which problems you face are signs of a lack of one sphere's influence or a surplus of another's.

Spheres and sphere workings

Manifestation	use to develop:	stability, realistic attitudes, capacity to focus, attention to everyday realities
	signs of excess:	anxiety, depression, mental rigidity, obsession with material things, a sense of "stuckness"
	balancing sphere:	Harmony
Foundation	use to develop:	vitality, joy, sense of oneness with the world, sensitivity to the emotional and energetic states of others
	signs of excess:	oversensitivity, confusion, lack of concentration, trouble maintaining boundaries between self and others
	balancing sphere:	Knowledge
Competence	use to develop:	intelligence, wit, mental agility, capacity to learn and apply knowledge, deftness, practical skills
	signs of excess:	overthinking, "paralysis by analysis," rigid intellectual schemes, flight from emotion
	balancing sphere:	Love
Desire	use to develop:	passion, artistic and creative talents, relationship skills, emotional healing
	signs of excess:	wallowing in emotional states, repeated indulgence in interpersonal drama, flight from thinking
	balancing sphere:	Power

(*Continued*)

(Continued)

Harmony	use to develop:	self-confidence, self-knowledge, vivid imagination, a clear sense of purpose and direction in life
	signs of excess:	self-centeredness, arrogance, detachment from the realities of everyday existence
	balancing sphere:	Manifestation
Power	use to develop:	will, discipline, self-control, strength, capacity to deal with challenges
	signs of excess:	mental or physical rigidity, hostility, defensiveness, inability to relax
	balancing sphere:	Desire
Love	use to develop:	benevolence, fairness, generosity, calmness, grace, a retentive memory
	signs of excess:	extravagance, laziness, overindulgence, tolerance of abusive and dysfunctional behavior in self or others
	balancing sphere:	Competence
Knowledge	use to develop:	clarity, spiritual insight, openness to the divine
	signs of excess:	isolation, narrowness, flight from the world
	balancing sphere:	Foundation

Even so basic a sphere working as the kind presented in this chapter can have powerful effects on human consciousness. Thus it is important not to overdo them, or you can very easily swing from one extreme to another without ever reaching the point of healthy balance in between! As a rule, once you have finished the seven workings of each of the temples described earlier in this section, never do more than three sphere workings in any one sphere without doing at least one working with the sphere that balances it.

At intervals, it is also wise to go through the whole set of temple workings from Manifestation up to Knowledge, giving one practice to each of the eight temples. This will bring through energies from all of the spheres in a balanced manner and help you avoid imbalances. These rules will become even more important when you include the more powerful practice of taking on the magical images of the spheres, as described in the next section.

Stage seven: the magical images

The magical images given to the seven spheres below the Abyss have more than one use in Cabalistic work. As symbolic images, they are worth close study while you are learning the correspondences of the Tree of Life. As you begin discursive meditation on the spheres, they make fine themes for meditation. In the imaginal temples you learned to build and work with in the previous section, the magical images—envisioned as statues in the center of each temple—are a core part of the imagery that helps you connect the temple with the sphere that it represents.

The most potent practice involving the magical images, however, involves a more challenging feat of imagination. In this next stage of the work, you will imagine yourself as each of the magical images. You will experience its body as your body, its mind as your mind, and the energy of the sphere that it embodies as the spiritual influence flowing into you. This is a simple form of the magical practice known as a body of transformation.

This form of practice is very ancient. In modern times it plays a central role in some of the most profound spiritual traditions of Asia, but it was also practiced in ancient Egypt, where priests and priestesses would take on themselves the images of gods and goddesses as part of certain rituals and esoteric practices. From Egypt it passed to Greek wizards influenced by Platonism, and from there passed into the body of Western magical tradition. Another echo of this form of practice is found in the Christian mystical practice of the imitation of Christ, in which the mystic uses memory, will, and imagination to live as Christlike a life as possible.

Here, just as before, you will be building on the work you have already done. Begin with music of the appropriate mode, if you wish. Then open your sanctum in the usual way, awaken the centers of the Tree of Life in and around your body, call on the two currents of energy from above and below, and use them to formulate a temple. The one difference in the temple is that there will be no statue representing the magical image of the sphere at the center. Instead, you will become each of the magical images. Whenever the magical image of a sphere includes a seat, a throne, or any other object for the figure itself to sit on, stand in, or hang from, imagine that, but see it empty and waiting for you.

Next, imagine yourself walking to the center of the temple and taking the place of the magical image. Become the magical image. See and feel its body in place of your own, clothed in its proper clothes and ornamented with whatever ornaments are assigned to it. Then fill your mind with the consciousness of the magical image, a consciousness focused on the affairs of the sphere it represents; use your imagination to fill in whatever details you wish. Finally, imagine the energies of the sphere flowing into your new body and mind, filling you with an intense awareness of the sphere's nature and power.

Once you are ready, release the influences you have called into yourself in the reverse order of their arrival; first, let go of the energies of the sphere, then clear your consciousness of the consciousness of the magical image, and then dissolve the body of the magical image and resume your own body. In your imagination, leave the center of the temple and return to your starting place. Then close the practice in the usual way. At first it is best to maintain the state of identity with the magical image only for a few minutes; later on, you can increase the length of time you stay in that state. The longer you spend in it, the stronger the effects will be.

Since this is a considerably more powerful way of invoking the influence of each sphere, the risk of imbalance is greater, so it is important not to get "stuck" on any one image. Thus you will begin with the tenth sphere and take on that magical image once. After that one practice, proceed at once to the ninth in your next practice and go from there, taking on each sphere's magical image only once before you go on to the next one. The one exception is the sixth sphere, which has three images; devote three sessions to this sphere, taking on one of the magical images each time.

Go through the entire sequence seven times. Once you have done this, you will be able to use the magical images of the spheres to give additional force to your sphere workings. Here again, though, be careful of becoming overbalanced in any one direction. Do three workings at most of the magical images of any given sphere before doing a working of the magical image of its balancing sphere, and go through the whole sequence regularly to maintain your balance in general.

The magical images of the spheres are listed below for your convenience. As noted earlier, you can add additional details so long as they do not conflict with the descriptions given. Some people have very precise visual or tactile imaginations and can build up magical images with a photographic level of realism. Others cannot, but their magical images can be just as effective as those of people with more gifted imaginations. Do your best and do not worry about whether your images are "good enough." If you take up the practice systematically and do at least one or two of these workings a week, you will find that they are quite effective.

Do each of these magical images seven times, in the sequence described above. Then you will be ready to begin the pathworkings in the next section of this book.

Tenth sphere

A young woman seated on a cube of black stone. She wears a plain black dress with a cord belt. Her hair is long, dark, and unbound, her feet are bare, and she sits with her knees together and her hands resting on her thighs. Hanging from a plain cord around her neck, an equal-armed cross of pure but roughly formed gold rests over her heart.

Ninth sphere

A beautiful naked man standing with his feet firmly planted on the ground and his arms raised in the posture of Atlas supporting the heavens. His hair is dark and he has a short beard. His muscles are well developed. He radiates a sense of great strength.

Eighth sphere

A young man in a short tunic of tawny fabric, with a headband of the same color and sandy hair. He stands firmly on his right foot but his left is rising as though taking a step; his legs are bare and he wears leather sandals. In his right hand he holds a short white staff or baton, the old emblem of a herald.

Seventh sphere

A beautiful naked woman standing in a meadow dotted with flowers. She wears a garland of flowers about her head but nothing else, and her long golden hair is unbound. Her arms are extended downward and out to the sides, as though inviting an embrace.

Sixth sphere

This sphere has three magical images. The first is a naked child standing and reaching up as though to a parent. The second is a young monarch in golden robes seated on a throne, with a sword in the left hand and a scepter in the right. The third is a sacrificed god, naked except for a loincloth, who is crucified or otherwise suspended above the ground. The gender of these figures is the same as that of the practitioner, as they represent his or her higher self.

Fifth sphere

A warrior queen in a chariot drawn by two roan horses. Her head is bare and her black hair streams out behind her. She wears a crimson cloak and armor of polished steel. In her right hand is a sword, and on her left arm is a round shield painted black with a red pentagram on it.

Fourth sphere

An old wise king upon a throne, dressed in blue robes, with a crown and belt of gold. His hair and beard are long and white. He holds a scepter of gold in his right hand, and, in his left, an orb with an equal-armed cross atop it.

Stage eight: pathworkings

The paths of the Tree of Life can be traveled in many ways. In some esoteric orders, the rituals of initiation include symbolic journeys along the paths, in which symbols of each path are presented to the new initiate as he or she is guided from a place that represents one sphere to a place that represents another. In others, practitioners are taught to do such journeys themselves in solo rituals. Guided meditations in which a group of people imagine themselves making a journey along a path while an experienced practitioner reads aloud from a prepared text, describing the scenes and incidents of the journey, are popular in some circles. When I was first studying the Cabala, you could purchase cassette tapes that provided narrations of this kind, complete with sound effects; nowadays you can download much the same thing as sound files from the internet.

The mode of pathworking that John Gilbert taught was a little different than these. He had his students use a combination of ritual and active imagination to travel the paths. This approach was not unique to him—there have been plenty of other teachers who taught the same thing before and since—but it fit well with the other practices he taught. This is the method we will be using in this chapter.

As before, all the preliminary steps are the ones you have already learned. You may begin with music of the appropriate mode if you wish. Then open your sanctum with the familiar ritual, go through the preliminaries of meditation, formulate the Tree of Life in and around your body, bring in power from the solar and telluric currents, and use that to formulate one of the temples you have learned to build. Once you are well established in the temple, you will rise in your imagination and go to one of the portals that leads from that temple to the temple of one of the other spheres. You will pass through the portal, make the journey, and reach the other temple, where you will take your seat. You will then close the working from within that temple.

After the work you have done in previous sections of this book, all this will be relatively easy. Experience has shown, however, that pathworkings done in this fashion have powerful effects on the body, mind, and spirit of the practitioner. They are, in every sense of the word, initiatory experiences. Done in the right way, they open up higher reaches of consciousness and human possibility as effectively as formal initiation in an esoteric order.

The sequence of initiation

It is important to begin this work in a balanced manner. Your first task in pathworking, then, is to work through the paths in numerical order, beginning with the first path. This will follow the upward dynamic of the way of initiation, though the path of the arrow itself is worked at a later stage.

Before you do each pathworking in this sequence, meditate on the symbols of the path and of the spheres at its beginning and end. For your first practice, that is, you will meditate on the first path, the tenth sphere, and the ninth sphere, reviewing their meanings and their symbols. If you wish, you may use the music of the Mixolydian mode to help place you in the inner temple of Manifestation.

Then, when you are ready, you will open your sanctum in the usual way, proceed through the steps you have already learned, and formulate the temple of Manifestation, establishing it as solidly as you can. Then, in your imagination, you will rise from your seat and go to the portal of the First Path, the one in the middle of the far wall. This portal is a vivid image of Trump I, the Magician. As you watch, the painting becomes a reality: you see before you a portal into the garden of the

Magician, which you have already entered in your work with active imagination.

As you did in that earlier work, pass through the portal into the Magician's garden and greet the Magician. Ask him to guide you along the first path to the temple of Foundation. Once he agrees to this, follow his guidance. He will take you on a journey through an imaginal landscape that begins in his garden and ends at the temple of the ninth sphere. Once you arrive at the temple, thank the Magician, go into the temple of Foundation, take your seat in it in the usual way, spend a little while imagining the temple of Foundation as clearly as possible, and then close the working in the usual way. In this sequence of workings, you do not go back down the path to the starting point—the goal is to establish an upward movement of attention and energy along the paths.

Meditate on the journey and on the symbols and events you encountered on your way from the tenth sphere to the ninth. When you have finished, meditate on the meanings and symbols of the second path, the tenth sphere, and the eighth sphere, and then do the next pathworking in the sequence, rising along the second path from the temple of Manifestation to the temple of Competence. Meditate on the journey as before, then on the third path, the ninth sphere, and the eighth sphere, and then do a pathworking along the third path from the temple of Foundation to the temple of Competence.

Continue in this way in order from the first to the 14th path, going always upwards—that is, from the sphere with the larger number to the sphere with the smaller number. (Thus you will work the sixth path from Competence to Desire, and the 14th path from Power to Love, rather than the other way around.) Finish by doing a pathworking on the 15th path from Harmony to Knowledge. Now repeat the whole sequence from the first to the 15th path again, and then a third time. This completes the sequence of initiation.

The sequence of creation

Now that you have opened up the paths on the Tree of Life as far as the human soul can reach, your next task is to carry the grace of the Divine down the paths from the three spheres of the reflected triad all the way back to the world of matter. This is done by traversing the same set of paths one at a time in reverse order, from the 15th path down to the first. In this sequence you are always moving from a sphere with a lower number to one with a higher number; thus you will travel the 14th path from the sphere of Love to that of Power, and the sixth path from the sphere of Desire to that of Competence.

The method is identical to the one you have already learned; only the direction changes. By the time you begin this sequence you will very likely know the symbolism of the spheres inside and out, due to your earlier meditations during the pathworkings of the sequence of initiation; simply meditate on each path before you descend it, and, of course, after each working you should meditate on your journey and each of the symbols and events you encountered on it.

The sequence of creation is not something to undertake lightly. Your life will change as the creative forces begin flowing more freely through the paths of your microcosmic Tree, and some of the changes may be unexpected and unsettling. Since this sequence works downward from above, furthermore, it tends to entangle you further in the world of everyday life, and you may need to work for a while to overcome this.

For these reasons it is best to do the sequence of creation once, and then do other forms of occult practice for at least a year before doing it again. Give the changes you are setting in motion time to work themselves out! The work is well worth doing, however. By doing pathworkings in the sequence of creation you are becoming, in however small a way, a co-creator with the Divine, helping to bring currents of life, blessing, and power from the shores of the Abyss to the world of everyday life. By doing this you help restore harmony and balance to your life and the life of everyone around you.

Practical applications

Like sphere workings, pathworkings can be done for practical purposes. Each path below the Abyss has certain effects when worked in an upward direction and a different set of effects when worked in a downward direction. When doing a pathworking in this way, it is done by itself, without placing it in a sequence with other pathworkings; it is therefore best to do this form of work only after you have completed the sequence of initiation at least three times, as specified above, and the sequence of creation at least once.

The method is the one you have already learned: open your sanctum, awaken the spheres of the Tree and the two currents, formulate the temple where you will be beginning the pathworking, then journey by way of the path to the temple where you will end the work, and close in the usual way. If you wish, you can state the intention for which you are doing the working after you open your sanctum and before you begin the awakening of the spheres, but this is optional.

The following table sets out a few of the many practical purposes for which pathworkings can be used. If your intention is not included in the table, discursive meditation on the intention you have in mind can be used to determine which path is best suited to it.

Path	Use going upwards to:	Use going downwards to:
1	overcome depression	become more grounded
2	become more wise	improve your memory
3	encourage creativity	resolve fertility issues
4	strengthen reasoning ability	take charge of your life
5	develop intuition	find a teacher
6	become better able to make choices	attract a love relationship
7	find your direction in life	attain success in your career
8	become more courageous	overcome your problems
9	cope with solitude	become a better teacher
10	get out of unwanted mental states	change your luck for the better
11	achieve inner balance	succeed with legal issues
12	become more aware of your inner life	recover from bad decisions
13	release your fears and worries	let go of unhelpful habits
14	transmute weaknesses into strengths	sort out truths from falsehoods
15	accelerate your spiritual development	achieve more freedom in your life

Just as you have been instructed to do three workings all the way up the way of initiation but only one descending on the way of creation, you should plan on doing at least three practical workings going upwards for every one you do going downwards. This helps maintain your focus on spiritual development, and keeps you from getting too deeply mired in the grubby details of the tenth sphere, but it also has an important practical dimension.

Harsh as it may seem to point this out, it is nevertheless true that the one thing all your problems have in common is you. Most people, caught up in the habit of projection discussed earlier, spend their whole lives convinced that their problems are all outside themselves, and flail about trying to change the world when their only hope of solving their problems is to change themselves. Thus they fail. To get past this trap, it's necessary to recognize that you can achieve your goals most effectively by shedding the attitudes and habits that get in the way of success.

The work of the way of initiation is one way to do this. Yes, there are some situations where you can also get good results by working to change the world around you, which is why the descending paths of the way of creation are discussed here. You will find, though, that the results will be better if your first response on encountering a problem is to ask yourself, "How am I contributing to this problem, and what changes can I make in myself to stop doing that?" Make those changes, and even if that does not solve the problem, you will find that changing the world outside you becomes much easier once you stop being part of the problem and become part of the solution.

The path of the arrow

Once you have worked through the pathworkings of the ways of initiation and creation, and experimented with pathworking for practical purposes, the next stage—the final step in the journey traced out in this book, and the first step in a much greater journey—is to use the pathworking experience as a way of bringing yourself into closer contact with the Divine. This is not something to take up lightly. Done correctly, it will challenge you to the depths of your being, and set in motion changes in your life that cannot be predicted in advance.

Before you begin this stage of the work, read through the description that follows and spend plenty of time in meditation and reflection, deciding if you are ready for the labor ahead. You and you alone can decide if you are ready for this work, and if so, how often you should perform this working, which follows the path of the arrow straight up the central axis of the Tree of Life from the sphere of Manifestation to the brink of the Abyss.

The pathworking of the path of the arrow is simple, though here as so often, "simple" is not the same thing as "easy"! You begin in the usual way, proceeding from the sanctum opening to the bridge of light, and then formulate the inner temple of Manifestation, the tenth sphere. Establish yourself in that temple in the usual way.

Then arise in your imagination and proceed to the portal of the first path. As you do so, concentrate on the idea that you are leaving your body in the temple of Manifestation. Everything that belongs to your material body stays behind, and so does everything that belongs to your life in the world of matter—your home, your job, your possessions, and the rest of it. You approach the first path stripped of all these things, just as you will have to let go of all of them when the time of your death arrives.

Proceed up the first path in the usual way, guided by the Magician. When you reach the temple of the ninth sphere, Foundation, thank the Magician for his guidance and proceed into the temple. Establish yourself there in the usual way.

Then arise in your imagination and proceed to the portal of the seventh path. As you do so, concentrate on the idea that you are leaving your ego in the temple of Foundation. Your ego and everything that belongs to it—whatever mix of pride, shame, guilt, self-love, self-hatred, and other thoughts and feelings gathers around your sense of who you are—remains behind. You approach the seventh path stripped of all these things, just as you will have to let go of all of them when you achieve enlightenment.

Proceed up the seventh path in the usual way, guided by the Charioteer. When you reach the temple of the sixth sphere, Harmony, thank the Charioteer for his guidance and proceed into the temple. Establish yourself there in the usual way.

Then arise in your imagination and proceed to the portal of the 15th path. As you do so, concentrate on the idea that you are leaving your individual identity in the temple of Harmony. What approaches the portal of the 15th path is pure awareness, without memory, will, imagination, desire, competence, or life force. You approach the 15th path stripped of all these things, returning to the essential spiritual core of yourself which exists outside of space and time, a gesture of the creative will of the Divine.

Thus there is no one for the Fool to guide up the 15th path. It is as the Fool himself that you ascend that path. As you reach the temple of Knowledge, the Fool dissolves around you, and it is as pure empty awareness that you enter into the empty space on the brink of the Abyss, the furthest point that the human individual can reach without dissolving completely back into the Divine.

Wait in the temple of Knowledge for a time, and see what happens. It is quite possible that nothing will happen. It is also possible, especially after multiple repetitions of this working, that certain spiritual experiences will occur. These will not be described here, as this might encourage your ego to fake them. Whatever does or does not happen, wait until you sense that the time is right to begin the descent, and then leave the temple of Knowledge and begin to descend the 15th path as the Fool.

When you reach the temple of Harmony, your sense of individual identity is waiting for you. Put it on, in much the same sense that you put on clothing when you get up in the morning. Establish yourself again in the temple of Harmony, and then rise and go to the portal of the seventh path. There the Charioteer is waiting for you. Allow him to guide you back down the seventh path to the temple of Foundation.

When you reach the temple of Foundation, your ego is waiting for you. Put it on, here again in much the same sense that you put on clothing when you get up in the morning. Establish yourself again in the temple of Foundation, and then rise and go to the portal of the first path. There the Magician is waiting for you. Allow him to guide you back down the first path to the temple of Manifestation.

When you reach the temple of Manifestation, your body is waiting for you. Once again, put this on, returning to an awareness of your embodiment and your life in the material world. Establish yourself again in the temple of Manifestation. When you are ready, close the practice in the usual way.

The first time you do this, you may get dramatic results, no results at all, or something between these two extremes. For most people, it takes repeated practice of the working to make the process of shedding body, ego, and individual existence, even in the imagination, more than a tentative gesture in the desired direction. Even that first gesture, however, can begin to teach you to draw the essential distinctions between body, ego, soul, and spirit, and to open yourself at least a little to the descending grace and blessing of the Divine. With regular repetition, the distinctions become clearer, the process of opening to the Divine more meaningful, and the chance of significant spiritual experiences at the peak of the working increases.

And then? As noted earlier, this is the end of one journey and the beginning of another. If you have worked your way through all the practices described in this book, you will have mastered an effective set of tools that can be used in many other branches of occult study. Where you apply those tools, however, is up to you, for the process of spiritual awakening does not end with this book.

Even if you have powerful spiritual experiences at various points along the way, the path of initiation rises up far beyond the human level. By working through the Cabalistic training given in these pages, you have taken an important step along that journey, but there are more steps ahead of you. The insights and experiences you have had in the work you have done, if you pay close attention to them, will guide you to the next stage on your journey—and beyond.

BIBLIOGRAPHY

Achad, Frater (2020). *The Anatomy of the Body of God*. n.p.: Global Grey (globalgreyebooks.com).
Ashcroft-Nowicki, Dolores (1987). *Highways of the Mind: The Art and History of Pathworking*. Wellingborough, UK: Aquarian Press.
Burkert, Walter (1972). *Lore and Science in Early Pythagoreanism*, trans. Edwin L. Minar Jr. Cambridge, MA: Harvard University Press.
Butler, W.E. (1964). *Magic and the Qabalah*. New York: Weiser.
Case, Paul Foster (2008). *Esoteric Secrets of Meditation and Magic*. Richardson, TX: Fraternity of the Hidden Light.
Case, Paul Foster (2008). *Occult Fundamentals and Spiritual Unfoldment*. Richardson, TX: Fraternity of the Inner Light.
Case, Paul Foster (1947). *The Tarot: A Key to the Wisdom of the Ages*. Los Angeles: Builders of the Adytum.
Case, Paul Foster (1985). *The True and Invisible Rosicrucian Order*. York Beach, ME: Weiser.
Corbin, Henry (1976). *Mundus Imaginalis, or the Imaginary and the Imaginal*. Ipswich, UK: Golgonooza Press.
Davies, Stevan L. (1983). *The Gospel of Thomas and Christian Wisdom*. New York: Seabury Press.
Deadman, Alison (2006). "Letter, Musical Pitch, and Color in the Work of Paul Foster Case." *The Esoteric Quarterly*, Spring 2006, pp. 9–18.

Dillon, John (1996). *The Middle Platonists*. Ithaca, NY: Cornell University Press.
Fielding, Charles (1989). *The Practical Qabalah*. York Beach, ME: Weiser.
Fort, Charles (1933). *Wild Talents*. n.p.: Global Grey (globalgreyebooks.com).
Fortune, Dion (1987). *Applied Magic and Aspects of Occultism*. Wellingborough, UK: Aquarian Press.
Fortune, Dion (1935). *The Mystical Qabalah*. London: Ernest Benn.
Frankl, Victor (1959). *Man's Search for Meaning*. Boston: Beacon Press.
Gray, William G. (1984). *Concepts of Qabalah*. York Beach, ME: Weiser.
Greer, John Michael (2013). *The Celtic Golden Dawn*. Woodbury, MN: Llewellyn Publications.
Greer, John Michael (2022). *The Ceremony of the Grail*. Woodbury, MN: Llewellyn Publications. (Cited as Greer 2022a.)
Greer, John Michael (2020). *The Dolmen Arch* (2 vols). Portland, OR: Azoth Press.
Greer, John Michael (2007). *The Druid Magic Handbook*. San Francisco, CA: Weiser.
Greer, John Michael (2022). *The Fellowship of the Hermetic Rose*, 4 vols. East Providence, RI: Creative Commons. (Cited as Greer 2022b.)
Greer, John Michael (1996). *Paths of Wisdom*. St. Paul, MN: Llewellyn Publications.
Greer, John Michael (2024). *The Way of the Four Elements*. London: Aeon Books.
Greer, John Michael (2021). *The Way of the Golden Section*. London: Aeon Books.
Guthrie, Kenneth Sylvan (1987). *The Pythagorean Sourcebook and Library*. Grand Rapids, MI: Phanes Press.
Hellman, Neal (1977). *Dulcimer Songbook*. New York: Oak Publications.
Hersey, George L. (1976). *Pythagorean Palaces: Magic and Architecture in the Italian Renaissance*. Ithaca, NY: Cornell University Press.
Hoeller, Stephan A. (1975). *The Royal Road*. Wheaton, IL: Theosophical Publishing House.
Jung, Carl (1960). *Synchronicity: An Acausal Connecting Principle*. Princeton, NJ: Princeton University Press.
Kingsley, Peter (1995). *Ancient Philosophy. Mystery and Magic: Empedocles and Pythagorean Tradition*. Oxford: Clarendon Press.
Knight, Gareth (1998). *Magical Images and the Magical Imagination*. Albuquerque, NM: Sun Chalice Books.
Lenain, Lazare (2020). *The Science of the Kabbalah*, trans. Piers A. Vaughan. Bayonne, NJ: Rose Circle Publications.

Lévi, Eliphas (2017). *The Doctrine and Ritual of High Magic*, trans. John Michael Greer and Mark Mikituk. New York: Tarcher.
Lewis, C.S. (1964). *The Discarded Image: An Introduction to Medieval and Renaissance Literature.* Cambridge, UK: Cambridge University Press.
Maryon, Edward (1924). *Marcotone: The Science of Tone-Color.* Boston: C.C. Birchard.
May, Dorothy (1984). *Dulcimer a la Mode.* Prairie Village, KS: Meadowlark Press.
Olsen, Christina (1994). *Carte da Trionfi: The Development of Tarot in Fifteenth-Century Italy.* Doctoral dissertation, University of Pennsylvania.
Origen (1885). *Contra Celsum*, trans. Frederick Crombie. In Robert, Alexander, ed., *The Ante-Nicene Fathers*, vol. 4. New York: Christian Publishing Co.
Patai, Raphael (1967). *The Hebrew Goddess.* New York: Ktav Publishing House.
Peeke, Margaret B. (1908). *Numbers & Letters, or the Thirty-Two Paths of Wisdom.* New York: Broadway Publishing Co.
Plato (1961). *Symposium*, trans. Michael Joyce. In Hamilton, Edith, and Huntington Cairns, eds., *The Collected Dialogues of Plato.* Princeton, NJ: Princeton University Press.
Regardie, Israel (2015). *The Golden Dawn.* Woodbury, MN: Llewellyn Publications.
Regardie, Israel (1938). *The Middle Pillar.* Chicago: Aries Press.
Robinson, James M., ed. (1988). *The Nag Hammadi Library.* New York: HarperCollins.
Sadhu, Mouni (1962). *The Tarot.* London: George Allen and Unwin.
Scholem, Gershom (1987). *The Origins of the Kabbalah*, trans. Allan Arkush. Princeton, NJ: Princeton University Press.
Theon of Smyrna (1979). *Mathematics Useful for Understanding Plato*, trans. Robert and Deborah Lawlor. San Diego: Wizards Bookshelf.
Westcott, William Wynn, trans. (1893). *Sepher Yetzirah: The Book of Formation.* London: Theosophical Publishing Society.
Whistlewood, Gwyneth (2013). "Muses, Modes, and the Music of the Spheres." *Feral Flute*, https://feralflute.blogspot.com/2013/08/muses-modes-and-music-of-spheres.html; accessed April 30, 2024.
Williams, Strephon Kaplan (1985). *The Jungian-Senoi Dreamwork Manual.* Berkeley, CA: Journey Press.
Yates, Frances A. (1966). *The Art of Memory.* London: Routledge & Kegan Paul.

INDEX

the Abyss, 8, 15
    and awakening to divine, 58–59
    crossing, 71–72
    paths above, 88–89
    paths below, 83–88
active imagination, 104–105, 106, 147
    beginning, 149–151
    Cabalistic dreamwork, 148–149, 154–157
    consciousness, 148
    and discursive meditation, 151–154
    dreams, 148
    imaginal world, 148
    and meditation, 151–154
    and tarot, 149, 155
    Trump I, 149–151
Against Celsus (Origen), xiv
archetype, 13
    decad, 17
    dyad, 15
    ennead, 17
    as foundations of meaning and cosmos, 14
    hexad, 16–17
    human consciousness, 14
    monad, 14
    numbers, 14
    octad, 17
    pentad, 16
    tetrad, 15
    of Tree of Life, 14
    triad, 15
art of memory, 180
Ashley, Juliet, xxii, 85, 113, 129
astral plane, 58
Atkinson, William Walker, 88
autotrophs, 43
autumn equinox ceremony, 143–144
awakening
    creative imagination, 58
    to divine, 58–59
    to first triad, 59, 60
    of human potential, 60–61
    second triad, 56–57
    self, 53–61
    to spiritual realm, 27

214 INDEX

of third triad, 54–56, 59
of will, 46–47
awakening to inner worlds, 53–61
    the abyss and awakening to divine, 58–59
    creative imagination, 58
    first triad, 59, 60
    human potential, 60–61
    second triad, 56–57, 60
    third triad, 54–56, 59
    three highest spheres, 59
    Veil of the Sanctuary, 56

Blavatsky, Helena, 109
bodhisattva, 38
body of transformation, 195
breathing, 116–117
Bridge of Light, 169
    descent of light, 169–170
    fusion into lunar current, 172–173
    as path of healing and blessing, 173–175
    union of two currents, 170–172
Buddhism, 38
Builders of the Adytum (BOTA) deck, 94
Burns, Robert, 105

Cabala practice methods, 104
    active imagination, 104–105, 106
    discursive meditation, 104, 106
    personalizing, 35–39
    Plato's teaching, 106–107
    practical side of, 104–106
    ritual, 105–106
    technical side of, 106
Cabala, xiii. *See also* Tree of Life
    correspondences, 64
    embodied, 159–161
    Gilbert's, xxii–xxiii, 11
    Gnostic and Greek origins, xiv
    Jewish Cabala, xiv, xx, xxi
    Lurianic Cabala, xvi–xvii
    myths of timelessness, xiii
    origins of, xiv, xvi
    philosophy of, 64

Pythagoras and Esoteric roots of, xviii
    symbolic tools of, 64–67
    universal simplicity of, 3–4
Cabalistic dreamwork, 148–149, 154–157
Cabalistic symbolism, 64
    of eighth sphere, 182
    elemental order and, 23
    experiential spheres on Tree of Life, 65
    integrating color, symbolism, and invocation, 166–168
    modernizing celestial symbolism, 64–65
    musical modes and planetary rulerships, 66
    of ninth sphere, 181
    of seventh sphere, 183–184
    spheres of primal triad, 65
    symbolic tools and preparatory practice, 66–67
    of tenth sphere, 180
    tradition and innovation in, 64
Carr-Gomm, Philip, 153
Case, Paul Foster, xiii, 101
celestial symbolism, modernizing, 64–65
Celsus, xiv
ceremonial invocation, 67
chakras, 65, 160
Christian Cabala, 35
Cicero, xv
Clement of Alexandria, 26
Competence, temple of, 182, 183, 201
consciousness, 14, 148
    balancing through breath, 116–117
    limits of, 71–72
conscious self, 46, 57
consecration rituals, 129–138
Corbin, Henry, 58, 148, 153
correspondences, 64
correspondences of paths, 81
    Divine grace and elemental correspondence, 88–89
    English alphabet and Cabala, 89–91

Fool and Divine, 84
14 statements of the Emerald Tablet, 87
letter-path attributions and numerology, 91
mystical paths and elemental connections, 88–89
paths above the abyss, 88–89
paths below the abyss, 83–88
reinterpreting planetary correspondences, 86–87
subjective paths, 81–83
symbolic correspondences of lower paths, 83–88
tarot attributions, 82
tarot-path correspondences, 82
correspondences of spheres, 69
crossing the abyss, 71–72
eighth sphere, 76–77
fifth sphere, 73–74
first sphere, 69–70
fourth sphere, 72–73
limits of consciousness and Lower World, 71–72
ninth sphere, 77–78
second sphere, 70
seventh sphere, 75–76
sixth sphere, 74–75
tenth sphere, 78–79
third sphere, 70–72
cosmic dualities, 7–8
creation, trinity of, 7–8
creative imagination, 58
Crowley, Aleister, 35

Daath. *See* Knowledge
decad, 17
deity invocation, 35–36
Desire, temple of, 183–184
Dillon, John, xvi
directed daydreaming. *See* active imagination
discursive meditation, 104, 106, 109
active imagination and, 151–154
for active life, 109–111
art of combinations and tracing thought, 120–122
balancing consciousness, 116–117
breathing, 116–117
closing self-massage, 113–115
dream imagery in, 155
Eastern meditation, 109–110
fourfold breath, 116–117
grounding body after meditation, 113–115
Lesser Ritual of the Pentagram, 112
meditation, 117–118
opening visualization, 112–113
physical stillness and inner awareness in, 111–112
posture, 111–112
practical requirements, 110–111
practice of relaxation, 115–116
preparing mind and space for, 110
releasing tension, 115–116
Sphere of Protection ritual, 112–113
themes for practice, 119–120
thinking with purpose, 117–118
Divine
ascending to, 204–207
awakening to, 58–59
Fool and, 84
grace and elemental correspondence, 88–89
linking with higher self, 162–164
personal conceptions of, 39
Plato's path to wisdom and, 106–107
triads, 37–39
doctrine of primal worlds, xvi
Dogme et Rituel de la Haute Magie (Lévi), 3
Do-In, 113
dreams, 148, 154. *See also* active imagination
Cabalistic dreamwork, 148–149, 154–157
dream imagery, 155
lucid dreaming, 157
dualities, cosmic, 7–8
dyad, 15

Eastern meditation, 109–110
ecology and Tree of Life, 42–43
elemental
    order and symbolism, 23
    symbols, 129, 132, 134, 136
elements, tetractys of, xix
English alphabet and Cabala, 89–91
ennead, 17
Enneads (Plotinus), xv

first triad
    awakening, 59, 60
    in microcosm, 59
    flaming sword, 28, 33
Fort, Charles, 120
Fortune, Dion, xiii, 28, 36, 81, 112
Foundation, temple of, 181, 182, 201, 205, 206
fourfold breath, 116–117
four material elements, 23
four worlds, 22, 23
    air, 23–24
    Clement's allegory of 42 scrolls, 26–28
    earth, 25
    fire, 25
    four material elements, 23
    four trees, 25
    in microcosm, 48–49
    tattwa symbols, 23, 24
    water, 24
14 statements of the Emerald Tablet, 87
42 sacred scrolls, 26
    awakening to spiritual realm, 27
    four worlds, 26–28
Frater Achad. *See* Jones, Charles Stansfield
Freud, Sigmund, 148

gematria, xiv, 91
geomancy, 86
geomantic figures, 86
Gilbert, John, xxii–xxiii, 4, 38, 48, 64, 66, 85, 86, 88, 89, 125, 129
    Bridge of Light, 169–175
    Cabala, xxii–xxiii, 11, 71

colors and spheres, 65
conscious self, 57
correspondences of the Paths, 83
English numerology, 91
pathworking, 199
tarot divination, 93, 96
teachings, 8, 23, 30, 51, 65, 93–95, 96, 112, 159
three highest spheres of Tree, 37, 39, 47, 59, 162
three realms, 36
Tree of Life, 30, 31
Gnostic Christianity, xv
Gnostic traditions, number 12, 27
Golden Dawn system, 30
Gray, William G., 82, 89
"guardian genius", 126
guided meditations, 199

Harmony, temple of, 184–185, 205, 206
Hebrew alphabet, xxi
The Hebrew Goddess (Patai), 38
Hermes Trismegistus, 26, 87
Hermetic Order of the Golden Dawn, founders of, 82
heterotrophs, 43
hexad, 16–17, 49, 51, 162–164
higher self
    linking Divine with, 162–164
    to primal triad, 47
Hinduism, modern, 38
Hoeller, Stephan A., 2
human microcosm, 43–44

imaginal temples, 195
    Competence, 182, 183
    constructing, 178, 179–180
    Desire, 183–184
    formulating inner temples, 190–194
    Foundation, 181, 182
    Harmony, 184–185
    Knowledge, 188
    Love, 187
    Manifestation, 180, 181
    Power, 185–186
imaginal world, 58, 148, 153

imagination, 51. *See also* active
    imagination
  creative imagination, 58
individuation, 57
inner
  barrier, 53–54
  journey, 53–61
  temples, 190–194
invocation
  ceremonial, 67
  deity, 35–36
  integrating color, symbolism,
    and, 166–168
  ritual, 129–132
isosephy, 91

Jewish Cabala, xiv, xv, xx, xxi, 8, 9, 35
  Hebrew alphabet, 89
  primal spheres, 37
  Sepher Yetzirah, 11
  Veil of the Sanctuary, 56
John the Baptist, 33
Jones, Charles Stansfield, 82
Jung, Carl, 5, 14, 47, 53, 191
  archetype, 13
  individuation, 57
  practice of active imagination,
    104, 105
  projection, 55

Knowledge, 11, 15
Knowledge, temple of, 179, 188,
    205, 206
The Kybalion (Atkinson), 88

Lao Tsu, 7, 15
Lesser Ritual of the Pentagram, 112
letter-path attributions, 91
Lévi, Eliphas, xxii, 3, 90, 129
lightning flash, 27, 28
Limit and the Unlimited, 7
Love, temple of, 187
lower self, 46
Lower World
  activating spheres of, 179–180
  limits of consciousness and, 71–72

lucid dreaming, 157
Lull, Ramón, 120
Luria, Isaac, xvi
Lurianic Cabala, xvi–xvii

macrocosm, 41–51
mage, 178
magical images, 195
  body of transformation, 195
  eighth sphere, 198
  fifth sphere, 198
  fourth sphere, 198
  ninth sphere, 197
  practice of transformative
    identification, 195–197
  seventh sphere, 198
  sixth sphere, 198
  tenth sphere, 197
Manifestation, temple of, 178, 180, 181,
    200, 201, 205, 206
mapping realms onto Tree of Life,
    36–37
*Mathematics Useful for Understanding
    Plato* (Theon of Smyrna), xviii
meditation, 117–118. *See also* discursive
    meditation
  and active imagination, 151–154
  and advanced visualization,
    169–175
  guided, 199
  practices, 104
  theme of, 117
meditative entry, 161–162
memory, art of, 180
Memory of Nature, 58
mesocosm, 177–178
Metatron, xiv
microcosm, 41
  ecology and Tree of Life, 42–43
  first triad in, 59
  four worlds in, 48–49
  hexad, 49, 51
  human microcosm, 43–45
  manifestation, proportion,
    and life force, 45
  on path of spiritual unfoldment, 51

218　INDEX

pentad, 50, 51
　second triad in, 56–57
　third triad in, 54–56
　Tree of Life in, 44, 53
　Upper World of, 47
middle pillar exercise, 159
Middle Platonism, xvi–xvii, 27
The Middle Platonists (Dillon), xvi
mind, 109
　in Cabalistic practice, 36
　preparing for discursive
　　meditation, 110
　realm of mind, 36
Mittraton. *See* Metatron
monad, 14
mountain dulcimer, 188–190
musical dimension, 188–190
musical modes, 66
mystical
　numerology, 91
　　paths and elemental connections,
　　　88–89
The Mystical Qabalah (Fortune), xiii, 28

nature, 41
　Memory of Nature, 58
Nichols, Ross, 105
numbers, 8, 13, 14, 89. *See also*
　archetype
numerology, mystical, 91

occult Cabala, 35, 38
"occultism", xvii
occult philosophy, xvii
octad, 17
On Isis and Osiris (Plutarch of
　Chaeroneia), xvi
On the Nature of the Gods (Cicero), xv
Origen, xiv
The Origins of the Kabbalah
　(Scholem), xiv

pandit, 109
Papus, xxii
Patai, Raphael, 38
path(s), 28–29, 30–31
　above the abyss, 88–89
　of arrow, 31–32, 33
　below the abyss, 83–88
　correspondences of, 81–91
pathworking, 104, 199
　ascending to divine, 204–207
　guided meditations, 199
　as initiatory journey on Tree of Life,
　　199–200
　of Manifestation, 201–202
　path of arrow, 204–207
　practical applications, 202–204
　rituals of initiation, 199
　sequence of creation, 201–202
　sequence of initiatory, 200–201
　shedding the self, 204–207
　threefold journey through fifteen
　　paths, 200–201
　transformation through intent
　　and direction, 202–204
pentad, 16, 50, 51
Phoenicians, xxi
pillars, three, 19
　flow of creation, 22–23
　three triads, 21, 23
planetary correspondences,
　reinterpreting, 86–87
Plato, 106–107
Platonism, xvi, xvii–xviii
Platonists, xvi, xviii
Plotinus, xv
Plutarch of Chaeroneia, xvi
posture, 111–112
Power, temple of, 185–186
"premeditated", 117
primal spheres, 37
primal triad, 8, 69
　higher self to, 47
　spheres of, 65
　visualizing, 161–162
primal worlds, doctrine of, xvi
"projection", 55
Pythagoras of Crotona, xviii, 2, 7

Rabbinic Tree of Life, 29
realm of mind, 36

reflected triad, 9, 47
Regardie, Israel, 159
relaxation, 115–116
religious dimension, 35–39
Rhodonn Starrus. *See* Shaw, Matthew
Rider-Waite deck, 94, 95
ritual(s), 105–106, 123
    consecration, 129–138
    foundations, 123–125
    of initiation, 199
    for protection and elemental purification, 126–128
    of purification and invocation, 129–132
    of release and gratitude, 128
    seasonal rituals, 138–146
    tools and space for ritual practice, 124–125, 128–129

salamanders, 129
sanctum, 123
sanctum ceremonies, 123
    autumn equinox ceremony, 143–144
    book of air, 129–132
    closing ceremony, 128
    cup of water, 134–136
    of equinoxes and solstices, 138–139
    foundations, 123–125
    four working tools, 128–129
    opening ceremony, 126–128
    pentacle of earth, 136–138
    protection and elemental purification, 126–128
    purification and invocation, 129–132
    release and gratitude, 128
    seasonal rituals, 138–139
    spring equinox ceremony, 139–141
    summer solstice ceremony, 141–142
    tools and space for ritual practice, 124–125, 128–129
    wand of fire, 132–134
    winter solstice ceremony, 144–146
sannyasin, 109
Scholem, Gershom, xiv

"scrying", 104
seasonal rituals, 138–139
    autumn equinox ceremony, 143–144
    spring equinox ceremony, 139–141
    summer solstice ceremony, 141–142
    winter solstice ceremony, 144–146
second triad
    awakening, 56–57
    in microcosm, 57
    three spheres of, 57
secular realm, 36
Sefer ha-Zohar (Leon), xiii
self
    awakening, 53–61
    -awareness and reality, 53–54
    conscious self, 57
    fourfold nature of, 48–49
    journey through, 47
    -massage, 113–115
    realms of self, 57
    subconscious, 46, 47
    unawakened, 46
Sepher Yetzirah, 11, 23
sephirah, xiv
sephiroth, xviii
seven chakras, 65
Shaw, Matthew, xxii, 173
Smith, Pamela Coleman, 94
sphere(s), 28–29, 33, 81
    activating spheres of Lower World, 179–180
    balancing, 190–194
    colors and, 65
    correspondences of, 69–79
    eighth sphere, 182
    fifth sphere, 185–186
    fourth sphere, 187
    harmonizing with, 188–190
    ninth sphere, 181
    primal, 37
    of primal triad, 65
    sacred representations of sixth, 184–185

seventh sphere, 183–184
and sphere workings, 192–193
tenth sphere, 180
Sphere of Protection ritual, 112–113
sphere workings, 177
    activating spheres of Lower World, 179–180
    art of memory, 180
    balancing spheres, 190–194
    Competence, temple of, 182, 183
    constructing imaginal temples, 178, 179–180
    Desire, temple of, 183–184
    eighth sphere, 182
    entering mesocosm, 177–178
    formulating inner temples, 190–194
    Foundation, temple of, 181, 182
    harmonizing with spheres, 188–190
    Harmony, temple of, 184–185
    Knowledge, temple of, 188
    Love, temple of, 187
    Manifestation, temple of, 180, 181
    musical dimension, 188–190
    using music and mountain dulcimer, 188–190
    ninth sphere, 181
    Power, temple of, 185–186
    practical applications, 190–194
    sacred representations of sixth sphere, 184–185
    seventh sphere, 183–184
    spheres and, 192–193
    symbolism and structure, 180–184
    tenth sphere, 180
    warrior queen of fifth sphere, 185–186
    wise king of fourth sphere, 187
spiritual development, 57
spiritual healing, 174. *See also* Bridge of Light
spring equinox ceremony, 139–141
Sri Aurobindo, 60
subconscious self, 46, 47

summer solstice ceremony, 141–142
symbolic tools of Cabala, 64–67

Taijitu, xv
Tao Te Ching, xxii
tarot, 93
    and active imagination, 149, 155
    attributions, 95, 100–101
    BOTA deck, 94
    Cabala and ceremonial initiation, 93–95
    deck, 177–178
    Fool's pilgrimage, 95–99
    foundations for practice, 100–101
    Gilbert's teachings, 93–95, 96
    layout, 96, 97, 98
    memorizing Trumps and correspondences, 100–101
    -path correspondences, 82
    Rider-Waite deck, 94, 95
tattwa symbols, 23, 24
Temple of Solomon, 19
tetractys, xviii, xix
tetrad, 9, 15, 47
Theon of Smyrna, xviii
third triad, 10
    awakening of, 54–56, 59
    and manifestation, 164–166
    in microcosm, 54–56
three highest spheres of Tree, 37, 39, 47, 59, 162
three pillars of Cabalistic practice, 104–107
three triads, 21, 23
Tortona, Marziano da, 93
Tree of Life, xiv–xv, xx, 2, 10, 71
    the Abyss, 8, 15
    animating, 166–168
    archetypes of, 14
    divine triads, 37–39
    in ecology, 42–43
    Gilbert's Tree of Life, 30, 31
    human microcosm, 43, 53
    Knowledge, 11, 15
    last spheres, 10–11
    lightning flash, 27, 28

lower spheres of, 9
mapping macrocosm and microcosm, 41–51
mapping realms onto, 36–37
in microcosm, 44
objectivity and subjectivity on, 28–29
and personal conceptions of Divine, 39
primal triad, 8
process of human action in, 12
Pythagorean perspectives, 2
qualities and quantities, 3
Rabbinic Tree of Life, 29
reflected triad, 9
symbolic structure, 3, 19
Taijitu, xv
ten spheres, 3, 69
tetrad, 9
third triad, 10, 54–56
three perspectives of, 2
upper spheres of, 8
Waite, 30
Tree of Life in the body, 159
animating Tree of Life, 166–168
embodied Cabala, 159–161
formulating hexad, 162–164
integrating color, symbolism, and invocation, 166–168
linking Divine with higher self, 162–164
meditative entry, 161–162
third triad and manifestation, 164–166
tree and chakras, 160
visualizing primal triad, 161–162
triad, 15
Trimurti, 38
trinity of creation, 7–8
The True Discourse (Celsus), xiv
Trump I, 149–151

unawakened Self, 46

Veil of the Sanctuary, 56
visualization and meditation, advanced, 169–175

Waite, Arthur Edward, 30, 82, 83, 85, 94
warrior queen of fifth sphere, 185–186
The Way of the Four Elements (Greer), 139
will, awakening of, 46–47
winter solstice ceremony, 144–146
Wirth, Oswald, xxii
wise king of fourth sphere, 187

Zhou Dunyi, xv

www.ingramcontent.com/pod-product-compliance
Ingram Content Group UK Ltd.
Pitfield, Milton Keynes, MK11 3LW, UK
UKHW021614180925
463049UK00009B/95